SIKH IDEOLOGY
POLITY AND SOCIAL ORDER

SIKH IDEOLOGY POLITY AND SOCIAL ORDER

From Guru Nanak to Maharaja Ranjit Singh

(Revised and Enlarged)

J.S. Grewal

MANOHAR
2007

First published 2007

ISBN 81-7304-737-5

Published by

Ajay Kumar Jain for
Manohar Publishers & Distributors
4753/23 Ansari Road, Daryaganj
New Delhi 110 002

Typeset at

Digigrafics
New Delhi 110 049

Printed at

Lordson Publishers Pvt. Ltd.
Delhi 110 007

To

TARA, SHARAN, RANBIR and MANEK

My Grandchildren

Contents

Part 3
SIKH POLITY

Part 4
SIKH SOCIAL ORDER

Preface

This is a new version of the *Sikh Ideology, Polity and Social Order* published in 1996. All the essays have been revised, some more and other less. Therefore, they reflect the present understanding of the author. The subtitle 'From Guru Nanak to Maharaja Ranjit Singh' has been added to indicate the period, and also the gradual development from the religious to the political concerns of the Sikhs.

This is also an enlarged edition. Six new essays have been added: Babarbani, Khalsa in the *Var* of Gurdas, Sikh Tradition of Martyrdom, Raj Karega Khalsa Anthem, The Sikh State, and Sikh Raj and the Sikh Social Order. The volume is divided into four parts. To suggest linkages between essays and parts, an Introduction has been added.

Mainly responsible for encouraging me to revise and enlarge this book are Professors Indu Banga and Gurinder Singh Mann. They would like me to believe that this short volume is the best introduction to the pre-colonial Sikh tradition for young researchers. I am thankful to them for their appreciation. Professor Banga has read the typescript and made valuable suggestions. The general reader should find it of great interest as it is based on contemporary sources. Shri Ramesh Jain and Shri Ajay Kumar Jain have readily agreed to publish this revised and enlarged edition. I am thankful to them.

A young scholar who has assisted me in preparing this edition for publication is Karamjit K. Malhotra. I am thankful to her. Amit Bansal has typed out the matter with great care. I am happy to acknowledge his help.

26 January 2007 J.S. GREWAL

Introduction

There are thirty essays in all in this volume, ranging from four to fourteen pages in print. The shorter ones generally relate to a single source or a minor theme. But each makes a few basic points. Nearly all the essays are based on contemporary evidence, which adds a certain depth to the treatment of all the themes. All the major themes are seen from more than one perspective. Ideology, polity and social order were interrelated: each had a close bearing on the other two. The intermeshing of ideas, politics, and society makes the subject rather fascinating.

Each essay is not necessarily a direct discussion of the broad theme of the part in which it is placed. There is overlap too in terms of information given in each essay. The book is not a formal treatment of the subject. However, each essay provides insights into ideology, polity or social order. The essays and the parts into which they are grouped are arranged in a broad chronological order, keeping in view their logical links. The basic objective is to depict the contours of the past in their complexity.

In the first part of this book there are six essays, all related to the ideas and attitudes of Guru Nanak. He looked upon the contemporary systems of religious belief and practice in terms of three traditions: the Brahmanical, the ascetical, and the Islamic. He assessed these three traditions on a set of theological, ethical and social criteria reflected in these essays.

Guru Nanak's experience at Sultanpur involved a kind of illumination or enlightenment, an intuitive understanding of the true purpose of life. He came to believe that he could guide his contemporaries on the right path. His contact with the representatives of orthodox and Sūfī Islam at Sultanpur proved to be important for assuming a position of transcendence. His message went beyond what was taught in the Islamic, the Brahmanical and the ascetical tradition. The essay on Bābarbāṇī reveals that Guru Nanak's concerns were not only religious and ethical but also political. This aspect of his concerns is generally ignored, resulting in a misunderstanding of his basic position, and that of his successors.

The essay on Islam in the service of the state shows that Guru Nanak's criticism of orthodox Islam was not confined to external observance as opposed to inner feeling; it embraced the realm of politics and administration. The representatives of orthodox Islam were closely associated with the state and acted as the agents of its oppression, injustice, and discrimination. The Sūfis were better than the *'ulamā* because of their devotional life. However, they too were aligned with the state, receiving *madad-i ma'āsh* from the rulers and praying for their long rule. Furthermore, they tended to presume that they had attained to the goal of life; they taught others how to reach the goal, and they authorized them to guide still others. There is no doubt that Guru Nanak appreciated the devotional theism of the Sūfis but his own position was markedly different from theirs. The general impression that Guru Nanak had an unqualified appreciation for the Sūfis is evidently based on a partial understanding.

Guru Nanak takes notice of the Gorakh Nāthīs as the most influential of the representatives of the ascetical tradition in his times, but without any appreciation for them. In the first place, the assumption of the Gorakh Nāthīs that one could attain to the state of bliss by one's own effort alone negated the idea of God's omnipotence and grace which was an essential feature of Guru Nanak's theology. Then, their aspiration to acquire supranatural powers appeared to have no spiritual or ethical value. Above all, Guru Nanak was opposed to celibacy and mendicancy, which formed the core of the ascetical tradition, whether Gorakh Nāthī or any other. Understandably, therefore, he did not approve of the renunciation of the Gorakh Nāthīs which amounted to renouncing social responsibility.

Guru Nanak's conception of God and valid way of worship was the basis of his criticism of Vaishnava *bhakti*. He did not subscribe to the idea of incarnation which was the cardinal belief of the worshippers of Rama and Krishna. The worship of their images was seen by Guru Nanak as spiritually futile and ethically neutral. The Vaishnava practice of dance and drama appeared to trivialize the divinity. To sing God's praises in congregation and to meditate on the Name and the Shabad were central to Guru Nanak's conception of God's adoration.

All the three traditions of his times were discarded by Guru Nanak on the basis of a common set of criteria to which he himself subscribed: unity of God, devotion to Him in love and fear, acceptance of His will, active participation in social life, ethical conduct, and service. Central to Guru Nanak's thought is his conception of liberation-in-life. It is not an inert state of bliss but an experience of God which enables the individual to participate in social life effectively for the welfare of others (*parupkār*).

These six essays in the first part indicate that Guru Nanak cannot be bracketed with any of the contemporary religious traditions. He does not recognize the authority of any known scripture. In fact, he invokes God's authority for what he says as His herald (*dhādī, tabal-bāz*). This is nothing short of claiming total originality for the faith he initiated. For a proper understanding of Sikhism and Sikh history it is necessary to understand that Guru Nanak founded a new faith, with a new conception of liberation-in-life.

In the second part, there are eleven essays, all related directly or indirectly to the Khalsa. The starting point is the expanding Panth of Guru Nanak in the sixteenth century, supported by the doctrine of the unity and continuity of Guruship, compilation of the Sikh scripture, and proliferation of the institution called the *dharmsāl.* All these three were based on Guru Nanak's decision to install his successor in his lifetime, the use of his own compositions for congregational worship, and the founding of a *dharmsāl* at Kartarpur for congregational worship and community meal. The message of Guru Nanak and his successors appealed to a wide range of social strata, from the Brahman to the Chandāl, but particularly to the trading communities, the artisans, and the agriculturists. The increasing number of Sikhs and an improvement in their economic position throughout the second half of the sixteenth century, coupled with the ideological and institutional aspects of the movement, made the Gurus increasingly important from a political point of view. This was the context in which Jahangir ordered the execution of Guru Arjan in 1606, on the plea of his blessings to the rebel prince Khusrau.

The essay on the cleavage in the Sikh Panth after the martyrdom of Guru Arjan, brings out the difference between the sixteenth and the seventeenth century situations. Guru Hargobind, the son and successor of Guru Arjan, adopted martial activity and came into armed conflict with the officials of the Mughal empire. Confrontation with the state resulted in a splintering of the Sikh community, bringing rival claimants to Guruship on the stage, like the followers of Prithi Chand and his descendants, called '*minas*' by the Sikhs of Guru Hargobind, the followers of Dhir Mal and his descendants, and those of Ram Rai and his successors. Unlike the Gurus of the central stream of the Sikh Panth, their rivals had no hesitation in accepting patronage from the state and supporting its authority. A political dimension was, thus, added to the situation more emphatically now than in the late sixteenth century. To look upon this position as 'militarization' of the Sikh Panth is to oversimplify the situation.

The martyrdom of Guru Tegh Bahadur in 1675 was the result of a sustained confrontation between the Mughal state and the central stream of the Sikh Panth. By accepting Guruship, he challenged the authority of the Mughal emperor to arbitrate in the matter of succession. Guru Tegh Bahadur's compositions reveal his commitment to the values of his predecessors. When Aurangzeb began to pursue a policy of coercion, Guru Tegh Bahadur decided to uphold the freedom of conscience. This was the basic reason for his martyrdom. It was not a sacrifice for the protection of Hindu *dharma,* or even the Sikh faith alone. What was essentially at stake was the freedom of religious belief as such, or the freedom of conscience. With the martyrdom of Guru Tegh Bahadur, the confrontation between the followers of the acknowledged line of Gurus and the Mughal state reached a point of no return.

An analysis of the *Bachittar Nātak* shows that this work was essentially a proclamation of war in the way of righteousness (*dharmyuddh*) to ensure the protection and promotion of the Sikh tradition with the use of physical force. Before the composition of this work, Guru Gobind had fought battles against the hill chiefs and the Mughal *faujdārs*. The declaration in the *Bachittar Nātak* was followed by the institution of the Khalsa, which made the bearing of arms and fighting for the righteous causes a religious duty. An almost inevitable conflict with the Mughal state resulted in the loss of Anandpur, the headquarters of Guru Gobind Singh. It was in this situation that he wrote the *Zafarnāma* in which he refers to the perfidy of Aurangzeb's officials, justifies his own stand, and blames Aurangzeb for supporting the wrong party, that is, the hill chiefs. The essay on the insistence on justice shows that Guru Gobind Singh's purpose in meeting Bahadur Shah and his stay near his camp, was meant to get Anandpur back for the righteous war from a place which was his rightful possession.

In the *Gursobhā*, written by Sainapat in 1711, removal of the *masands* to establish direct link of the Sikhs with the Guru is presented as the necessary prelude to the institution of the Khalsa which was meant to make the Sikh Panth openly a political community. The essential features of the Khalsa were: baptism of the double-edged sword (*khande kī pahul*), keeping the *kesh* uncut, wearing arms to fight and to die fighting if necessary, bearing the epithet 'Singh', and having no association with the followers of the *masands* and those who did not regard Guru Gobind Singh as the only true Guru. The ultimate purpose was to establish the rule of the Khalsa as a sovereign entity. Before his death, Guru Gobind Singh announced that Guruship was vested henceforth in the Khalsa and in Shabad-Bāṇī. In the *Vār* of Gurdas (different from Bhai Gurdas), written towards the end of the eighteenth century, Guru Gobind Singh is praised for being both the Guru and the disciple at the same time (*āpe gur-chelā*), and the Khalsa are praised for establishing a just and sovereign rule that ensures the freedom of conscience. The distinct identity of the Khalsa, the essential continuity of the Singhs with the Sikhs, and the basic importance of their religious life are underscored in both the works.

The essay on the Khalsa in later historiography shows that the Persian chronicles of the late eighteenth and the early nineteenth century, which were generally commissioned by the British, were not really based on any earlier sources. By and large, they reflected the traditions which had developed by the time of their writing. The greater importance of the contemporary and near contemporary evidence thus gets underlined. This evidence establishes the essential features of the Khalsa, including all the items of the '5Ks', even though the formulation of '5Ks' appeared in the late nineteenth century.

The essay on the Sikh tradition of martyrdom shows that martyrdom was linked to Sikh ideology and not to the Punjabi tradition of heroism. The precolonial Sikh literature makes martyrdom central to the Sikh tradition. To regard it as a part of the Punjabi heroic tradition, or as an invention of the Singh Sabha Movement, is to miss its real significance.

The last essay in this part shows that the idea of the 'Rāj Karegā Khālsā' had become current in the early eighteenth century. The phrase '*rāj karegā khālsā*' goes back to the days of Guru Gobind Singh. The final form of the anthem, in which the idea of Guru Granth is given greater importance than the idea of Guru Panth, appears to have come down from the period of Sikh rule, especially the early nineteenth century.

The third part of the book has eight essays on Sikh polity. Ahmad Shah of Batala in his *Tārīkh-i Hind* gives great importance to the *misl* as a unit of organization in Sikh polity. He states that the number of Sikh chiefs was very large but the most important were those who were associated with one or another of the unit called *misl*. The leader of the *misl* was the first among equals. His leadership was voluntarily accepted by others. They occupied territories collectively but divided them among the individual members to govern and administer. Ahmad Shah's evidence shows that the individual members acted independently of others not only in their administration but also in their political relations with other rulers, whether Sikh or non-Sikh. The importance of the *misl*, therefore, lay essentially in the concerted action of its members for territorial occupation. The *misl*, obviously, was a combination of leaders primarily for conquest.

Ganesh Das in his *Chār Bāgh-i Panjāb* talks of *misldārs* as subordinate to the *sardār* of the *misl*. In other words, the *misl* was not a combination of equals. Nevertheless, the association of the *misldār* with the *sardār* was voluntary. More even than Ahmad Shah, Ganesh Das emphasizes the independence of the Sikh chief in his own territory and in his political relations with other rulers, whether Sikh or non-Sikh. Ganesh Das looks upon sovereignty as the political objective of the Khalsa and invokes no other ideology. He looks upon the Sikh chiefs as individuals who acquired power and exercised it without any formal constraint. Between them and Maharaja Ranjit Singh there was a difference only of degree. The monarchical form of government emerged as the norm in the time of Sikh rule.

However, the eighteenth century Sikh polity was conceptualized by J.D. Cunningham as 'theocratic confederate feudalism' and some other historians have accepted or merely modified his basic formulation. The inscriptions on the Sikh coins struck at Lahore and Amritsar, the doctrines of Guru Panth and Guru Granth, the meetings of the Sarbat Khalsa and their resolutions (*gurmatas*), the action of the Dal Khalsa, and the institutions of Rākhī and Misl are cited in support of this view. It has been shown, however, that the *misl*, the *rākhī*, the *dal khālsā*, and the *gurmata*, which played a crucial role in the occupation of territories, were not exactly relevant for governance and administration. The doctrine of Guru Panth was uncompromisingly egalitarian, and it could serve as the basis of a republican or even a democratic polity. Actually, however, it was seen as ensuring the equal right of the individual Singh to fight and conquer and rule: 'rulership for every Khalsa horseman' was a prophecy attributed to Guru Gobind Singh. No institutional arrangement was evolved for a collective functioning of the chiefs on the basis of equality between them. We are left with the inscriptions on the coins which derive sovereignty from Guru Nanak and Guru Gobind Singh through God's grace. There is no doubt that this declaration made for the sovereignty of the Khalsa Panth. By the same token, however, it made every Khalsa ruler sovereign in his own place and independent of all other rulers, whether Sikh or non-Sikh. On the authority of the Gurus, the individual Sikh chief ruled in the name of the Khalsa. The position of each 'Singh Sahib' or 'Khalsa Ji' was inherited by his heirs. Sons succeeded to the position of the founders of principalities as a matter of routine.

Detailed evidence on one of the most important leaders of the Khalsa in the eighteenth century, Jassa Singh Ahluwalia, leaves no doubt that he exercised political power as an individual without any formal or informal check on his power. Indeed, he was seen as 'the *pātshāh* of the Panth' by the Sikhs themselves. But he was not alone. There were many other Sikh rulers in his time who exercised power in their individual capacity. There was a difference only of degree between Jassa Singh Ahluwalia and Maharaja Ranjit Singh. This comes out in the essay on 'Sarkar Khalsa', or the government and administration of 'Singh Sahib' Ranjit Singh, who was popularly referred to as the Maharaja. He claimed to rule in the name of the Khalsa, like all his eighteenth century predecessors. The government of Ranjit Singh was far more elaborate than that of his predecessors but the major planks of his government were the same and he exercised political power as an individual with no other constraint than that of his conscience. The epithet 'Maharaja' referred to his monarchical status without making him more sovereign than the 'Singh Sahib' or the 'Khalsa Ji' – the epithets used for him till nearly the end of his life.

Suzerain-vassal relationship, in which a more powerful ruler exercised political control over subordinate rulers who were allowed to administer their autonomous territories, was an important feature of Indian polity since at least the time of Harsha. The Mughal rulers had made an effective use of this relationship in establishing their political control over territories much beyond the directly administered areas. Significantly, the eighteenth century Sikh leaders tried to use this tradition more or less successfully. Maharaja Ranjit Singh made use of suzerain-vassal polity on a large scale, making no distinction between Sikh and non-Sikh chiefs. Most of the Sikh chiefs were treated as vassals before their territories were taken over. The only Sikh chief to survive as a vassal was Fateh Singh Ahluwalia. The change from an independent ruler to a vassal in his case is discussed in an essay included in this part.

A number of Muslim chiefs were also treated as vassals before their territories were annexed to the dominions of Ranjit Singh. After the conquest of Multan and Kashmir there was no Muslim vassal of any consideration. In the Punjab hills, however, a considerable number of Rajput principalities were allowed to survive. But even in the hills, the rulers of Kangra and Jammu were made subordinate first and then removed from power. The Rajput Muslims also suffered the same fate. A considerable number of hill chiefs were made subordinate to the new Rajas created by Maharaja Ranjit Singh. The essay on the Jamwals – Raja Gulab Singh, Raja Dhian Singh, Raja Suchet Singh, and Raja Hira Singh – illustrates this process. Eventually the creation of these new Rajas loosened the control of the successors of Ranjit Singh over the hills, and paved the way for the creation of the state of Jammu and Kashmir after the first Anglo-Sikh war in 1845-46 as a vassal state of the British empire.

The last essay in this part relates to the Sikh state as a political institution. Three important phases of Sikh history are considered: the time of Banda Bahadur, the so-called Misl period, and the time of Ranjit Singh. In the first phase, the inscriptions used on the seal and the coin show that the Khalsa declared their sovereign status and derived it ultimately from Guru Nanak through God's grace. Sikh ideology is clearly the basis of this declaration. These inscriptions were used in the late eighteenth century coins struck at Lahore and Amritsar, and continued by Ranjit Singh, known appropriately as the Nanak Shahi coins. In some of the Sikh principalities of the Sutlej-Jamuna Divide, the coin struck by Ahmad Shah Abdali remained current, carrying the implication that his suzerainty was acknowledged as the source of legitimacy. In 1809, these states came under the 'protection' of the British but continued to strike the Ahmad Shāhī coin.

Thus, sovereign power and authority in most of the Sikh states was sought to be derived from the Gurus and God; in a few of them authority was derived from a sovereign ruler. In the latter case, Sikh ideology had no relevance for the acquisition of power. For the exercise of power at any rate, Sikh ideology found no constitutional expression in any of the Sikh states. The government of the Sikh rulers, with the *jāgīrdārī* system and the system of state patronage through *dharmarth* (*madad-i ma'āsh*) as its salient features, was similar to the government of the Mughals. The operation of Sikh ideology was left to the discretion and conscience of the Sikh ruler.

Five essays in the fourth part have a bearing of the Sikh social order. The first relates to the doctrines of Guru Panth and Guru Granth, with their origins in the sixteenth century. However, a decisive enunciation was made by Guru Gobind Singh before his death that Guruship henceforth was vested in the Khalsa and Shabad-Bāṇī. The end of personal Guruship did not mean the end of Guruship itself. The continuity was ensured by the crystallization of the doctrines of corporal and scriptural Guruship. The doctrine of Guru Panth was uncompromisingly egalitarian, and it played an important role in the eighteenth century, with a close bearing on the contemporary Sikh social order. The doctrine of Guru Granth too was egalitarian , but rather in the sphere of religion. With the establishment of Sikh rule, which curtailed the role of the idea of equality, the doctrine of Guru Granth became more important than the doctrine of Guru Panth. It was suited more to the increasing differentiation of the Sikh social order in which partial equality could exist side by side with social inequalities.

The essay on the city of Sikh pilgrimage outlines the emergence of the city of Amritsar in the late eighteenth and the early nineteenth century due to the religious roots of the town of Ramdaspur . The institution of Akal Takht made it the rallying centre of Sikh struggle for political power during the early eighteenth century. This historical process in turn added sanctity to the institutions of the Harmandir (later the Golden Temple) and the Akal Takht. All the Sikh rulers thought of rendering service to Amritsar as a matter of religious merit and the Sikhs began to look upon it as the foremost centre of Sikh pilgrimage. With the Harmandir and the Akal Takht, Amritsar came to be seen as a symbol of the unity of the Sikh Panth.

The essay on Kesar Singh Chhibber's *Bansāvalīnāma* and Ratan Singh Bhangu's *Gurū Panth Prakāsh* seeks to bring out the views of the authors on the Sikh social order. Both subscribed to the distinct identity of the Khalsa and the idea of equality. Chhibber's ideal of equality was restricted to the sphere of faith; he advocated the continuance or re-introduction of the traditional *jati* norms for connubium and commensality. Bhangu visualized a more egalitarian social order, extending commensality to all the four castes, though not to the former untouchables. On the whole, the contemporary social order appears to have been more egalitarian and liberal than what Chhibber, a Brahman by birth, wanted it to be, and less egalitarian than the ideal of Ratan Singh Bhangu.

The essay on a theory of Sikh social order is a brief analysis of the Rahitnama known as the *Prem Sumārg Granth.* It is believed to be a late eighteenth century work, based in part on some earlier sources. The author equates the Sikh with the Khalsa and looks upon the Khalsa as both distinct from and superior to Hindus and Muslims. Their unique faith was meant to replace all previous dispensations. The author advocates that there should be no distinction of caste and gender in the Khalsa Panth. Because of the strongly ingrained prejudices of the people, however, some temporary compromises could be made for matrimony and commensality. Some of the ideas of the author are extremely conservative: he advocates that there should be no change in the occupations of craftsmen, and he accepts the popular notion that women were devoid of intelligence and prone to excessive sexual urge. Nevertheless, he upholds no social hierarchy, advocates re-marriage of widows in certain situations, and gives the right of inheritance to daughters in the absence of male heirs. His ideal Sikh state is ruled by an autocrat who is a devout Sikh. There is a good deal of emphasis on justice and welfare of the poor and the indigent. The Sikh 'Maharaja' or 'Padshah' should work in the interest of the Khalsa and the Sikh faith. In its main features, the ideal Sikh state resembles the Mughal state more than the state of Maharaja Ranjit Singh. It functions in a manner that reinforces differentiation in the Sikh social order on the basis of the differential in the economic means of its various sections and their social prestige. On the whole, the author's conception of the Sikh social order is a compromise between Sikh ideology and empirical realities. The ideal social order is not totally egalitarian but it is more egalitarian than the Sikh social order of the time of Sikh Raj.

The last essay on Sikh Raj and Sikh social order is based on the contemporary evidence of the Gurbilas literature, the *Var* of Gurdas, Rahitnamas, the chronicles in Persian and Gurmukhi, and the early British writers. What emerges from this evidence is the predominance of the Khalsa Singhs in the Sikh community, their distinct identity, importance of the ideas of Guru Granth and Guru Panth, claims of some Sodhis and Bedis to be *gurūs*, equation of the *Ādi Granth* with Guru Granth, veneration for the *Dasam Granth*, belief in One God combined with other entities at different levels and for different purposes, the Gurdwara as by far the most important religious institution of the Sikhs, pilgrimage to Sikh sacred places, limited role of Brahmans in Sikh ceremonies and rites, commensality among the four castes, traditional patterns of matrimony, social differentiation based on the varying economic means, and the extension of state patronage to all religious communities with a preference for the Sikhs.

Part 1

GURU NANAK'S IDEAS AND ATTITUDES

1

The Experience at Sultanpur

For over five hundred years, the town of Sultanpur has been associated with the life of Guru Nanak. Traditions regarding his stay in this town are unquestionably early and strong. Though Bhai Gurdas does not refer to Guru Nanak's residence in Sultanpur, he does refer to Daulat Khan Lodhi as a disciple of the Guru, which would indicate that Bhai Gurdas simply assumed that Guru Nanak had stayed in Sultanpur. It was a fact of common knowledge.[1]

Indeed, the town was associated with an important phase of Guru Nanak's life by the contemporaries of Bhai Gurdas. In the *Purātan Janamsākhī,* for instance, a good deal of attention is given to Guru Nanak's stay in Sultanpur. His brother-in-law, Jai Ram, was the steward (*modī*) of Daulat Khan Lodi. On Jai Ram's recommendation and request, Guru Nanak was given employment by Daulat Khan. The *Purātan* tradition refers to Guru Nanak's simple life at Sultanpur and to his charities; it refers also to his life of devotion to God. Much more important than these is Guru Nanak's ascension to the Divine Presence where the nectar of God's Name (*amrit*) is given to him and he is asked to return to the world for the propagation of the Divine Name. [2]

An account of Guru Nanak's stay in Sultanpur is given also by Sodhi Miharban, Guru Arjan's nephew, in the *Pothī Sachkhand.* The meeting of Guru Nanak with God is presented as the culmination of a spiritual crisis and the nature of the resolution of this crisis is also indicated. After this experience, Guru Nanak appeared to be a changed man and people asked him about his new religion. He replied, 'There is neither Hindu nor Musalman

– whose path should I follow? God is neither Hindu nor Musalman and the path which I follow is God's'. In both the *Purātan* tradition and the *Pothī Sachkhand* Guru Nanak's triumph in his contest with the representatives of Islam is given in some detail.[3] This evidence carries the implication that Guru Nanak's experience at Sultanpur was of crucial significance for his later life. It resulted in his conviction that he had been called to proclaim divine truth to the world. Thus, at Sultanpur he made the discovery of those ideals to which he would later give utterance and practical expression.

To understand the full significance of Sultanpur in the life of Guru Nanak we have to turn to the context in which his experience of 'illumination' took place. In the last decade of the fifteenth century, when Guru Nanak lived in Sultanpur as an employee of the Afghan administrator of that area, there was nothing exceptional about a Khatri of the Punjab accepting service under the contemporary administration. In fact many a Khatri of the Punjab had learnt Persian with an eye on government service.[4] The fact that Guru Nanak was regarded as competent for service must be seen in relation to his early education. In spite of the conventional image of Nanak as a young man who refused to learn anything from either a *pandit* or a *mullā*, it may be suggested that his teachers performed their task well and Guru Nanak improved upon their instruction through his own genius. It may be safely assumed that before he came to Sultanpur, he was an educated young man according to the ideas of his time. [5]

There are frequent references in Guru Nanak's compositions to one or other aspect of government or administration: the court, the throne, the crown, the army, palaces, royal canopy, elephants, armour, cavalry, trumpets, salary, mint, taxes, and grants of revenue-free land, for example. In fact the entire governmental structure is covered by the phrases used by Guru Nanak in one context or another: *sultān, hukm* or *amr, wazīr, dīwān, nā'ib, umarā, khān, malik, shiqdār, qāzī, chaudharī, muqaddam,* among others.[6] We need not insist that this familiarity with contemporary government and administration inevitably resulted from his life in Sultanpur, but his preoccupation with the details of administration is clear and much of this experience would have been acquired at Sultanpur. Just as his earlier experience would certainly have familiarized him with the *patwārī*, the *chaudharī* and the *muqaddam*, his experience of Sultanpur was bound to bring the *shiqdār* and the *qāzī* within the range of his personal observation.

Indeed we can appreciate the justness of this inference if we keep in mind the administration of the Lodhis. The highest official in the primary unit of administration was the *shiqdār*, and this office was generally entrusted to an Afghan noble with the title of *khān* or *malik*. He held quite substantial power in his hands and commanded a considerable number of troops. In his personal life he tried to imitate the ruler.[7] We may be sure that the *shiqdār* of Sultanpur was an important administrator. Indeed, when we know that this office was held by Daulat Khan Lodhi, we need not entertain any doubt about his importance. Daulat Khan's father, Tatar Khan, had been among the most important governors of Sultan Bahlol Lodhi, holding in his charge the territories of Lahore, Dipalpur and Sirhind. He was killed in a battle against Prince Nizam (later, Sikandar Lodhi) in the 1480s and his son Daulat Khan was given the charge of Sultanpur. Daulat Khan's importance is indicated also by the fact that soon after 1500 he was made the governor of Lahore by Sikandar Lodhi.

It can be safely assumed that Daulat Khan Lodhi at Sultanpur was assisted by important officials such as the *'āmil* or the *amīn*, the *qānūngo*, and professional writers (*navīsandas*). The department of justice would be represented by the *qāzī*, assisted by an expounder of the law (*muftī*). They were representatives also of Muslim orthodoxy, paid by the state through grants of revenue-free land. On the whole, at Sultanpur Guru Nanak could have acquired first-hand knowledge of Lodhi administration at the regional level. Sultanpur in those days was on the highway between Lahore and Delhi, and Guru Nanak is most likely to have observed the caravans of trade and Afghan troops passing through the town.

The importance of Sultanpur as a town with a considerable Muslim population must be taken into account to appreciate the significance of Guru Nanak's experience. He had come in contact with a few Muslims earlier but here for the first time he could meet the learned and also probably the mystics of Islam. With his inclination towards religion, he would certainly have taken interest in the religious beliefs and practices of the residents of Sultanpur and would have met the leaders of religious opinion. In his compositions, Guru Nanak reveals great familiarity with Islam in its orthodox and Sūfi forms. These compositions cannot be related literally to his experience at Sultanpur, but it is quite certain that his deep understanding of contemporary Islam had much to do with his life there.

Guru Nanak had come to the town of Sultanpur with a background marked by spiritual searching. His association with itinerant *sādhs* and *sants* around his village (Nankana Sahib in the present district of Sheikhupura in Pakistan) had been perhaps the richest experience of his early life. This experience had resulted in serious yearning after truth. With this background, his contact with Muslim beliefs and practices in Sultanpur comes to have an importance of its own. Before that time his dissatisfaction related chiefly to contemporary forms of Hindu belief and practice. But at Sultanpur he found Islam too wanting in what he was looking for.

Coming after his contact with contemporary Islam, Guru Nanak's 'enlightenment' at Sultanpur is indeed of utmost significance. In his later life he appears to have believed that he had discovered a path for himself, a path which he was anxious to show to others as well. Guru Nanak's mission was interpreted by his followers as transcending all previous dispensations, including the Indic and the Islamic. There is enough justification for this interpretation in the works of Guru Nanak. Transcendence was built into Guru Nanak's discovery of the truth for himself at Sultanpur after he had come to know the Islamic and the Indic systems.

NOTES

1. Bhai Gurdas, *Vārān Bhāī Gurdās*, ed., Giani Hazara Singh, Amritsar: Khalsa Samachar, 1962, Vār 1: pauṛī 13.
2. *Purālan Janam Sākhī Sri Gurū Nānak Dev Jī*, ed., Bhai Vir Singh, New Delhi: Bhai Vir Sahit Sadan, 1999, pp. 37, 38, 39, 40.

3. *Janam Sākhī Sri Gurū Nānak Dev Jī*, eds. Kirpal Singh and Shamsher Singh Ashok, Amritsar: Khalsa College, 1962, p. 93.
4. J.S. Grewal, *Guru Nanak in History*, Chandigarh: Panjab University, 1969, pp. 29-30.
5. *Janam Sākhī Sri Gurū Nānak Dev Jī*, eds. Piar Singh, Amritsar: Guru Nanak Dev University, 1974, pp. 33, 34, 35, 41. Incidently, in the *B40 Janamsākhī*, Jai Ram refers to Nanak as a well educated person.
6. Grewal, *Guru Nanak in History*, p. 147.
7. Ibid., pp. 24-5.

2

Bābarbāṇī

Only four *shabads* of Guru Nanak are generally regarded as Bābarbāṇī: Asa 39, starting with '*khurāsān khasmāṇā kiā*'; Asa Ashtpadi 11, starting with '*jin sir sohan pattiān*'; Asa Ashtpadi 12, starting with '*kahā su khel tabelā*'; Tilang 5, starting with '*jaisī mai āvai khasm kī bāṇī*'. These *shabads* contain no more than seventy-one lines, but their significance is crucial.

Bābarbāṇī figures in the Janamsākhīs. The *Purātan Janamsākhī*, for example, refers to Baba Nanak's visit to Saidpur at a time when the Pathans of the town were preoccupied with the celebration of weddings. They refused to give food to the hungry *faqīrs* accompanying Baba Nanak. Annoyed with their indifference, he recited the Tilang *shabad* as a prophecy of doom. A Brahman of the town brought a tray of fruit and requested Baba Nanak to withdraw his curse. He was told that the utterance could not be withdrawn, but he could save himself and his family by going to a particular place about 12 *kos* from the town. On the following day Babur attacked Saidpur, and all that was prophesied now came to pass. Hindus and Muslims were massacred even in the villages around.

Baba Nanak and Mardana were among the people made captive. Mir Khan, the Mughal, ordered them to march along with others. He saw that the burden which the Baba carried did not touch his head; the horse that Mardana was supposed to lead by the bridle was following him on its own. On hearing this report Babur remarked that he should not have sacked the town of such *faqīrs*. When the captives were asked to grind corn, the grindstone moved without its handle being touched by the Baba. When Babur came to witness all this, Baba Nanak uttered the Asa

Ashtpadi 11. At the end of this recitation, Babur seems to have asked for a miracle, and Baba Nanak sang another *shabad* (not in the *Guru Granth Sahib*).

When Baba Nanak expressed surprise at what had happened, Mardana remarked that it happened in accordance with the Baba's *bhāṇā.* Then Baba Nanak sang the Asa Ashtpadi 12. The Asa 39 *shabad* does not figure in the *Purātan Janamsākhī.*[1]

Teja Singh places Ashtpadi and Tilang *shabads* in 1521 as the year of Babur's attack on Eminabad (Saidpur).[2] Sahib Singh dates all the four *shabads* to 1521.[3] The inference is based on the assumption that 'Sammat 1578' is referred to in the Tilang *shabad.* W.H. McLeod has argued, however, that the Bābarbāṇī verses cannot be associated with a specific event like the sack of Saidpur. Read independently of the Janamsākhīs they do not necessarily point to his presence at the sack of Saidpur. The assumption that one of the *shabads* is addressed to Bhai Lalo, a carpenter of Saidpur, is not necessarily correct. Lalo as a person appears only in the later Janamsākhīs. The initial meaning of Lalo ('O beloved') was a common form of poetic address, and could easily be changed into a proper noun after the story of Bhai Lalo and Malik Bhago had become current.[4]

The Asa Ashtpadis appear to refer to the invasions of 1524 and 1525-26. Saidpur is not mentioned and the descriptions hardly accord with the limited nature of the earlier excursion which, according to Beveridge, was undertaken in 1520. Indeed the implied destruction of Lodhi authority, together with the nature of the warfare described, plainly suggest that these two *ashtpadis* were composed after 1526. They were not prompted by a single event but rather by the series of events that culminated in the overthrow of the Lodhi dynasty. The remaining two *shabads* could also come after the fall of the Lodhis, since in these too there is the theme of God's *hukam* which is common to all the four *shabads.* McLeod comes to the conclusion that all the four *shabads* were probably composed after 1526 in response to the repeated invasions, rather than in response to any single event within the series. If one *ashtpadi* appears to suggest a specific event, it could be the capture of Lahore in 1524 rather than the sack of Saidpur in 1520. Guru Nanak must have personally witnessed devastation caused by Babur's troops. In his description of agony and destruction, there is a vividness and a depth of feeling which can be explained only as expression of a direct, personal experience.[5]

In the *Purātan Janamsākhī*, Baba Nanak's annoyance with the Pathans of Saidpur who are indifferent to the hungry *faqīrs* is the cause of destruction. The curse of the Mahan Purkh was effective because God listens to the *faqīrs* who are devoted to Him. He listens to their wishes, and acts accordingly. The compiler goes on to describe the characteristics of true *faqīrs* and to advise the householders to serve those who don the garb of *faqīrs*, irrespective of their caste and with total disregard to whether they are Hindu or Muslim, or even thieves and robbers. This could include the *faqīrs* who professed to be the followers of Guru Nanak. [6]

The *shabad* recited by Baba Nanak after the first *ashtpadi* induced Babur to fall at the Baba's feet. He asks Baba Nanak to accept something from him as a token of his submission. The Baba asks Babur to release the captives. After the second *ashtpadi* there is no comment. The *ashtpadi* itself contains several general statements of great moral significance. The person who is led astray is first shorn of his goodness. Much later, Mardana asks Baba Nanak why innocent people had been killed along with the guilty. The Baba asks him to go and sleep under a particular tree. There, when an ant bites him, he kills several others too without being aware of it.[7] On the whole, the import of the Bābarbāṇī verses in the Janamsākhī is religious and moral.

Teja Singh sees the Asa 39 *shabad* as a denunciation of the Afghans.[8] In the two *ashtpadis*, the import is moral as well as political: to forget God is to invite misfortune; nations are made or unmade not by armies or the lack thereof but by moral strength or the lack thereof. These *shabads* also show that Guru Nanak was equally sympathetic to Hindus and Muslims. The rulers of the day ignored their essential duty to protect their subjects and indulged in luxury and sensuality.[9] Teja Singh assumes that the Tilang *shabad* is addressed to Bhai Lalo. The Mughal soldiers make no distinction between Hindu and Muslim in their harsh treatment of women and the violation of their honour. The reference to 78 and 97 is taken to refer to the coming of Babur in 1521 and the expulsion of Humayun in 1540. Made in the time of

Babur, it is a bold statement. Finally, there is the moral import about heedlessness.[10]

Sahib Singh looks upon the use of 'dogs' as a reference to the Mughals who have destroyed the best of men and women. However, the Mughals are the instrument of God for punishing those who had forgotten Him in their life of luxury in India.[11] In the first *ashtpadi,* God reveals His ordinance in the dramatic change that comes about in the fortunes of the beautiful women of the ruling class.[12] In the second *ashtpadi,* the men of the ruling class suffer the same fate, reinforcing the idea that God can create and destroy in a trice. The Afghan rulers asked many *pīrs* to use their spiritual powers in their favour but they could do nothing. The women who suffered were both Muslim and Hindu. A part of their plight was widowhood. God's will is operative in the world, and human beings receive reward or punishment in accordance with their deeds.[13]

The Tilang *shabad* according to Sahib Singh was addressed to Bhai Lalo. Babur is forcibly taking over India as a 'bride'. The metaphor of marriage is used actually to depict rape and slaughter. Hindu and Muslim women of all castes and classes are ill-treated. The *shabad* demonstrates the truth that God has engaged all mankind in the pursuit of *māyā*: He alone is detached and watches the play. India would never forget the justice of God as demonstrated in Saidpur. Sahib Singh looks upon 78 and 97 as marking the advent of the Mughals and the expulsion of Humayun from India on the assumption that the reference is to Sammat 1578 and 1597. Even in the midst of these changes the best thing to do is to continue to sing God's praises.[14] The significance of the Bābarbāṇī is mainly religious and moral but also somewhat political.

According to W.H. McLeod, the 'rulers' and 'princes' of the *ashtpadis* were the Lodhis. The change from Afghan to Mughal rule is the basic historical theme, a change that expresses for Guru Nanak a religious truth. It is an illustration of the truth that God's justice cannot be ignored, that the divine order (*hukam*) cannot be defied, that unrighteousness will be punished.[15] Indeed, the pursuit of salvation is mankind's paramount concern; Guru Nanak's comment on contemporary conditions relates almost exclusively to attitudes, customs, and institutions which obstruct this quest. Political, social, and economic issues find expression in his works only in so far as they relate to the pattern of religious salvation which he upheld, or to contemporary patterns which he rejected. Details relating to such issues can be gleaned from his works; the effect of his teachings extends far beyond a recognizable religious context.

Nanak was not uninterested in human joy or suffering. The Bābarbāṇī verses make it abundantly clear that the wretchedness inflicted by Babur's army had evoked deep compassion in him. There remained, however, the conviction of a condition transcending the misery and decay of this life. Guru Nanak's concern was accordingly for salvation, for personal salvation and for the salvation of others.[16]

There is no doubt that Babur's invasions called for comment as the most important political events in the life of Guru Nanak.[17] For a proper appreciation of Guru Nanak's response to the events in question, the Bābarbāṇī verses must be considered together.[18]

Guru Nanak mentions the suffering caused by war. In Tilang, for instance, occur the following lines, believed to have been addressed to Lalo:

> With the marriage-party of sin, he has come from Kabul and demands charity (*dān*) by force. Honour and morality have hid themselves and falsehood struts in the van. Not the *qāzīs* or *brahmans* but Satan presides over the rites of marriage.

In these lines, the primary emphasis is on rape, committed obviously by the Mughal troops. In Asa Ashtpadis also, Guru Nanak refers to this unfortunate aspect of war: 'The robes of some are torn from head to foot'. Or, 'they have been carried away, having been dishonoured'. Guru Nanak also observes that rape was committed indiscriminately. In Tilang, the reference to this is indirect: Muslim women invoke God in despair and the Hindu women of all castes find themselves in a similar plight. In Asa Ashtpadis the women who suffered are specifically referred to as many a Hinduāṇī, Turkāṇī, Bhattiāṇī and Thākurāṇī.

The suffering caused by war was obviously not confined to rape. It involved death and murder. In Tilang, the reference to 'blood' is general: 'the paeans of murder are sung and the saffron-mark is of blood'. In Asa Ashtpadis there is a reference to those who died in the field of battle and left wailing widows behind. Many buildings, including strong mansions, were burnt and even 'princes' were cut into pieces and rolled in the dust. Guru Nanak was particularly pained to see the suffering of the weak, presumably ordinary people who had little to do with politics and war: 'If the mighty destroy only one another, one is not grieved. But if a mighty lion falls upon a herd of cows, the master is answerable.' Indeed, Guru Nanak asks God, 'At this suffering and lamentation, did not You feel compassion?' With a firm belief in God's omnipotence, Guru Nanak sees the will of God behind these events. This is evident from some of the verses in the Bābarbāṇī. In Asa Ashtpadi there is the line, 'You alone join and You alone separate – such is Your greatness.' And there is also the line, 'This world is Yours; You alone are the Master.'

In a single moment God creates and destroys. If He Himself acts and causes others to act, to whom can one complain? If suffering and happiness are dispensed by Him, to whom can one go and cry? His is the command that prevails and men receive what is ordained by Him. 'It is for Him to bestow greatness or to chastise.'

Obviously, Guru Nanak's question about human suffering is addressed to God who is omnipotent. On this belief, Guru Nanak exposes the pretention of many a *pīr* to miraculous powers. 'No Mughal became blind and none performed a miracle.'

The pursuit of temporal power and riches at the cost of righteousness brings its nemesis.

> Where are those sports, those stables and horses, those trumpets and clarions? Where are those sword-belts, those chariots and those scarlet tunics? Where are those mirrors and those handsome faces? They are nowhere to be seen.
> Where are those houses, mansions and palaces? and those seraglios? Where are those soft beds and those beautiful women whose sight banished sleep? Where are those betels and those *harams*? They have vanished.

Guru Nanak's explanation of this change is retribution for the blind pursuit of wealth and riches. Because of wealth, it went hard with many; wealth cannot be amassed without sins and it does not accompany the dead. Indeed, 'He who is misled is first deprived of his virtue!'

It is clear that Guru Nanak's response to war, and to suffering caused by war, is an expression of his anguish, but there is a moral dimension also to the situation. There is no outright condemnation of the conqueror or the conquered, but there is no appreciation for either. Guru Nanak's moral judgement is not confined to the rulers:

> They who wore beautiful tresses and vermillion in the parting of their hair, their locks have been shorn and dust rises to their necks. They used to dwell in 'palaces' and now they cannot find even a place to sit. When they were married, their spouses adorned their sides; they came in palanquins, adorned with ivory bangles; they were ceremoniously received, amidst glittering fans, and immense money was bestowed upon them; they relished nuts and dates and enjoyed their conjugal beds. But now on their necks are halters, and broken are their strings of pearls.

Guru Nanak observes that wealth and beauty which served as the source of pleasures have now become their enemy: they have been dishonoured. He goes on to add 'Had they paused to think in time, they could have escaped punishment.'

The senseless pursuit of pleasure by the rulers is contrasted with the helplessness of the 'princes' after Babur's ascendancy. In their common plight, Muslim and Hindu women could not attend to *namāz* or *pūjā*; the Hindu women were unable to perform their routine observances. They had never remembered Ram and now they cannot invoke Khudā. Their heedlessness has brought about this retribution. Thus, all the suffering involved in war was not wholly undeserved. For all his sympathy with the sufferers, Guru Nanak does not regard them all as completely 'innocent'.

As we have seen, the Janamsākhīs were concerned with the moral and religious import of the Bābarbāṇī verses. Teja Singh underscores the political dimension more than the moral and the religious. Sahib Singh gives greater importance to the religious and moral dimensions than to the political. W.H. McLeod too gives primacy to Guru Nanak's religious concern.

Like the other compositions of Guru Nanak, the Bābarbāṇī verses reflect the socio-economic environment of Guru Nanak. The lion is mentioned as falling upon the herd of cows. Dogs, which could be domesticated or relatively wild, were a more familiar sight. The horses and elephants kept in stables were surely domesticated, and used in war and peace. There are products of nature which reflect material culture, like gems, pearls, and gold. There are artifacts used in war, like guns and swords. There are palaces, mansions, and tents. Trumpets and clarions indicate the high status of those for whom they are played. There are *sarāis* for travellers to stay in. There are articles of food which indicate luxury, like dry fruits and betel leaf. There are things associated with women, like vermillion, *hidolī*, ivory bangles, fans studded with bright objects, *ārsī* used as a mirror, saffron, and the bridal bed. On the whole, the salient features of the life of the ruling class are well depicted.

The society of the times in reflected in the Bābarbāṇī. Several categories of people are mentioned. There are Muslims and Hindus, Mughals and Pathans, Bhattis and Thakurs. There are others who belong to the lower castes and people who are still lower in social scale. Marriage parties accompany bridegrooms, and brides are given in charity through ceremonies performed by Brahmans. The Qāzīs perform *nikāh*. Polygamy is a feature of the *harams* of the affluent individuals. There are women in the *harams* who serve betel nuts. Some women veil themselves in public and travel in palanquins. The married women adorn their heads with vermillion in the parting of the hair. Songs are sung at the time of marriage. Saffron is used for putting auspicious marks. After the wedding, brides are carried to their husband's home in palanquins, and lakhs of rupees are spent on ceremonials for their sake. They wear pearl necklaces and ivory bangles. Muslim women pray and Hindu women perform *pūjā*. There are *pīrs* who claim to possess suprnatural powers. It was not uncommon to send written messages. The paper carrying the sad news of a death was torn at one end. The dead were cremated, and mourning was observed.

The political comment is no less important. Guru Nanak refers to the rulers who had lost all sense of duty in the pursuit of pleasure. They lived in palaces, kept large *harams*, owned stables of horses, commanded troops, and amassed wealth at the cost of others. There was contest for power between the Mughals and the Afghans. In a decisive battle, the Mughals used guns and the Afghans used elephants. A large number of men were killed in the battle. The *pīrs* who prayed on behalf of the Afghans were utterly ineffective: no harm came to the Mughals. The writ of Babur began to run. Before this decisive battle, however, Babur raided Hindustan and his soldiers massacred unarmed men and raped women of all castes and classes, irrespective of their religious affiliation. Men and women were made captive, presumably to be sold as slaves. Guru Nanak has no sympathy with either the Mughals or the Afghans. The former's atrocities were matched by the negligence of the latter. Elsewhere in the *bāṇī* of Guru Nanak, contemporary rule is denounced as discriminatory, unjust, and oppressive.[19] Therefore, the question of Guru Nanak's sympathy with the Afghans does not arise. Incidentally, the view presented by the *Purātan Janamsākhī* that Guru Nanak's annoyance with the Pathans of Saidpur for their preoccupation with merry-making in weddings to the point of ignoring the *faqīrs* was the reason for their punishment by Babur, is a specific application of the general attitude of Guru Nanak towards the Afghan rule. The political comment made by Guru Nanak is important in itself.

This does not mean, however, that the moral or religious dimension of the *Bābarbāṇī* is less important. These dimensions are quite obvious. Babur is God's instrument for punishment. Whoever arrogates greatness to himself and indulges in pleasures is only a grain-picking ant in the eyes of God. The Lord exalts and casts down as He likes. If men contemplate God beforehand they might escape punishment. The Hindus who never called on Ram are not allowed now to invoke *Khuda*. Those whom the Creator casts off are deprived of their goodness first. God alone can join and unjoin, such is His power. The real achievement is to die to one's own self in order to live by the holy Name. Wealth and beauty, used for indulgence in sensual pleasure, turn out to be enemies. Wealth is not amassed without sin, and it does not go with anyone. All happens as God wills. His is the world and He is the Master; He can make and unmake in a moment.

Suffering and joy lie in His will. His Ordinance operates in the universe, and one receives what is ordained. He sits apart and dispenses justice which is always true. Guru Nanak is deeply moved by the agony and suffering of the people, especially of those who appeared to suffer for no fault of theirs. Guru Nanak's faith in God, and in His justice, enable him to reconcile himself to this mystery.

Political comment is not diluted by the declaration of faith in God. The prophecy about political change is not easy to interpret in specific terms.[20] Faith in God enables Guru Nanak to face change in the world about him. His moral, political, theological, and spiritual concerns are not mutually exclusive.

NOTES

1. *Purātan Janam Sākhī Sri Gurū Nānak Dev Jī*, ed. Bhai Vir Singh, New Delhi: Bhai Vir Singh Sahit Sadan, 1999 (rpt.), pp. 116-25.
2. *Shabdārth Sri Gurū Granth Sāhib Jī*, 4 vols, Amritsar: Shiromani Gurdwara Prabandhak Committtee (standard pagination of *Ādi Sri Gurū Granth Sāhib*), notes on pp. 360, 417, 722.
3. Sahib Singh, *Sri Gurū Granth Sāhib Darpan*, 10 vols., Jalandhar: Raj Publishers, notes in vol. III, pp. 77, 376; vol. V, p. 314.
4. W.H. McLeod, *Gurū Nānak and the Sikh Religion*, New Delhi: Oxford India Paperback, 2003 (third impression), pp. 7, 86-7. Gurbachan Singh Talib suggests that 'Lalo' may refer to God: *Sri Guru Granth Sahib in English Translation*, Patiala: Punjabi University, vol. II, p. 1502, note.
5. Ibid., pp. 135-6, 137-8.
6. *Purātan Janam Sākhī*, pp. 117-18. Curiously, the followers of Guru Nanak in the garb of *faqīrs* could be Udasis.
7. Ibid., pp. 123, 124, 125, 127, 128-29 n. The moral import of the Mardana episode is not clear. Is punishment a mystery, or does it raise the question of identification with a whole class or a group?
8. *Shabdārth*, p. 360 n 28.
9. Ibid., general note on page 417 and n 15.
10. Ibid., general note on page 723 and note 35; p. 723 nn 4,5.
11. Sahib Singh, *Sri Guru Granth Sahib Darpan*, vol III, pp. 76-8.
12. Ibid., pp. 372-4.
13. Ibid., pp. 374-8.
14. Ibid., vol. V, pp. 313-16.
15. W.H. McLeod, *Gurū Nānak and the Sikh Religion*, pp. 135-6.

16. Ibid., pp. 162-3.
17. J.S. Grewal, *Guru Nanak in History,* Chandigarh: Panjab University, 1969, p. 159.
18. Ibid., pp. 159-65.
19. Ibid., pp. 153-9.
20. The reference to '78' and '97' in Tilang is generally interpreted as the coming of Babur in 1521 and the expulsion of Humayun from India in 1540. However, none of these years can be taken literally as marking the two events. What is even more important, the easy assumption that Guru Nanak could forecast the future does not accord with his own belief in the inscrutability of God's will in these very verses.

3

Islam in Service of the State

Although the influence of Islam on Guru Nanak has been emphasized by a number of writers, his attitude towards the Islam of his day has not been seriously studied. Contrary to the impression of some scholars,[1] Guru Nanak's familiarity with Islam was by no means superficial or second-hand. One of his verses contains reference to Allah and his attributes, to prophets and *pīrs,* and to the various categories of religious men among Muslims. Even a hundred poets cannot adequately describe God's greatness. Salvation cannot be ensured by the fact of belonging to a particular creed. Made actually in response to some of the beliefs current among the contemporary Muslims, this entire statement carries the import that God's grace cannot be bestowed on Muslims simply because of their faith in the Prophet; God's grace is not necessarily denied to those who are not Muslim. God does not consult anyone when he creates or destroys, when he gives or takes away; only He knows His power, and He does what He likes; He sees everyone with kindness but He bestows His grace on whomever He likes. Here, Allah is redefined in Islamic terminology but in terms of Guru Nanak's own conception of God.[2]

Guru Nanak's attitude towards the *Qur'ān,* which was regarded as the last and final revelation by contemporary Muslims, is not without significance. At one place, the *Qur'ān* is one of the books (*katebā*) due to God's *qudrat* which is all-embracing.[3] We can argue that here the veracity of the *Qur'ān* is clearly recognized but we have to admit that no particular importance is being attached to it; the *Qur'ān* is only one item among thousands which testify to God's *qudrat.* In another verse, it is in accordance with God's will that a person reads the *Qur'ān* and becomes a *mullā* or a *shaikh*.[4] But whatever anyone is or does, is so or does so in accordance with God's will. This verse occurs in the context of the universal operation of God's *hukam*. The safest inference that we can draw from these verses is that even if Guru Nanak did not question the veracity of the *Qur'ān* he did not give it an exclusive veractity. In fact, he explicitly states that the *Qur'ān*, like the Veda, does not lead one to the realization of the Only True God.[5] Guru Nanak's attitude towards the prophet of Islam is quite similar. Muhammad was a *paighambar* but not the seal of the prophets. On this last point his difference with the orthodox Muslims of his day is fundamental.

There is one belief, however, which Guru Nanak broadly shares with his contemporary Muslims: the belief in the One, Only God. As he does not believe that their faith in their God is genuine, however, their conception of God is not the same as his own. For instance, if one really believes that God alone is eternal, one cannot treat worldly things as if they are to last for ever.[6] The *jogī* and the *mullā* tend to stick to their places as if they were permanent.[7] Both the *jogī* and the *mullā* forget that God alone is everlasting. The upholders of the *sharī'at* do not actually offer genuine submission and devotion to God.[8] The *qāzīs*, who comment profusely on the *Qur'ān*, know nothing of the mystery of God's creation (though they profess to know).[9] The *shaikh* as well as the *qāzī* is bound to remain chained to the wheel of transmigration if he does not realize that only virtuous deeds are rewarded.[10]

On the criteria of genuine faith and real virtue, Guru Nanak castigates his contemporary Muslims and invites them to follow the right path. The *qāzī* speaks falsehood and eats unlawfully earned food: but only he who dies to self through the Guru's grace is the real *qāzī*; only he who cleanses his heart is the real *dānishmand* and a real Musalman.[11] Talk by itself does not lead to Paradise; ill-gotten food does not become lawful by being spiced; falsehood begets nothing but falsehood. Instead of the five daily prayers, the real Musalman appropriates truth, earns lawfully, wishes well of all, cleanses his mind of all extraneous thoughts by way of adoring the Lord; his virtuous conduct is his confession of faith (*kalma*).[12]

Guru Nanak's criticism of the respresentatives of Islam in these verses is not merely a criticism of external forms (as it is generally but wrongly believed). Those forms are surely set aside. What is more important to realize, Guru Nanak invites his Muslim audience to adopt new values and new ethics. The metaphorical use of the mosque, the prayer carpet, the *qāzī*, the *Qur'ān*, the *sunnat*, fasting, the *ka'bah*, the *pīr*, the *kalma*, *namāz*, and the *tasbīh* in his verses should not so overwhelm us as to lead us astray from its positive import. Guru Nanak is obviously insisting on the adoption of *mihr*, *sidq*, *haqq* and *halāl*, *saram*, *sīl*, *karanī*, *sachch*, *karam* and *lāj*.[13] And these are the ethical values he was offering to all his contemporaries, irrespective of their creed. This may be an obvious point, but it is of crucial importance for our understanding of Guru Nanak's attitude towards Islam.

Guru Nanak's offer is not confined to matters of virtuous conduct. It embraces doctrines as well. The *qāzī* and the *shaikh* both need the True Guru for salvation,[14] and the Word and the Truth as well.[15] The *qāzī* is he who adopts the Name.[16] Here, the True Guru, the Word (*shabad*), the Truth (*sachch*), and the Name (*nām*), four of Guru Nanak's basic concepts, are offered as the means of genuine faith and liberation.

Contrary to the generally held impression that Guru Nanak had great appreciation for the Sūfis and their interior faith as opposed to the external piety of the '*ulamā*, we find him speaking of the *shaikh* and the *mullā* in the same strain. Occasionally, however, he appears to give preference to the *dīn* of the *walīs* over the practices of the orthodox. He refers to *aul-dīn* (the way of the *auliyā*) and appreciates the indifference of the Sūfis to earthly possessions, their absolute trust in God, willing acceptance of His will, clear recognition of His omnipotence, and compassion for all.[17] Moreover, these ideas are expressed in terms that would be immediately understandable to the Sūfis. This passage embodies an invitation to genuine faith which is extended to the *shaikh* in Sūfi terms. At any rate, Guru Nanak specifically disapproves of the identification of the *shaikhs* with the government of the times.[18] He denounces their dependence upon the state on moral grounds.

Guru Nanak refers to the tax imposed on gods by the government established by the followers of Islam, and the *shaikhs* are mentioned as the chief representatives of Islam.[19] Elsewhere his denunciation of the contemporary government and administration is quite unequivocal.[20] We may infer, therefore, that the identification of the *shaikhs* with the government of the times is not appreciated by Guru Nanak.

The dependence of the Sūfis upon government grants is clearly condemned by Guru Nanak in a passage which has passed unnoticed. There is direct reference to a common practice of the *shaikhs* of the times, the practice of authorizing their disciples to initiate others into the Sūfi path. Guru Nanak denounces the presumption of these *pīrs* that they have realized God. Then there is indirect reference to their subsistence on the *madad-i ma'āsh* grants of land given by earthly rulers, in contrast with Guru Nanak's complete dependence upon the true Name which he has received from the Divine Court. [21] Thus, not only the *'ulamā* but also the Sūfi *shaikhs* were criticised by Guru Nanak for their association with and dependence on the state.

NOTES

1. Cf. W.H. McLeod, *Gurū Nānak and the Sikh Religion*, London: Clarendon Press, 1968, pp. 158, 159. Also, W.H. McLeod, 'The Influence of Islam upon the thought of Guru Nanak', *History of Religions*, vol. VII. No. 4 (May 1968), pp. 302-16.
2. *Ādi Sri Gurū Granth Sāhib Jī* (Sri Damdami Bir, various printed editions, standard pagination), p. 53.
3. Ibid., p. 464: *Qudrat Ved Purān katebā, qudrat sarb vīchār.*
4. Ibid., p. 145: *Ja tudh bhavey ta paṛhey katebā mullā saikh kahāvey.*.
5. Ibid., p. 1153. Realization of the only God is what matters and not any sectarian garb or practice, or the knowledge of the Vedas or the *Qur'ān.*
6. Ibid., p. 24. One is a true *mullā* or *qāzī* only if one realizes God.
7. Ibid., p. 64. 'The *jogī* sticks to his *āsan* and the *mullā* to his *muqām.*'
8. Ibid., p. 465.
9. Ibid., p. 4.
10. Ibid., p. 1169.
11. Ibid., p. 662.
12. Ibid., p. 141:

    One cannot go to paradise by mere talk. Liberation comes through the appropriation of truth. Unlawful food does not become lawful if you add spices to it. Falsehood begets falsehood. There are five daily prayers, each with its own specific name and time. The first is appropriation of Truth; the second is lawful earning; the third is trust in God; the fourth is right inclination; and the fifth is singing of God's praises. The *kalma* of a Musalman is good conduct. He who is untrue reaps falsehood.

13. Ibid., pp. 140-1:
Kindness is the mosque, and steadfastness is the prayer mat; lawful earning is the *Qur'ān*. Labour with one's hands is *sunnat* and satisfaction with what one receives from God makes one Musalman. Good conduct is the *ka'bah*, Truth is the *pīr*, and grace of God is the *kalma*. Being accepted by one who protects one's honour is the rosary.
14. Ibid., p. 227:
The *qāzī* and the *shaikh* don the dress of *faqīrs*. In search of earthly greatness, they suffer from *haumai*. Death does not spare anyone who does not take refuge in the True Guru.
15. Ibid., pp. 23-4:
Let good actions be your field and the word your seed. Irrigate it regularly with the water of Truth. Be trustful like a farmer. Then you will know the difference between heaven and hell.
16. Ibid., pp. 23-4.
17. Ibid., p. 141:
It is difficult to be a Musalman. Appropriate the path of *walīs* first, and cleanse the mirror of your heart. Die unto yourself while you are alive to follow the path of true submission. Accept what is done by God, recognizing Him and not yourself as the doer. Be merciful towards all human beings. Then you will be a Musalman.
18. Ibid., pp. 1190-1.
19. Ibid., p. 1191:
The Primal Being is called Allah now that the turn of the *shaikhs* has come. Gods and goddesses are taxed: such is now the custom. There is now the pot of water, call for prayers, prayer-mat and prayer; God himself is dressed in blue. The word *miān* is current in every home and the speech of the people has changed. Everywhere is the greeting of *salām* and this is how God is praised. Charity, rosary, and pilgrimage have little reward. I cherish the Name as the source of all honour.
20. J.S. Grewal, *Guru Nanak in History*, Chandigarh: Panjab University, 1979 (2nd edn.), pp. 157-8.
21. *Ādi Sri Gurū Granth Sāhib Jī*, p. 1286:
They who bestow caps on others are crazy; they who receive them obtain no honour. They are like the rat which is too fat to enter the hole and yet attaches a winnowing basket to its tail. They who pray for others themselves die, they also depart for whom prayers are offered.

They who do not recognize God's *hukam*, where will they go? The word is my spring harvest and the True Name is my crop in autumn. I have received a piece of revenue-free land from the court of the Great Master. There are many who sit at the doors of earthly masters; there are innumerable beggars who spend their lives in begging and then depart without honour.

4

Renunciation of the Gorakh Nāthīs

In an early nineteenth century drawing in the Government Museum and Art Gallery, Chandigarh, Guru Nanak is shown absorbed in serious debate with a group of *jogīs*. This dramatic and tense depiction by a well-known artist was meant to serve as an 'illustration' for a Janamsākhī.[1] With or without such illustrations, Guru Nanak's encounters with *jogīs* have remained a favourite theme of Sikh literature for nearly four centuries. This tradition was well established in the time of Bhai Gurdas in whose Vārs we have one of the earliest interpretations of Guru Nanak's attitude towards the *jogīs*.[2]

In the *bāṇī* of Guru Nanak there are several passages which easily could and did serve as the basis of the later tradition. Some of the modern writers too have noticed these passages as significant. It has been noted, for instance, that in the *bāṇī* of Guru Nanak there is frequent use of the terminology of the *jogīs*.[3] It has been also suggested that Guru Nanak was deeply influenced by them.[4] More recently, it has been argued that the *hath-yoga* of the Nāth *jogīs* had come to form an integral part of the synthesis evolved by the *sants* of northern India by the time of Guru Nanak who was much indebted to this Sant tradition.[5] However, Guru Nanak's attitude towards the contemporary beliefs and practices of the *jogīs* has not received the attention it deserves.

The conspicuous presence of *jogīs* in northern India during the time of Guru Nanak may be gathered from some of the references made to them by the contemporaries. Ibn Battuta describes their supranatural feats in the presence of Sultan Muhammad bin Tughluq.[6] In the Sūfi literature of the fourteenth and fifteenth centuries, there are several references to contests of some great *shaikhs* with the *jogīs*. There are also some appreciative references to their ideas and practices.[7] In the Punjab itself, several of the well-known centres of the *jogīs* had come into existence by the late fifteenth and early sixteenth centuries.[8]

The premier *jogī* establishment in the Punjab was the Tilla of Gorakh Nath, and nearly all *jogī* establishments were connected with it. These establishments were not the only monastic orders in the country but they were perhaps the best organized. Succession to the *gaddī* at the Tilla and elsewhere was regular and quite formal; it had to be recognized by all the heads of the various establishments. The strength of the *jogī* order in the Punjab appears to have consisted partly at least in its organization. Thus, the movement initiated by Gorakh Nath several centuries earlier had come to acquire momentum by about 1500, and individual *jogīs* were popular amongst the common people. Perhaps they were also feared because of the common belief that they possessed supranatural powers.

The *jogīs* of the Gorakh Nāthī order presented a striking appearance. Those who went through the last stage of initiation had their ear-lobes pierced for large rings (*mundrās*). They generally used the epithet *nāth* with their names and were commonly called *kanpātās*. They smeared their bodies with ash, wore a loin-cloth and used a particular kind of cloak. They generally carried with them a staff, a begging bowl and the blowing horn called *singī* or *nād*. Some of them stayed in cremation grounds. At their centres, fire was kept constantly burning (*ḍhūṇī*), and they ate from a common *bhandār*. They saluted one another with the epithet *ādes*.

In their religious practices, the *jogīs* attached great importance to preliminary purifications and depended on meditation (*tāṛī*) and the techniques of *abhyāsa* and *prānayāma* for attaining to the state of supreme bliss (*sahaj*) which for them was the ultimate goal. This could be achieved in a *jogī's* lifetime and, consequently, he became *jīvan-muktā* or liberated-in-life. The possession of supranatural powers, or *siddhī*, was regarded as a sign of the *jogī's* perfection. It was believed that he could then become as small or as large as he liked; he could become heavy or light at will; he could walk on the edge of a razor or on the bridge made of a hair; he could walk on water and fly in the air; he could know the minds of others; he could change shape and form; and he could command the natural elements. These powers were generally attributed to the adept among the *jogīs*. Their interest in herbs and medicines too was widely known and they were believed to possess alchemical knowledge.[9] They all believed in the existence of eighty-four *siddhs* and nine *nāths*, the immortal demigods who lived in the Himalayas.

Turning to the *bāṇī* of Guru Nanak, we observe his thorough familiarity with the beliefs and practices of the *jogīs*, a familiarity which could be the result only of personal observation and of contact with some of the representatives of the Gorakh Nāthīs. He refers to their ear-rings (*mundā* or *mundrā*), their loin-cloth (*jangotā*), the ash they used on their bodies (*bhasam, bhabūt*), the cloak (*khinthā*), staff (*dandā*), begging bag (*jholī*) and blowing horn (*singī*). He refers also to their object of concentration (*samyā*), their meditation (*tāṛī*) and their objective of gaining supranatural powers (*siddhī, riddhī*). He was familiar with their medicinal and alchemical interests, their mode of salutation (*ādes*), and with their terminology: *sunya-smādh, anhad shabad, sahaj, mahāras, shivnagrī,* for instance. There are references also to their meal (*bhugat*), joint meals (*bhandār*), and their twelve orders (*bhekh-bārā*). In fact, Guru Nanak appears to know more about the Gorakh Nāthīs than what is known to the present-day students of Nāthism.

At any rate, the number of passages relating to the *jogīs* in the compositions of Guru Nanak is larger than the number of those given to any other religious group of the times. This surely is a measure of his preoccupation with them: it is also a measure of their importance and popularity. The *jogīs* were his most formidable opponents.

Far from being a token of appreciation, Guru Nanak's preoccupation with the *jogīs* is a proof of his differences with them. Almost every passage relating to the *jogīs* contains an explicit or implicit disapproval of their practices. When Guru Nanak uses their terminology, it is only to express his own message in terms which they were believed to understand. Invariably, he makes only a metaphorical use of their concepts.

This is an essential feature of Guru Nanak's attitude towards the *jogīs*. And since this point is of vital importance, we may give a few characteristic examples for illustration. In Rag Dhanasari, God in the beginning (or before the beginning) of time is referred to as Jogī.[10] Similarly in Rag Asa, Guru Nanak refers to the *shabad* as God's revelation and cherishes this truth in terms which can be easily misinterpreted in favour of his appreciation of *jog*.[11] In Rag Parbhati, the *jogī* as well as the *sanyāsī* is presented as following the wrong path.[12] Similarly, practices such as the smearing of the body with ash, begging from door to door, and staying in cremation grounds are condemned as false humility, or a source of pain, or ignorance.[13] Guru Nanak has no sympathy with the *jogī* aim of gaining supranatural powers.[14] In fact real honour with God is any time preferable to the status of being a *siddh* in the eyes of men. [15] For Guru Nanak, the primary objective is to realize the divine presence within oneself by purifying the mind and restraining sensual desires.[16] Similarly, the true begging bowl is the effort to earn honour with God, and the true reward is the gift of the Name (*nām*).[17] True meditation means being really detached.[18] The true *mundrā* is the *shabad* of the Guru and the true cloak is forgiveness; the true *jog* is to accept the will of God.[19] Notwithstanding the use of *jogī* terminology in many a verse, what is being expressed in them is the truth as it was conceived by Guru Nanak. The divinity within man is revealed by the Guru and man recognizes God in a state of supreme bliss.[20]

We may safely conclude that Guru Nanak's differences with the *jogīs* were fundamental, in matters both of belief and of practice. His conception of loving devotion to God as the best form of worship was opposed to the use of psycho-physical techniques of the *jogīs*. Rejecting the idea of God's grace they appeared to be rather presumptuous in their advocacy of self-effort as the sufficient means of liberation. Guru Nanak's ideal of social commitment clashed with the *jogī* ideal of renunciation. Consequently, he had much, but nothing commendable, to say about the followers of Gorakh Nath. Guru Nanak's denunciation of the *jogīs* was in fact a part of his rejection of all ascetic traditions of India which placed renunciation at the centre.

NOTES

1. This drawing is ascribed to a well known hill artist, Ranjha, and is reproduced in J.S. Grewal, *Guru Nanak in History*, Chandigarh: Panjab University, 1969, p. 219.
2. Bhai Gurdas, *Vārān Bhāī Gurdās*, ed. Giani Hazara Singh, Amritsar: Khalsa Samachar, 1962, Vār 1: pauṛīs 28-31, 39-44. These verses reveal Bhai Gurdas's view of the *jogīs* and their encounters with Guru Nanak. The first encounter, at Mount Sumeru, takes place with the *siddh mandalī* of eighty-four *siddhs*, all of Gorakh Nath's stature. They try to win over Guru Nanak to their order by miraculously turning water into precious stones but the Guru prefers his own path of loving devotion over the supranatural powers of *siddh jogīs*. The second encounter is placed at Achal, near Batala in the Gurdaspur District of the Punjab, where at the time of Shivratri festival the *jogīs* dislike Guru Nanak's popularity with the people and feel offended even more when he unmasks their hypocrisy. Bhangar Nath taunts Guru Nanak for his having adopted the life of a householder in preference to that of a renunciant and Nanak in turn chides him for begging from householders. The *jogīs* then use their supranatural powers and turn into ferocious tigers and hissing cobras; they fly in the air and catch the stars. They ask Guru Nanak to show his miraculous powers, but Guru Nanak offers the True Name as his miracle, and the *jogīs* are vanquished in the encounter.

   It may be pointed out that in pauṛī 43, Bhai Gurdas paraphrases a passage from the *bāṇī* of Guru Nanak in which a clear preference is shown for the True Name against the attainment of supranatural powers: *Ādi Sri Gurū Granth Sāhib Jī* (Sri Damdami Bir, various printed editions, standard pagination), p. 147.
3. Sohan Singh, *The Seeker's Path*, Bombay: 1959, p. 78.
4. Sher Singh, *The Philosophy of Sikhism*, Lahore: 1944, p. 103.
5. W.H. McLeod, *Gurū Nānak and the Sikh Religion*, London: Clarendon Press, 1968, p. 152.
6. Gibb, H.A.R. (tr.), *Ibn Batuta: Travels in Asia and Africa 1325-54,* London: Routledge & Kegan Paul, 1953 (third impression) pp. 225-6.
7. As in the *Fuwāid al-Fuād*, the *Siyar al-Auliyā*, the *Jawāmi'al-Kilam* and the *Bahr al-Hayāt*.
8. For instance, Gorakh-hatri, Tilla Balgundai, Achal and Kahnuwan. Some of the other *jogī* establishments were at Makhad, Katas, Kirana, Kohat, Bohar, Bawana, Bhera, Pehowa and Jakhbar. B.N. Goswamy and J.S. Grewal, *The Mughals and the Jogis of Jakhbar*, Simla: Indian Institute of Advanced Study, 1967.
9. Zafar Hasan (ed.), *Khulāsat ut-Tawārīkh*, Delhi: 1918, p. 24. Sujan Rai mentions their ability to transmute ash into gold, and the efficacy of

their medicines, their longevity, clairvoyance, and the power to fly in the air, and to walk on water.

10. *Ādi Sri Gurū Granth Sāhib Jī*, p. 685:
The Jogī sitting in the void (*sunn-mandal*) is neither male nor female, and hence the problem of how to refer to that Being.
11. Ibid., p. 351.
12. Ibid., p. 1332.
13. Ibid., p. 477: 'He lives in wilderness in the cremation grounds, unaware of his ignorance; he regrets in the end'; p. 879: 'He begs for food and clothes. He is miserable here and he will suffer pain hereafter'; p. 1189: 'Pride is not removed by smearing the body with ash. This is not the path of true union'.
14. Ibid., p. 14: 'If I were to be the master of all *siddhīs* and *riddhīs,* appear and disappear at will, and people were afraid of my power – I would rather stick to your Name than have all these.'
15. Ibid., p. 17: 'If offerings were to come to me and I were to be regarded as a *pīr*; if I were to obtain all earthly things; if I were to be famous and looked upon as *siddh* – all this would be futile without honour with God.'
16. Ibid., p. 155: 'There is a ring within the ring and the body itself is the cloak. Control the five senses O Jogī so that your mind becomes the supporting staff.'
17. Ibid., p. 877: 'The word is my *surt* and sākhī is my *singi.* I blow it and people hear. Honour is my *jholī* for begging, and I receive alms of the Name.'
18. Ibid., p. 634: 'In this concentration on the divine within, the *bairāgī* is indifferent to hope and despair.'
19. Ibid., pp. 359-60: 'The word of the Guru is the ear-ring in the mind and mercy is the cloak. Accept what he does as the best so that you receive the gift of the union.'
20. Ibid., p. 436:
'By concentration day and night my *bairāgī man* has discovered the Eternal Being within myself. The beloved Primal Being, the unseeable, has been shown to me by the True Guru. By meditation I have found the One unchanging Lord. I have become one with the Name and hear the music of bliss.'

5

Idolatry in Vaishnava Bhakti

The religion of Guru Nanak is generally believed to have a basic similarity with the cult of *bhakti,* the dominant religious mode in medieval India. For J.N. Farquhar, Guru Nanak's religion was 'practically identical' with the systems of Vaishnava sects which arose during the medieval period.[1] Almost unconsciously, however, Farquhar contradicts himself by noticing Guru Nanak's protest against the practice of idol-worship and belief in incarnation. Farquhar appears to assume that the similarity between the *bhakti* cult and the religion of Guru Nanak was more fundamental than the differences between them.

However, this view ignores Guru Nanak's attitude towards the contemporary forms of Vaishnava belief and practice. In his writings there is little appreciation for any particular form of religious belief and practice, whether Hindu or Muslim.[2] His positive appreciation is reserved for *sādhs* and *sants.* But this approval is expressed in general terms. No individual from amongst his contemporaries or from the preceding few centuries is mentioned. It is clear in any case that Guru Nanak's *sādhs* and *sants* were not the devotees of Rama and Krishna.

It is remarkable indeed that in the writings of Guru Nanak there is explicit disapproval of some Vaishnava beliefs and practices. In the first place, Vishnu for Guru Nanak is a mere creature of God.[3] Like everything else created by God, he is subject to annihilation.[4] His existence is recognized but he is deprived of all functions. When Guru Nanak uses the epithet Narain, Hari, or Gobind for his God we may be absolutely sure that he does not refer to Vishnu as a supreme deity.[5]

Furthermore, rejection of the idea of incarnation implies

rejection of Rama and Krishna as the *avtars* of Vishnu. They add nothing to God's greatness.[6] In fact Guru Nanak's attitude to Krishna is by no means respectful. In one place Krishna is referred to as the seducer of Chandraval with whom he amused himself in Brindaban.[7] Krishna is not a deity for Guru Nanak[8] and adoration of Krishna springs from a wrong kind of belief. For Guru Nanak, God alone is the true object of worship and, though He is revealed in His creation, He is not contained in the universe. He cannot be confined by space and time. As may be expected logically, Guru Nanak disapproves of idol-worship.[9] 'The gods and goddesses whom you worship and to whom you pray, what can they grant? You wash them yourselves and (were you to leave them in water) they would sink'.[10]

The worship associated with Vishnu is specifically rejected by Guru Nanak.[11] Similarly, he disapproves of the practices connected with the adoration of Krishna and Rama. For instance,

> The disciples play and the *giānīs* dance; they shake their feet and they roll their heads; dust arises and falls over their head; people are amused, they laugh and they return home; the performers beat time perfectly but only for bread and the dancers dash themselves to the ground. They sing as *gopīs* and the *kānh*; they sing as Sita and Ram.[12]

It may be evident from these lines that some of the most fundamental beliefs and cherished practices of the Vaishnava *bhaktas* are rejected by Guru Nanak. He does not appear to see any affinity between their religion and his own. We may be sure that Guru Nanak does not accord special treatment to the representatives of the *bhakti* cult in his attitude towards the contemporary forms of religious belief and practice.

Nevertheless, Guru Nanak's emphasis on *bhakti* is quite unmistakable.[13] It may be safely asserted in fact that, in his view, there can be no liberation without *bhakti.*[14] The *bhakti* of his conception therefore must be more meaningful and valid than the contemporary Vaishnava *bhakti.* It has been said, indeed, that Guru Nanak's *bhakti-mārga* becomes 'a fourth way of salvation' which is more effective than any or all the other three.[15] This view does find support in the attitude of Guru Nanak towards the Vaishnava *bhakti* and its disapproval in his writings. It is necessary therefore to understand the significance of *bhakti* in relation to the religious thought of Guru Nanak.

There are numerous passages in the writings of Guru Nanak which clearly indicate that for him *bhakti* is primarily 'loving devotion'. The ideas of love and dedication are inseparable in his conception of *bhakti*.[16] However, this basic similarity is qualified first by an equal insistence on the idea of 'fear' (*bhai* or *bhau*). In fact Guru Nanak uses *bhai-bhakti* or *bhai-bhāv* as almost a single epithet.[17] This juxtaposition of 'fear' with devotion suggests an equal emphasis on both. At one place he makes it quite explicit that only those who have fear (*bhai*) can have devotion (*bhao*).[18] The idea of 'fear' in the religious thought of Guru Nanak is intimately linked with his conception of God's omnipotence and His grace (*nadar*).

The significance of *bhakti* for Guru Nanak is inseparable from his understanding of the nature of God. All the basic concepts of his theology have a direct bearing on his conception of *bhakti*. God in His absolute nature is without attributes and He alone is eternal. He is revealed through His creation, which is subject to change and annihiliation. To realize this immutable distinction between God and His creation is to perceive the Truth (*sachch*). God is the sole creator, the sole sustainer and the sole destroyer of the universe; He is the omnipotent, the omniscient and the omnipresent Lord. His manifestation in His creation is the expression of His *hukam*, which comprehends everything that happens in the moral and the physical world. The acceptance of God's *hukam* and a willing submission to it form an essential part of the devotion of Guru Nanak's thinking. Another essential element in his conception of *bhakti* is contemplation on God's revelation with awe and wonder (*vismād*) as a way of adoring His ineffable greatness. It is in this context that Guru Nanak uses the concepts of the Name (*nām*) and the Word (*shabad*). Thus, Guru Nanak's *bhakti* involves a great deal of reflection upon the macrocosm. It involves also a good deal of introspection to perceive the element of divinity within oneself, by eradicating self-centredness (*haumai*) and by pursuing the highest ideals of moral conduct. In this way one may recognize the Divine Preceptor (Guru) who, among other things, is the divine voice within oneself.

Of crucial importance in the religious thought of Guru Nanak is his concept of God's grace (*nadar*). In a certain sense His grace finds expression in the revelation of God through His creation. But no amount of reflection upon this revelation is sufficient to lead man to liberation. In fact no amount of human effort by itself can 'earn' salvation. It is to be bestowed upon man by God. The bestowing of salvation, or even of the means to salvation, is an expression of God's grace. The concept of *nadar* upholds the omnipotence of a personal God who is also compassionate. The devotee must tread the path of loving devotion in utter humility, for his salvation depends not on himself but on God's grace.

From this brief overview it may be suggested that Guru Nanak's disagreement with the Vaishnava *bhaktas* can be ignored only at the cost of clear conceptualization. His insistence on *bhakti* does not equate him with Vaishnava *bhaktas.* Differences within devotional theism, arising out of the differences in the conception of God, the goal and the path, carried social implications which made the differences far more important than any verbal or emotional similarities. Guru Nanak's rejection of idol worship and belief in incarnation was a part of his rejection of all Brahmanical traditions.

NOTES

1. J.N. Farquhar, *Modern Religious Movements in India,* London: 1929, p. 336.
2. J.S. Grewal, *Guru Nanak in History,* Chandigarh: Panjab University, 1969, pp. 232-3.
3. *Ādi Sri Gurū Granth Sāhib Jī* (Sri Damdami Bir, various printed editions, standard pagination), p. 7.
4. Ibid., p. 1153. Like the whole universe, Brahma, Vishnu and Shiva suffer from the disease of mortality.
5. Ibid., pp. 503-4. It may be added that Guru Nanak is not the only religious figure to use multiple epithets for God without compromising the conception of the Oneness of God. In fact 'unity' is sought to be reinforced by the 'multiplicity' of epithets in the composition of Shaikh Farid, Kabir, and Shah Husain as well as Guru Nanak.
6. Ibid., pp. 350-1. Rama killing Ravana, and Krishna overpowering the serpent Kali or killing Kansa do not add anything to God's greatness.

7. Ibid., p. 470.
8. Ibid., pp. 73, 75.
9. Ibid., p. 68.
10. Ibid., p. 637.
11. Ibid., p. 1171. The reference here is to *sālagrāma*, the rosary of *tulsī*, and the worship of Rama, amounting to cultivating saline soil and plastering a wall of mud.
12. Ibid., p. 465. Singing of God's praises is meritorious but not playing the part of the *gopīs* and Krishna, or of Sita and Rama.
13. Ibid., pp. 228, 413, 418, 420, 1172, 1320.
14. Ibid., p. 413.
15. J.C. Archer, *The Sikhs in Relation to Hindus, Muslims, Christians and Ahmadiyas: A Study in Comparative Religion*, Princeton: Princeton University Press, 1946, p. 133.
16. Grewal, *Guru Nanak in History*, pp. 258, 275-7; W.H. McLeod, *Gurū Nānak and the Sikh Religion*, London: Clarendon Press, 1968, p. 213.
17. *Ādi Sri Gurū Granth Sāhib Jī*, p. 357. The frequent use of these epithets is important.
18. Ibid., pp. 465, 1188.

6

Liberation-in-Life

The basic ideas and concerns of Guru Nanak are embodied in his compositions which form the bedrock of the *Ādi Granth* as the sacred scripture of the Sikhs. The scope of his compositions is comprehensive enough to include matters social and political. His message of liberation, though seemingly religious, has social and political implications too.

Guru Nanak evolved a discipline which from his viewpoint was the most efficacious for liberation and he offered this path to everyone, irrespective of creed, caste, or gender. Some of his ideas may appear to be similar to what we come across in medieval Indian literature, but even the familiar terms and concepts undergo significant change and acquire new meaning in his theological thought.

Guru Nanak's emphasis on the unity of God is well known. In his compositions he often uses the phrases: 'He is one', 'He is the only true Lord', 'There is no other'. Guru Nanak also underlines that the one God is the only proper object of worship: 'I worship only the one; I know no other'. Furthermore, God in His primal aspect has no attributes. He is absolute, the eternally unchanging formless one (*nirankār*). God's absolute nature cannot be comprehended by human beings: He is inscrutable, boundless, self-existent, beyond time, and ineffable. He is completely detached from His creation. However, God has revealed Himself in His creation. He is the sole creator, the sole sustainer, and the sole destroyer of the universe. The phrases makes-and-unmakes, creates-and-destroys, and builds-and-demolishes occur frequently in Guru Nanak's compositions. God is also the nourisher of every living being. He is the One Sovereign Lord.

His *qudrat* is at work in both the physical and the moral world. The one True Lord is everywhere. He pervades the microcosm and the macrocosm. 'The ocean is in the drop, and the drop in the ocean; 'He is the tablet and the pen and the writing'.

The idea of revelation is of crucial significance. The terms which relate to divine self-revelation are Name (*nām*), Word (*shabad*), Divine Preceptor (*gurū*) and Divine Order (*hukam*). The Name refers essentially to both the primal and manifest states of God, and the Word refers to the manifest state. The Divine Preceptor is both the manifest God and His presence within man. The Divine Order is the power that controls the working of the universe and the moral world. Recognition of this Divine Order and its acceptance is an essential part of the discipline propounded by Guru Nanak. The frequent occurrence of these interrelated concepts in the *bāṇī* of Guru Nanak underlines the importance he attached to the idea of divine self-revelation. Equally important is his claim that his own compositions are a form of revelation.

The idea of divine revelation has a close bearing on Guru Nanak's idea of *bhakti*. The connotation of *bhakti* in his works is not the same as in medieval Vaishnavism. In the first place, Guru Nanak's *bhakti* is addressed to God and not to any incarnation of God. In fact, the idea of incarnation stands rejected. The most important aspect of his *bhakti* is meditation on God's revelation as the only way of understanding His nature and His attributes. The *bāṇī* of Guru Nanak is also helpful. God's fear is closely associated with *bhakti* as a direct corollary of His inscrutable omnipotence. It cannot be presumed that loving devotion to God would inevitably lead to liberation. Though gracious and compassionate, Guru Nanak's God is also the all-powerful God. His grace is expressed in His revelation which is accessible to all. However, what decides the issue of liberation is God's grace (*nadar*). Obviously, liberation is 'bestowed' by God, not 'achieved' by man. This conception of God's grace repudiates all presumption to liberation by mere human effort. God's *nadar* and God's *hukam* are two sides of the same theological coin.

Contextually, Guru Nanak can speak of *karma* as a term easily understandable to his contemporaries. Essentially, however, *karma* is replaced by God's *hukam* which is not an impersonal causal phenomenon, but an expression of God's omnipotence and grace: 'He can wash away millions of sins in a moment'. The law of *karma* is set aside. Ethical conduct is redefined in the context of his own discipline.

The universe as God's creation is real and, as His revelation, it helps man to understand His nature. But God alone is eternal and He is clearly distinct from His creation. There can be no conciliation between man's allegiance to God and his affiliation to His creation. Everything other than God is *māyā*. Thus, the conception of *māyā* gets transformed in the religious thought of Guru Nanak. In contrast with God's truth, His creation is false. What keeps man in bondage to *māyā* are his low passions and sensual appetites. This bondage obliges him to remain a stranger to God. Realization of the distinction between the creator and his creation can loosen the bondage.

Haumai or self-centredness stands in opposition to God as the only and omnipotent reality. The man who does not turn to God is *manmukh*, the self-willed fool who attributes things to himself in opposition to the omnipotence of God and His *hukam*. Unless the true nature of this self-centredness is realized, the way of liberation cannot be recognized. Without this realization man remains entangled in the net of *māyā*. Therefore Guru Nanak emphasizes the necessity of subduing the *man*, that is, both the heart and the mind. The *man* is conquered by the realization of God's *hukam*. With the *man* rightly attuned one may experience God within oneself.

The purpose of human life is liberation through an experience of God. Meditation on God's revelation all around and the *bāṇī* of Guru Nanak, total devotion to God, ethical living, service of others and, above all, God's grace lead to this experience in life. In the Realm of Truth, the dwelling place of the Formless One, there is perfect harmony with His *hukam*. After this experience, one lives in complete accordance with God's *hukam*.

With this goal in view, Guru Nanak exhorts men to discard heedlessness, depicts the dread of death and punishment in the life hereafter, dwells on sinfulness, offers humble devotion to God, and he adores Him by singing the praises of His ineffable greatness. It is this goal that he offers to others, irrespective of their caste, creed or gender. Liberation is experienced in human life itself. The term used for the person who has this experience is *jīvan-mukt.* He dies to self (*jīvat-marnā*) and subsists in God's will. Remaining detached in attachment (*anjan mahe niranjan*), he becomes a recluse in the home (*ghar hī mahe udās*). The liberated-in-life works for the welfare of others (*parupkār*). This is the essence of all wisdom.

The compositions of Guru Nanak reveal his familiarity with contemporary society. There is hardly an important aspect of the life of his contemporaries that is not directly or indirectly mentioned in his works. The range of his experience of contemporary society is strikingly comprehensive. Much of his comment is contextual, but the metaphors used and the situations depicted reveal the nature of his concerns. He was keenly aware of Muslim presence in the Punjab but he does not think in terms of 'Hindu' and 'Muslim' communities. He does not identify himself with any community or caste. This attitude was closely connected with his firm belief that the light of God shines in every human being, and that every human being is equal before God.

Earthly pursuits are not commendable as an end in themselves. The world is false in contrast with the Truth of God:

> False are palaces and mansions and those who dwell in them. False are gold and hoards of riches; false the body, the raiment and beauty. False are the husband and wife; false indeed is all earthly attachment.

What sanctifies earthly pursuits is dedication to God in pursuit of liberation:

> One may profit by millions; one may hoard millions; one may spend millions; immense wealth may pass through one's hands; (but) if one receives no honour (in God's court) one has no place of honour. One may master all the Shastras and read all the Puranas (but) if one receives no honour (in God's court), all one's learning is of no account.

Beliefs and practices that do not lead to liberation are of no value. The distinctions of caste are invidious. The distinctions based on birth become invidious when they imply denial of opportunity to a large number of people: 'There is no caste in the next world'. One does not become 'high' before God by regarding oneself 'high' in the social order. He who forgets the Master is of 'low caste'. Genuine piety and devotion to God are more important than anything else. God bestows greatness irrespective of one's caste. The fact of one's belonging to a high or a low caste is totally irrelevant to liberation.

Guru Nanak's rejection of caste had its own implications. Just as every human being was equal before God so every individual who accepted the path of Guru Nanak was equal before the Guru, and all his followers were equal before one another. So also Guru Nanak explicitly rejects the idea that woman is inferior to man. From his point of view, woman is on a par with man, just as the Shudra is on a par with the Brahman. Universality and equality, both, spring from Guru Nanak's conception of God.

Guru Nanak's compositions reveal his familiarity with nearly all aspects of contemporary government and administration. The pursuit of temporal power as an end in itself is not commendable:

> Were I to be a *sultān*, to raise armies and to set my foot on the throne; were I to possess regal command – all this would be worthless O Nanak, if I were to possess all these and to forget God.

Temporal power, like youth, beauty and high caste, can be a hindrance in the path of liberation. As in the case of society so of politics, Guru Nanak's denunciation springs partly from his moral values. Contemporary polity is denounced by Guru Nanak as much as the caste system:

> The rajas are lions and the *muqaddams* dogs; they fall upon (the *ra'iyat*) day and night; their agents inflict wounds with claws (of power) and the dogs lick blood and relish the liver.

This general denunciation of injustice and oppression is frank and forceful. Guru Nanak specifically denounced the discriminatory imposition of pilgrimage tax. By implication, the rulers may appear to be castigated because they are 'Muslim'. But what is condemned essentially is their discriminatory policy. The foremost obligation of the ruler is to be just and benign to all. A functionary of the government should be considerate of the common people. Indifference to their welfare and pursuit of personal interests are denounced as immoral.

The liberated-in-life works for the welfare of the people, in both the social order and the political realm. The state of liberation is not a state of blissful inactivity but of detached action for the good of all. Because of this commitment, to tread the path of liberation is to walk on the sharp edge of the sword. [1]

NOTES

1. Much of what is said in this short essay appears in my *Guru Nanak in History*, Chandigarh: Panjab University, 1969, but not the present perspective. W.H. McLeod's understanding of revelation is limited to divine self-expression, and his conception of liberation to an innert state of bliss. The essential clue to Guru Nanak's position lies in his conception of liberation-in-life which is central to his whole thought.

Part 2

THE KHALSA

7

The Nānak-Panthīs

As the culmination of a deep spiritual search amidst deep knowledge of the contemporary forms of religious belief and practice, Guru Nanak experienced 'illumination'. He was convinced that he had been called to proclaim divine truth to all men and women, irrespective of their caste or creed. For at least fifteen years he acted as guide to his regular disciples at Kartarpur (Dera Baba Nanak) and preached to those who visited the place. These years were the most important years of his life in terms of his posthumous influence, and he now gave practical expression to his ideals. The idea of equality before God found expression in the congregational worship (*sangat*) of the community at Kartarpur and in a common kitchen (*langar*) maintained by voluntary contributions in cash, kind, and service. Even more significant was Guru Nanak's decision to use his own compositions for the purpose of worship. It meant an unequivocal rejection of the known scriptures and their authority. It also lent, logically, a unique importance to his compositions in the eyes of his followers for whom they came to serve as a permanent source of inspiration. Equally important was his decision to install a successor from amongst his disciples before his death in 1539.

In the writings of Guru Nanak's successors during the sixteenth century, there is a clear insistence on the uniqueness and universality of Guru Nanak's message.[1] The belief that the truth discovered by Guru Nanak, and preached to others, is superior to any other is shared alike by his successors and by the writers of the Janamsākhīs of Guru Nanak. This belief is expressed in several ways. The most characteristic and the most comprehensive of such statements are that Nanak is the Preceptor of the World (*jagat-gurū*); he is the Manifest Guide (*zāhir pīr*); and he is the Guru of the modern age (*kaliyuga*). Behind the universality and uniqueness of Guru Nanak's message, his followers and successors saw the direct sanction of God, and Nanak the Guru stands in a special relationship with Him, sharing the traits of an *avtār* and a prophet but distinct from each. This conception of Nanak's position as the Guru was facilitated by his own concept of Guru as the Divine Preceptor. The epithets which he used for the Guru could easily be applied by his followers to Guru Nanak. For him, the Guru was equated with God in the macrocosm and within the human heart; for his followers and successors this function of guidance was vested in him. He who was qualified to instruct others by means of his exalted perception of the Divine Truth through a personal experience.

The uniqueness of Nanak the Guru had to be reconciled to the continuity of his work under his successors and this conciliation resulted in the idea of the unity of guruship. The appropriate metaphor of light mingling with light is the characteristic expression. Angad is simply Nanak the second, Amar Das is Nanak the third (and so on), for Nanak the Guru had become Angad the Guru and Amar Das the Guru (and so on). The office of Guru is not only distinct from but also superior to the person. In this way was safeguarded not only the distinctive position of the founder but also the authority of his duly nominated successors who were enabled legitimately to take vital decisions by virtue of their office. This legitimacy made their decisions essentially an 'extension' of Guru Nanak's work in the eyes of his followers.

Equally fertile was Guru Nanak's concept of the Word (*shabad*). In his compositions the *shabad* is one of the several crucial terms which refer to divine self-revelation. It is the medium of communication between man and God. For the followers of Guru Nanak, this function is performed by the divinely inspired *shabad* or the *bāṇī* of Guru Nanak and of his successors by virtue of their office. Thus the compositions of the Gurus came to have a unique importance and the compilation of a scripture, the Granth, by Guru Arjan in 1604, becomes a logical step from the rejection of known scriptures by Guru Nanak.[2] Furthermore, the Word is equated by Guru Nanak himself with the Guru. Thus, the Granth becomes an alternative to the personal Guruship of his successors.

By the early part of the seventeenth century, the followers of Guru Nanak were becoming conscious of their distinct identity. Guru Nanak had used the term *panth* simply for 'path'. This term came to be applied both to the distinctive path shown by Guru Nanak and to those who followed that path. In an early Janamsākhī this growing awareness of the nature and function of the followers of Guru Nanak as a distinctive *panth* is clearly reflected: 'Go Nanak', says God, 'your *panth* will flourish'. The name of this *panth* in the Janamsākhī is the *panth* of Nanak. The Nānak-Panthīs have their distinct form of salutation and their distinct places of worship; their purpose is to spread the true religion of Guru Nanak among mankind. The distinct identity of the *panth* of Nanak is unmistakable.

In the early seventeenth century, the followers of Guru Nanak often conceive of his position in terms of sovereignty. In fact all the Gurus are the 'true kings' before whom temporal authority fades into insignificance. As the true sovereigns, the Gurus are entitled to exclusive allegiance; those who do not submit to them are 'rebels'.

In the compositions of Guru Nanak there are numerous references to contemporary government and administration. In the comprehensive range of his observations, there is a good deal of emphasis on oppression and the corruption practised by the officials of the government, and an insistence on the ideal of justice. These two aspects of Guru Nanak's utterances on politics are emphasized in the early seventeenth century in the *Vārs* of Bhai Gurdas and the Janamsākhī of Guru Nanak compiled by Sodhi Miharban.[3]

The logical connection between the work of Guru Nanak and its interpretation by his successors or followers is clear, and so is the relevance of these ideas to the growth and development of the *panth* of Guru Nanak during the sixteenth century. They provide insight into the beliefs and psychology of the followers of Guru Nanak as members of a new socio-religious group. The consciousness of being distinct from the rest of their contemporaries did not necessarily mean hostility. In fact, in the writings of the successors and followers of Guru Nanak there is as much insistence on amicable coexistence as on the superiority of their faith. To be a true Sikh of the Guru was to be far above the considerations of caste or creed or community, including their own.

For the position of the Nanak-Panth in the early seventeenth century, we may turn to the evidence of Bhai Gurdas who was closely connected with several Sikh Gurus. He was a nephew of Guru Amar Das (1552-74), and therefore a cousin of the wife of Guru Ram Das (1574-80) and a maternal uncle of Guru Arjan (1580-1606). He remained closely associated with Guru Hargobind (1606-44). He witnessed the peaceful days of the reign of Akbar, the martyrdom of Guru Arjan in the beginning of Jahangir's reign, the reaction of Guru Hargobind to this event, and his armed conflict with the Mughal *faujdārs* in the reign of Shah Jahan. Thus, he lived through a long phase of Sikh history that was marked by an important transition.[4]

Bhai Gurdas was familiar with the Sikhs at Goindval and Ramdaspur. He refers to several other *sangats* also in the Punjab, notably those of Lahore, Patti, and Sultanpur. But the Sikh *sangats* were not confined to the province of Lahore: there were eminent Sikhs in Sirhind, Thanesar and Delhi. There were prominent Sikhs also in Kabul and Kashmir, in Agra and Allahabad, in Bihar and Bengal, in Rajasthan, Malwa, and Gujarat. Bhai Gurdas refers to Chaddhas, Sehgals, Handas and Nandas in Agra, to Sonis in Gwalior, to Dhirs in Ujjain, to Wadhawans in Burhanpur and to Behls in Raj Mahal. They were all Khatris, traders. Bhai Gurdas refers to Bhabhra Sikhs in Gujarat who too were traders. In the light of the polity and economy of the Mughal empire we may expect traders moving into the cities and towns of the Mughal empire in search of better opportunities. What is remarkable is the good number of Sikhs among them. Bhai Gurdas is jubilant: where there is one Sikh there is a Sikh; where there are two Sikhs there is an association of Sikhs; where there are five Sikhs, there is the veritable presence of God. And there are thousands of Sikhs in every city, and lakhs in every country.[5] There may be some exaggeration but it is a measure surely of Bhai Gurdas's feeling of gratification.

In the Punjab, the Khatris formed the most important constituency of the Nanak-Panth. Many Sikhs belonged to the well known Khatri subcastes of the Punjab: Sehgal, Ohri, Uppal, Julka, Bhalla, Passi, Khullar, Vohra, Vij, Kapur, Chaddha, Behl, Kohli, Marwaha, Mehra, Soni, Jhanji, Sodhi, Beri, Nanda, Wadhawan, Tuli and Puri. There are several other less familiar subcastes of the Khatris. However, there were prominent Sikhs belonging to other *varnas* and *jātis*. There are some Randḥawa, Khaira, Dhillon and Pannu Jatts. Among the Brahman subcastes are Tiwaṛī and Bhardwaj. There are Sūds and Aroras. Then there are Lohārs, Nāīs, Chhīmbās, Māchhīs, Dhobīs, Kumhārs, Telīs, masons and goldsmiths, and even a Chandal.[6] At one end of the scale there are rich merchants, *seths* and *sarrāfs* in cities and towns and *chaudharīs* in villages; on the other, there are labourers and slaves, with artisans and craftsmen, petty shopkeepers and peasants in between. In terms of the social background of the Sikhs there was a wide range, and the economic means of the members of the Panth varied from occupation to occupation and from person to person.

In the *Vārs* of Bhai Gurdas tension appears in the form of dissent. Prithi Chand is called *mīṇā* (a dissembling rogue). Virtually a whole *Vār* of twentyone stanzas relates to the *mīṇās*. In more than half of this *Vār* they are denounced in strong terms. They have blackened their faces by turning away from the true Guru. They are false and dishonoured. They eat carrion. They are bound for hell. Association with them is a source of suffering. Their path is dishonoured. Those who join them die without any hope for the life hereafter. They carry black marks on their foreheads; they are like false coins. They claim to be Gurus though they possess no merit. They are like the enunch who poses as a mighty warrior but who cannot deceive his wife. There is no salvation without the true Guru.[7]

Bhai Gurdas supports the claim of Guru Hargobind with extraordinary vehemence. The critics of Guru Hargobind refer to his deviation from the practices of the former Gurus: he does not stay in one place; he was sent to the fort of Gwalior by the king; he roams from place to place and knows no fear; he keeps dogs and hunts; he does not recite Gurbāṇī and does not listen to its recitation; he gives precedence to outsiders over his disciples.

But the true Sikhs, like Bhai Gurdas, are still enamoured of Guru Hargobind; they know that he is bearing an unbearable burden. The new measures of Guru Hargobind are not a deviation but an addition: an orchard is protected by the hedge of *kīkar* trees. The outward appearance is a test of the disciple's faith. It is a hard test, but those who have understanding remain firm in their faith. There is no Guru but Hargobind, the only legitimate successor of Guru Arjan, Guru Ram Das, Guru Amar Das, Guru Angad, and Guru Nanak.[8]

It is important to note that the polity and economy of the Mughal empire, which made it possible for the followers of Guru Nanak and his successors to move into distant cities and towns, widened their awareness of the contemporary world, an awareness which is reflected in the *Vārs* of Bhai Gurdas. He talks not only of Hindus and Muslims but also of Buddhists and Jains, Christians and Jews. Among the Muslims, he refers not only to the *mullās* and the Sūfis, or to the Sunnīs and the Shi'as, or to the four schools and the seventytwo sects of Islam, but also to the Rafizīs, the Malāhida, and the Manāfiqa. He refers not only to the Mughals, the Pathans, the Turks, and the Sayyids but also to the Armenians and the Rūmīs, the Habshīs and the Firangīs.[9]

With his horizons thus widened, the claims of Bhai Gurdas for the universality of the message of Guru Nanak become trenchant. Guru Nanak is the Guide Manifest (*jāhar pīr*), the Teacher of the World (*jagat-gur*). His message transcends all earlier dispensations. The Mullā and the Brahman have missed the Truth in wrangling about Ram and Rahim, about the four schools and the four *varnas,* the Ganges and the Ka'bah, the circumcision and the sacred thread. Neither Hindus nor Muslims have recognized the Truth. Guru Nanak's triumph over the custodians of *tīraths* and over the Siddhs is as patent as is his triumph over the custodians of Mecca and the Qādirī Pīr Dastgīr of Baghdad. Guru Nanak has shown the highway (*gādī rāh*) to all, from the king to the beggar. He has potentially saved all the nine regions of the earth in all the four directions. He is the only saviour of the *kalijuga.*[10]

It is significant that Bhai Gurdas broadens the highway of Guru Nanak by identifying kindred spirits not only of the present age but also of the previous ages. He finds the element of *bhau-*

bhaktī as a common feature of their lives: Dhruva, Prahlad, Raja Bal, Ambrik, Janak, Hari Chand, Bidr, Daropadi, Sudama, Ahaliya, Balmik, Ajaimal, Putana, among others. Included among them are also Jaidev, Trilochan, Namdev, Dhanna, Beni, Kabir, Ramanand, Sen, Ravidas and Sadhna. The compositions of all the *bhagats* of the Kaliyuga mentioned here were included in the Granth compiled by Guru Arjan. However, Bhai Gurdas extends the line to the mythical past. Nevertheless, he feels more concerned about the medieval *bhagats*, particularly those who emerged from the lower castes, like Dhanna who was a Jatt, Namdev who was a tailor or a calico-printer, Kabir who was a weaver, Sen who was a barber, Ravidas who was a cobbler, and Sadhna who was a butcher. The devotees of God have no caste.[11] Conversely, caste is no bar to become a devotee of God.

According to the evidence of Bhai Gurdas, the pure (*nirmal*) Panth in the early seventeenth century consisted of members coming from both the high and the low castes, including in fact the outcastes. Bhai Gurdas insists that the social background of the Sikhs did not matter. Guru Nanak had addressed himself to all the four *varnas*, and individuals from all the four *varnas* could accept his path; they all met in the *sangat* as equals. A true Sikh of the Guru does not bother about the distinctions of caste. Just as betel leaf, areca-nut and lime produce one colour, so the individual members coming from different backgrounds acquired one colour in the Sikh *sangat*. The Guru transmutes eight metals into one. All the four *varnas* become one and acquire the *gotra* of Gurmukh. The eight metals become gold with the touch of *pāras*.[12] The ideal of equality ennobled the low castes who entered the Panth of Guru Nanak.

The emphasis of Bhai Gurdas on the unity of Guruship is partly a reflection of the situation of dissent. The successors of Guru Nanak were not different from him. He made the stream reverse its course when in his lifetime he installed Angad as the Guru. Imparting his light to Angad, he changed his form. This transformation was a wonder of wonders. What Angad received from Guru Nanak was transferred to Amar Das: the gift (*dāt*) of the light (*jot*) bestowed greatness upon Guru Amar Das. It passed on to Guru Ram Das and Guru Arjan. Then, Guru Arjan changed form and became Guru Hargobind. The form was different but the light was the same. Furthermore, it was not an ordinary succession. Angad was a Sikh of Guru Nanak, but when he became the Guru, Nanak became his Sikh. The Guru became a Sikh and a Sikh became the Guru. Being the first, Guru Nanak was the Guru of Gurus. The interchangeable position of the Guru and the Sikh, the idea of indistinguishability of the Gurus, and the unity of Guruship are emphasized at many places in the *Vārs* of Bhai Gurdas. Because of his emphasis, the ideas crystallize. This crystallization provided an unqualified support to Guru Hargobind. Prithi Chand and his successors could invoke heredity, and also the line of succession from Guru Nanak. In fact they did subscribe to the idea of continuity and indistinguishability. The only claim which they could not put forth convincingly was that of nomination implied in the Guru-Disciple-Guru syndrome. This syndrome is emphasized by Bhai Gurdas more than any other idea. In conjunction with the ideas of continuity and indistinguishability, this syndrome becomes the most important contribution of Bhai Gurdas. He is clear about the importance of the syndrome: Angad, Amar Das, Ram Das, Arjan and Hargobind were Sikhs of the Guru before they became Gurus, but Prithi Chand was not and his successors were not. They were not given the gift (*dāt*) and they could not have the light (*jot*). Thus, there was no Guru other than Hargobind.[13]

The Guru was all the more important for being the only legitimate Guru. Guru Nanak is *pār brahm, pūran brahm.* And so are his successors. A Sikh should regard the Guru as God. In fact, the Guru and God are one. The equation between God and the Guru is there in the compositions of Guru Nanak. But in the *Vārs* of Bhai Gurdas the greater emphasis is on the Guru. Similarly, in Guru Nanak's compositions God is the true king but in the *Vārs* of Bhai Gurdas, the Guru is the true king. By comparison, the earthly rulers are 'false'. Guru Hargobind, as much as Guru Nanak or Guru Angad, is the king of *dīn* and *duniā.* There is only one king; all other men and women are his subjects, whether Hindu or Muslim; there is only one Guru in the world; all other men and women among the followers are his Sikhs. Hargobind is the true king; the *mīṇās* are not his Sikhs. They are 'rebels', and rebels have no place in the realm of the king; they have lost their place in this life and the life hereafter.[14]

In the *bāṇī* of Guru Nanak, *shabad* refers to divine self-revelation. For Bhai Gurdas also, God reveals the true *shabad*. However, this shabad is the *bāṇī* of Guru Nanak and his successors. The *bāṇī* of his successors surely is Gur-shabad. This Gurbāṇī is recited and sung in the *sangat*. It is more efficacious than the Vedas and the revealed Books. The Gur-shabad is the Guru. Bhai Gurdas is not the first to postulate this equation. But after the compilation of the Granth by Guru Arjan in 1604 the equation acquires a new meaning. Bhai Gurdas does refer to the fact in one of his *Vārs*. While the possibility of equating the Granth with the Guru is opened, the door to the compositions of the *mīṇās* being treated as Gurbāṇī is closed.[15]

The emphasis on exclusive affiliation to the true Guru and the true Panth is partly related to the occurrence of dissent. The 'other affiliation' arises out of ignorance; it is obliterated by the Guru. Recognize no other; a Sikh has no other affiliation. Outside the dispensation of the true Guru there is no salvation. All other dispensations are like a house without any door. Those who remain immune to the Guru's message do not know their own interest; they are fools. They who do not give their exclusive affiliation to the true Guru cannot be saved. There are those who turn away from the true Guru; they are doomed, like an abandoned woman or a dead tree. Lastly there are those who speak ill of the true Guru; they are ungrateful wretches who have lost their place in the universe.[16] Allegiance to the Guru is the criterion for drawing the line between the true and the spurious.

NOTES

1. These writings consist of the compositions of Guru Angad, Guru Amar Das, Guru Ram Das, Guru Arjan and Guru Tegh Bahadur, all of which are to be found in the standard editions of the *Ādi Sri Gurū Granth Sāhib*. The compositions of Guru Gobind Singh are included in the *Dasam Granth*. Then there are the Vārs and Kabitts and the Savvyyas of Bhai Gurdas, the *Purātan Janamsākhī* and the Janamsākhīs compiled by Sodhi Miharban and his descendants, and the Vārs of the Bhatts who attended upon the Sikh Gurus.
2. The fact that Guru Arjan included the compositions of several devotional theists in the Granth he compiled has sometimes been interpreted in terms of Kabir's influence on Sikhism, or even on Guru Nanak. Though

his verses are the largest in number, Kabir is one among many, including a *shaikh* like Farid. The proportion of their compositions put together remains rather small and they are nowhere included in those parts of the *Granth Sahib* which are used for liturgical purposes. The compositions of some of the Bhatts who served the Gurus are also included in the *Granth Sahib.* Guru Arjan's decision to include the compositions of devotional theists in his compilation appears to be an attempt to assimilate that tradition to Sikhism. This, however, was one but not the sole criterion for the inclusion of compositions other than those of the Gurus.

3. *Janam Sākhī Sri Gurū Nānak Dev Jī*, ed., Kirpal Singh and Shamsher Singh Ashok, Amritsar: Sikh History Research Department of Khalsa College, 1962 and 1969.
4. For biographical information, Ratan Singh Jaggi, *Bhāī Gurdās: Jīwan te Rachnā*, Patiala: Punjabi University, 1974; Trilochan Singh, *Guru Tegh Bahadur*, Delhi: Gurdwara Parbandhak Committee, 1967; W.H. McLeod, *Gurū Nānak and the Sikh Religion*, London: Clarendon Press, 1968 pp. 14-30.
5. Bhai Gurdas, *Vārān Bhāī Gurdās*, ed., Giani Hazara Singh, Amritsar: Khalsa Samachar, 1962, Vār 8: pauṛī 23; Vār 11: pauṛīs 16, 21, 22, 23, 25, 26, 27, 29, 30, 31.
6. Ibid., Vār 13: pauṛī 19; Vār 11: pauṛīs 13-25.
7. Ibid., Vār 11: pauṛīs 14, 16, 21, 25; Vār 26: pauṛīs 31, 32; Vār 36: pauṛīs 1, 2, 3, 4, 5, 6, 7, 8, 9, 11.
8. Ibid., Vār 26: pauṛīs 25, 26; Vār 35: pauṛīs 16, 20, 21, 22, 23; Vār 36: pauṛīs 14, 15, 16; Vār 38: pauṛī 20; Vār 39: pauṛīs 2, 3, 12.
9. Ibid., Vār 1: pauṛīs 18, 19, 20, 21; Vār 8: pauṛīs 6, 13, 16; Vār 38: pauṛī 11; Vār 39: pauṛī 10.
10. Ibid., Vār 1: pauṛīs 21, 23, 25, 26, 27, 28, 29, 30, 31, 32, 33, 35, 37, 39, 42, 43, 44; Vār 8: pauṛī 6; Vār 21: pauṛī 4; Vār 23: pauṛī 16, 17; Vār 24: pauṛīs 2, 3, 4; Vār 33: pauṛīs 2, 4; Vār 38: pauṛī 9.
11. Ibid., Vār 10: pauṛīs 1-23; Vār 12: pauṛī 15; Vār 23: pauṛī 15; Vār 25: pauṛīs 5, 6-12.
12. Ibid., Vār 1: pauṛī 23; Vār 3: pauṛī 16; Vār 6: pauṛī 6; Vār 7: pauṛīs 1, 5; Vār 9: pauṛī 1; Vār 11: pauṛīs 7, 10; Vār 12: pauṛī 12; Vār 14: pauṛī 2; Vār 15: pauṛī 12; Vār 16: pauṛīs 13, 18; Vār 18: pauṛī 14; Vār 23: pauṛī 15; Vār 24: pauṛīs 2, 5; Vār 26: pauṛī 18; Vār 27: pauṛī 4; Vār 29: pauṛīs 1, 5.
13. Ibid., Vār 1: pauṛīs 6-25, 44, 45, 46, 47, 48; Vār 3: pauṛī 11, 12; Vār 9: pauṛī 16; Vār 13: pauṛī 25; Vār 20: pauṛī 1; Vār 24: pauṛīs 6-25; Vār 26: pauṛīs 34; Vār 38: pauṛī 20.
14. Ibid., Vār 1: pauṛī 17; Vār 5: pauṛīs 13, 20, 21; Vār 7: pauṛī 1; Vār 13: pauṛī 25; Vār 15: pauṛī 1; Vār 19: pauṛīs 3, 13; Vār 20: pauṛīs 4, 21; Vār 26: pauṛīs 2, 32, 33; Vār 36: pauṛī 1; Vār 39: pauṛīs 2, 3, 4, 11.

15. Ibid., Vār 1: pauṛī 1, 3, 38, 42; Vār 5: pauṛī 21; Vār 6: pauṛī 1, 3; Vār 7: pauṛī 20; Vār 12: pauṛī 17; Vār 13: pauṛī 21; Vār 18: pauṛī 14; Vār 20: pauṛī 6; Vār 24: pauṛīs 4, 19, 25; Vār 32: pauṛī 2; Vār 39: pauṛī 17.
16. Ibid., Vār 11: pauṛī 16; Vār 27: pauṛī 11; Vār 32: pauṛīs 4-7, 10-20; Vār 33: pauṛīs 11-22; Vār 34: pauṛīs 1-4, 6-21; Vār 35: pauṛī 1, 2, 4, 6-12, 14-16, 18; Vār 36: pauṛīs 1-21; Vār 37: pauṛī 28.

8

Cleavage in the Panth

Of the two sons of Guru Nanak only the elder, Sri Chand, is believed to have opposed Guru Angad after his installation by Guru Nanak as the successor in 1539. Very little is known of Sri Chand from contemporary evidence. Bhai Gurdas refers disapprovingly to his celibacy and his decision to construct a *dehura* of Guru Nanak at Kartarpur (Dera Baba Nanak) which he apparently used as the centre of his activity.[1] In the *bāṇī* of Guru Angad there is no direct reference to Sri Chand's celibacy or the *dehura* at Kartarpur. But this may be only because Guru Angad had a more serious charge against him. 'What kind of a gift is this that is received from oneself', asks Guru Angad, and he adds, 'The miracle is to receive it from the Master'.[2] Not to accept the Guruship of Angad was Sri Chand's gravest fault. His 'disobedience' was proof of his 'ignorance'. If he was not faithful to Guru Nanak he could not be faithful to his message either. The principle of nomination is the criterion of judgement.

In 1552 Guru Angad installed Amar Das as his successor. Dasu and Datu, the sons of Guru Angad, refused to accept Amar Das as the Guru. In the *bāṇī* of Guru Amar Das they are included among the *manmukh* who speak falsehoods and can never be saved except by the Guru.[3] They are also the detractors of the Guru and his Sikhs.[4] Bhai Gurdas refers to the pretensions of Dasu and Datu in acting as Gurus.[5] They wanted to control the establishment at Khadur; as the sons of Guru Angad, they had a legal claim to this.[6] Guru Amar Das had to move to Goindval, just as Guru Angad earlier had to leave the establishment at Kartarpur (Dera Baba Nanak) to the legal heirs of Guru Nanak.

Dasu and Datu had violated the principle of nomination, demonstrating their built-in 'ignorance'.

In 1574 Guru Amar Das nominated his son-in-law, Ram Das, as his successor. Mohan and Mohri, the sons of Guru Amar Das, did not acknowledge Ram Das. Their position appears to be similar to that taken by Dasu and Datu. They claimed the establishment at Goindval for themselves, which they could easily do as legal heirs, as is indicated by Bhai Gurdas.[7] In fact, Guru Amar Das appears to have anticipated their opposition. The decision to found a new centre for his successor was taken in the time of Guru Amar Das. In the *bāṇī* of Guru Ram Das, the sons of Guru Amar Das are bracketed with the sons of Guru Angad and Guru Nanak. They are all greedy, false and accursed.[8] Their opposition to the Guru is clearly reflected in Guru Ram Das's preoccupation with the opponents in his *bāṇī*. It is extremely probable that some of the dissenters had started making misrepresentations to the government functionaries during the time of Guru Ram Das.

In 1581 Guru Ram Das nominated his youngest son, Arjan, his successor. The eldest son of Guru Ram Das, Prithi Chand, opposed this. The detail of Prithi Chand's opposition clarifies the position of the earlier dissenters as well. He is believed to have made a representation to a local Mughal official that he and his brother Mahadev had not been given their due share in the property of their father. Guru Arjan is believed to have given them 'house-rents' and custom duties of Chauk Passian in Ramdaspur. This arrangement worked well for several years, in fact till 1595 when Hargobind was born.[9] Prithi Chand's intrigues and his opposition even after 1595 did not bear much fruit. He was never able to control the establishment at Ramdaspur.[10] Unlike the earlier successors of Guru Nanak, Guru Arjan had as much legal claim to a share in Ramdaspur as Prithi Chand or Mahadev. Hereditary claims to a share in Ramdaspur as much as the principle of nomination was the source of strength for Guru Arjan.

Indubhusan Banerjee attributes the difference between Prithi Chand and the earlier dissenters to the principle of hereditary succession introduced by Guru Ram Das.[11] But the principle of nomination was never discarded by the successors of Guru Nanak. Guru Ram Das introduced the principle of familial succession not to replace nomination, but in addition to that principle. These two principles in combination undermined the strength of the hereditary principle which had been implicit in the attitude of the heirs of Guru Nanak, Guru Angad, and Guru Amar Das. Therefore, we have to look elsewhere for the changed tone and character of dissent in the seventeenth century.

The historical situation changed radically not before but after the martyrdom of Guru Arjan. His son and successor, Guru Hargobind, reacted to that event by adopting a militant policy; he came into armed conflict with the Mughal authorities, and eventually left the Mughal territories to found a new centre at Kiratpur in the territories of a vassal chief of the Mughals. The opponents of Guru Hargobind criticised him for his departure from the style of his predecessors. They maintained that:

> The former Gurus used to stay at their *dharmsāls* but he does not stay at any one place. Kings used to visit them, but he was imprisoned in a fort by the king. The Sikhs cannot think of one resort now that he runs from place to place undaunted. The former Gurus used to gratify the Sikhs with discourses from their *manjīs,* but he keeps dogs to hunt. They used to compose *bāṇī,* to recite it and to hear it recited, but he neither composes, nor recites, nor hears it recited. He does not keep *sikh-sevaks* with him; he has befriended the enemies and oppressors.[12]

But this is not what Bhai Gurdas himself believes. He is critical of the opponents who are trying to influence the Sikhs against Guru Hargobind. For Bhai Gurdas he is the only true Guru, and the true Sikhs are still enamoured of his lotus feet. We may be sure that the opponents of Guru Hargobind are primarily the dissenters and their supporters.

Bhai Gurdas is explicitly critical of all the opponents of the successors of Guru Nanak:

> Sri Chand remained celibate and established a *dehura* of Baba Nanak. Lakshmi Chand's son Dharm Chand, though a grandson of Baba Nanak, thought more of himself. Dasu and Datu established their own centres. Mohan went mad and Mohri made his own residence a place of sanctity. Prithia became crooked (*mīṇā*) and spread falsehood through his devious ways. Though close to the source of fragrance, they imbibed no fragrance, like bamboo in the proximity of sandalwood.[13]

The last to be mentioned here is Prithi Chand, who is called *mīṇā.* This may be with reference to the time of Guru Arjan.

Elsewhere Bhai Gurdas devotes ten stanzas to *mīṇās* in the plural. They are 'black-faced', because they have turned away from the true Guru. They wear 'black' *tikkās* on their foreheads as pretenders to Guruship and as the rivals of the true Guru. They are trying to make false coins current, and their *panth* is dishonoured. They and their followers are bound for hell.[14]

The strong language used by Bhai Gurdas against the *mīṇās* as well as his preoccupation with them may be taken as a measure of the gravity of the situation during the time of Guru Hargobind.

Today we happen to know more about the *mīṇās* than what was known to Indubhusan Banerjee. Prithi Chand lived for over a decade after the martyrdom of Guru Arjan. However, neither he nor his son Miharban was able to occupy Ramdaspur until Guru Hargobind left the Mughal territories and Ramdaspur in the 1630s. Miharban then established control over the town before his death in 1639, and his son, Harji, remained in occupation of Ramdaspur until his death in 1696. Thus, an indirect result of Guru Hargobind's conflict with the Mughal government was the loss of Ramdaspur.[15]

With the most important Sikh centre under their control, Miharban and Harji tried to consolidate their position. An elaborate exposition of the *bāṇī* of Guru Nanak was prepared by Miharban and his sons, Harji and Chaturbhuj, in the form of voluminous Janamsākhīs, by 1652. This could establish their credentials as inheritors of the original Sikh tradition. To each exposition they added their own compositions with the obvious implication that, unlike Guru Hargobind, they too could compose *bāṇī.* Furthermore, they recognized the line of succession upto Guru Arjan. While doing this, they did not forget Prithi Chand: he was treated as the sixth Guru. Miharban became *mahala satvān* and Harji *mahala aththvān,* using the pen-name 'Nanak' in their compositions.[16] Clearly then, they accepted and advocated the idea of the unity of Guruship. What they were trying to by-pass was the principle of nomination in its application to Guru Hargobind and his successors. The claims of the *mīṇās* were thus much broader than the claims of heredity. They were presenting themselves as the bearers of the early Sikh tradition, not only against Guru Hargobind and his successors but also against the other dissenters nearer home.

The activity of the *mīṇās* proved to be contagious in the historical situation of the seventeenth century. Before Guru Hargobind died in 1644, he installed Har Rai, the younger son of his eldest son Gurditta, to be his successor because Dhir Mal, the elder son, showed no inclination to bear the burden. He had already received revenue-free land in Kartarpur, near Jalandhar, from the Mughal emperor Shah Jahan 'by way of *in'ām*'.[17] Furthermore, Dhir Mal refused to acknowledge Guru Har Rai, and established his own centre at Kartarpur which had been founded by Guru Arjan and inherited by Guru Hargobind and which, consequently, Dhir Mal could claim as his share of inheritance. He is reputed to have possessed the original Granth prepared by Guru Arjan, which could buttress his position.[18] He recognized the line of succession upto the sixth Guru, claiming to be the seventh to start a new line of succession.

The case of Ram Rai presents a broad parallel to that of Dhir Mal. Guru Har Rai is believed to have thought of assisting Dara Shukoh against Aurangzeb, and Aurangzeb called him to Delhi. Har Rai sent his elder son Ram Rai who compromised himself by suggesting an alternative reading of a verse of Guru Nanak.[19] Guru Har Rai decided to nominate his younger son, Harkrishan, as the Guru. This decision was contested by Ram Rai through a representation to Aurangzeb. Guru Harkrishan too was called to Delhi. Before long he died of small pox. He is believed to have indicated that his successor was to be the Baba at Bakala. Tegh Bahadur was accepted as the Guru by an influential body of Sikhs. Ram Rai refused to acknowledge Tegh Bahadur as the Guru, just as he had refused to acknowledge Guru Harkrishan. Eventually, through Auranzeb's patronage, Ram Rai received revenue-free land and settled down in a place which came to be called Dehradun. He acknowledged the line of succession upto the seventh Guru just as the *mīṇās* had acknowledged it upto the fifth and Dhir Mal upto the sixth.

In the sixteenth century, the descendants of the Gurus had sought to control the established religious centre on the basis primarily of their legal claims. But they had failed to make the principle of heredity more effective than that of nomination. They had not invoked any new doctrines in support of their position. They had presented a threat to the position of the Guru not due to the number of their followers so much as because of their hobnobbing with local officials. In the seventeenth century, the dissenters adopted a more clearly pro-establishment attitude precisely when the Gurus of the central stream were adopting an anti-establishment stance. The dissenters also accepted the early Sikh tradition and tried to make use of the idea of the unity of Guruship. Long residence in Ramdaspur and Kartarpur enabled the *mīṇās* and the Dhir Mallias to move the *masands* as well as Sikhs away from the nominated Gurus. Consequently, the Bari and Jalandhar Doabs were virtually lost to the successors of Guru Hargobind.

NOTES

1. Bhai Gurdas, *Vārān Bhāi Gurdās*, ed. Giani Hazara Singh, Amritsar: Khalsa Samachar, 1962, Vār 6: pauṛī 33.
2. *Ādi Sri Gurū Granth Sāhib Jī* (Sri Damdami Bir, various printed editions, standard pagination), pp. 474-5.
3. Ibid., p. 753.
4. Ibid., p. 517.
5. Bhai Gurdas, *Vārān Bhāī Gurdās*, Vār 26: pauṛī 33.
6. The legal dimension of the situation has not been noticed by the historian. Indubhusan Banerjee, for instance, is struck by the fact that every one of the first three successors of Guru Nanak left the place of his predecessor and sought out a new one for himself. This, according to Banerjee, could be explained only on 'the supposition that each of these Gurus found the place of his predecessor extremely uncomfortable owing to the undisguised hostility of the latter's descendants', Indubhusan Banerjee, *Evolution of the Khalsa*, Calcutta: A. Mukherjee and Co., 1963, vol. 1, p. 262.

   For the existence of proprietary rights in general and the application of the state law to Muslims and non-Muslims alike in matters of property, see J.S. Grewal 'The Qazi in the Pargana', *Studies in Local and Regional History*, Amritsar: Guru Nanak Dev University, 1974, pp. 1-36. For a study of legal documents executed in the court of the *qāzī* of Batala, see J.S. Grewal, *In the By-Lanes of History*, Shimla: Indian Institute of Advanced Study, 1975.
7. Bhai Gurdas, *Vārān Bhāī Gurdās*, Vār 26: pauṛī 33.
8. *Ādi Sri Gurū Granth Sāhib Jī*, p. 307.
9. Indubhusan Banerjee, *Evolution of the Khalsa*, vol. 1, p. 191.

10. In the circumstances leading to the martyrdom of Guru Arjan two elements are emphasized: the hostility of Chandu Shah and Guru Arjan's meeting with the rebel prince Khusrau.
Jahangir gives the impression that he was looking for an opportunity to act against Guru Arjan even before the rebellion of the prince. *Tuzuk-i Jahangiri* in *Sikh History from Persian Sources,* eds. J.S. Grewal and Irfan Habib, New Delhi: Tulika/Indian History Congress, 2001, p. 57.
In the Sikh tradition the intrigues of Prithi Chand are emphasized.
11. Indubhusan Banerjee, *Evolution of the Khalsa,* vol. 1, p. 262.
12. Bhai Gurdas, *Vārān Bhāī Gurdās,* Vār 26: pauṛī 24.
13. Ibid., Vār 26: pauṛī 33.
14. Ibid., Vār 36: pauṛīs 1-8. In the first pauṛī of Vār 36, Bhai Gurdas asserts that the Guru is the true Guru and the *mīṇās* are 'black faced'. The import of the pauṛī is that they have learnt nothing from the Gurus in spite of being so close to them. In the second pauṛī, the *mīṇās* are compared to the jackal who passes as a lion after having been accidentally dyed in the dyer's vat, but is exposed by its howl. The falsehood of the *mīṇās* shall make them suffer in God's court. In the third pauṛī they are compared with the thief whose nose and ears are cut off. They live on carrion. In the fourth pauṛī, the *mīṇās* stand bound for hell because they are trying to vie with the creator. In the fifth pauṛī, the *sangat* of the *mīṇās* is presented as essentially false. In the sixth pauṛī, the false path of the *mīṇās* is compared to a mirage: those who associate themselves with the *mīṇās* leave the world with all their hopes unfulfilled. In the eighth pauṛī, the *mīṇās* are presented as crows pretending to be nightingales; they are the detractors who have turned away from the true Guru to mark their foreheads with black *tikkās* to strike false coins. They have been cursed by the Guru.
In the ninth pauṛī of Vār 36, *mīṇās* are not mentioned, but the import is clear that they claim to be Gurus without possessing any merit. The tenth pauṛī underlines the uselessness of the *simmal* tree which lures parrots; the implication, again, is clear enough. In the eleventh pauṛī, the self-styled meritless *gurūs* are compared to the enunch who wishes in vain to act like a husband.
15. The Janamsākhīs compiled by Prithi Chand's son Miharban and the latter's sons, Harji and Chaturbhuj, have been published with introductory essays by several scholars as *Janam Sākhī Sri Gurū Nānak Dev Ji,* eds. Kirpal Singh and Shamsher Singh Ashok, Amritsar: Khalsa College, 1962 and 1969.
16. The compositions of Miharban and his sons are given in the third appendix to the first volume and in the appendix to the second volume. In one of his compositions, Miharban denounces those who are proud of their Guruship.

In some other ways also, the compilers of the Janamsākhī try to reinforce their claim. In the Goshti Miharban Ji ki, attributed to Harji, Guru Nanak is made to prophesy that the seventh Guru shall reveal the true meaning of his *bāṇī*. *Janam Sākhī Sri Gurū Nānak Dev Jī*, vol. 1, pp. vii, x, 25, 39.

17. A *farmān* of Shah Jahan issued on 29 November 1643 contains reference to revenue-free land given in Kartarpur in the Pargana of Jalandhar in the province of Lahore in perpetuity by way of *in'ām*. *Mākhaz-i Tawārīkh Sikhān*, ed., Ganda Singh, Amritsar: History Society, 1949, pp. 51-2.
18. The descendants of Dhir Mal at Kartarpur are still believed to be in possession of the original Granth. It has been seen by several scholars and detailed comments on the Granth have also appeared in print. A few scholars have questioned its authenticity.
19. According to the Sikh tradition, Ram Rai substituted *be-īmān* for *musalmān* in a verse of Guru Nanak's *Āsā dī Vār*. Indubhusan Banerjee, *Evolution of the Khalsa*, vol. II, pp. 51-2.

9

In Defence of the Freedom of Conscience

The historians of Guru Tegh Bahadur have generally relied on later Persian chronicles, little realizing that the Persian chronicles are not reliable for the time of Guru Tegh Bahadur. A close analysis of all these chronicles has revealed that most of the elements in them come actually from the tradition current during the last quarter of the eighteenth century. No written source in Gurmukhi was available to the authors of the chronicles and they had to depend largely upon those who had heard or read Gurmukhi texts. Information at second-hand was then refracted through the mind of the chronicler.[1] Though the Sikh tradition is more reliable than the Persian chronicles, it is not so valuable as the compositions of Guru Tegh Bahadur. His compositions indicate that his basic problem was to uphold the claims of conscience in a trying situation.

We may notice, first, that Guru Tegh Bahadur wrote within the parameters evolved by Guru Nanak and his sixteenth-century successors. His profound link with the founders of the Sikh Panth is evident from his *bāṇī* which propounds the same theology, the same spiritual message, and the same path as enunciated by Guru Nanak. Guru Tegh Bahadur uses a score of epithets for God. The most frequently used epithets are Rām and Harī, followed by Prabhū and Gobind. Occassionally, he refers to God as Swāmī, Devā, Mādho, Niranjan, Murār, Dīnā Nāth, Brahm, Prītam, Bhagwant, Dīn Bandhu, Nārāin, Chintāmaṇī, Kanhāi, Bhagwān, Raghūnāth, and Gosāīn. This multiplicity underlines the unity of God perhaps more than anything else. God, for Guru Tegh Bahadur, is transcendent as well as immanent: He is *aginat, apār, alakh, niranjan, nirlep, alep, niārā*. He is also *nānārūp* and *sarbnivāsī*. God is within man as well as in the universe. God is the creator of everything; He alone is eternal. He is perfect, almighty, merciful. He is the remover of fear, the protector of his devotees.[2]

The universe is God's creation (*rachnā*) and is subject to annihilation. Whatever is visible is subject to annihiliation 'like the shadow of a cloud'. The universe is God's *māyā*: it is a 'mountain of smoke', a 'wall of sand'. In contrast with the truth of God's eternity, the universe is false precisely because it is not everlasting. Similarly, the human body is false (*jhūth, mithiā*); only 'Rām' within is true (*sācho*).

However, man is attracted by *māyā*, which includes almost everything except God. His bondwoman, *māyā*, is like a mirage for man, ever-present but always elusive. Attachment to perishable things like riches, power, human ties, the body and its pleasures serves as a snare for man who remains engrossed in *māyā* because of his five adversaries: *kām, krodh, lobh, moh*, and *hankār*. They stand in his way of understanding God's omnipotence and his own nothingness.

Engrossment in *māyā*, aided by the inner adversaries of man, keeps man chained to the cycle of death-and-rebirth, and he does not attain to liberation. Guru Tegh Bahadur uses various synonyms for liberation: *muktī, jīvan-muktī, pad-nirbān, nirbhai pad*, for example. Occasionally the epithets *baikunth* and *giān* are also used for the state of liberation which is the supreme purpose of life. Human existence is a rare opportunity for realizing that purpose. The person who does not know the purpose is asleep, not awake; he is *durjan, mūrakh, gawār*, and *agiānī*, steeped in ignorance (*durmat, kummat*). Opposed to *durmat* or *kummat* is Gurmat, and he who is attuned to Gurmat is Gurmukh. For such a person two other epithets are used by Guru Tegh Bahadur: *sādh* and *sant*. Those who have adopted the path of liberation (*muktī-path*) are addressed as brother (*bhāī*) and friend (*mīt*). An ordinary person is addressed as *prāṇī, nar*, or *jan*. But everyone is invited to follow the path of liberation.

To discard heedlessness and indifference, to be aware of the transmigratory noose of death, is the first step on the way to liberation. To refrain from evil acts (*pāp*) is another. To join the *sādh-sangat*, to take refuge with the Guru, to listen to his instruction and seek knowledge from him is to ensure one's progress on the path. Sensual pleasures are to be renounced by cultivating a high degree of detachment from *māyā*. The idea of detachment is given primacy by Guru Tegh Bahadur: man should not simply escape the stranglehold of *kām, krodh, lobh, moh, hankār*, riches, goods, power and the comforts of *māyā*, he should also remain psychologically indifferent to joy and sorrow, praise and blame, happiness and suffering, honour and dishonour, nectar and poison, gold and dust, love and fear. He should remember the omnipotent and omnipresent Lord, and offer loving devotion (*prīt, bhaktī*) to Him through *simran, kīrtan* and *bhajan* and by appropriating the Name (*nām*). He should seek God within himself. Through God's grace, then, he may attain to liberation.

In the *bāṇī* of Guru Tegh Bahadur we find echoes of all the primary concerns of Guru Nanak. If there is no reference to contemporary forms of religious belief and practice, it is precisely because Guru Tegh Bahadur, as a successor of Guru Nanak, takes for granted his evaluation of those beliefs and practices as futile in terms of liberation. There is, however, a certain shift of emphasis. Political power for Guru Tegh Bahadur is a part of *māyā*; it is a 'wall of sand'; in the hands of others, it is not a source of fear for him. God annuls all fear (*bhai-bhanjan*). The state of liberation for Guru Tegh Bahadur is a state of fearlessness (*nirbhai pad*). His own maxim, 'I do not cause terror to anyone; nor do I entertain fear of any', exemplifies his life as the prophet of assurance in a grave historical situation.[3]

Towards the end of March 1664, Guru Harkrishan died in Delhi after indicating to the Sikhs present that his successor was 'the Baba at Bakala'. Some of the prominent Sikhs of Guru Harkrishan arrived in Bakala in August to request Tegh Bahadur to assume the Guruship in accordance with his nomination by Guru Harkrishan. He accepted the office. It is safe to assume that Guru Tegh Bahadur knew that he was assuming a difficult office. He had seen much in life. Born at Ramdaspur in April 1621, he had received education and training under the direct supervision of his father, Guru Hargobind. Theology, music, horsemanship, and the use of arms occupied much of his time before he participated in the battle of Kartarpur in 1635. For nine years then he stayed in Kiratpur, where Guru Hargobind had lived in his customary grandeur, maintaining hundreds of trained horsemen and matchlock men until his death in 1644. The eldest son of Guru Hargobind had died in his lifetime and he chose his younger grandson, Har Rai, as his successor, ignoring the elder Dhir Mal. This nomination was not accepted by Dhir Mal who had established himself at Kartarpur as a Guru. In contrast with Dhir Mal, Tegh Bahadur accepted the nomination of Har Rai with grace and moved to Bakala with his wife, Mata Gujari, and his mother, Mata Nanaki.

Guru Har Rai died in 1661 after nominating his younger son, Harkrishan, as his successor, ignoring the elder Ram Rai who had tried to ingratiate himself with Aurangzeb during the lifetime of his father. Guru Harkrishan was called to Delhi by the emperor and both the brothers were there in March 1664. Guru Harkrishan died of small pox while the issue of Guruship was still unresolved. Tegh Bahadur was well aware that to accept the Guruship of the Sikhs in 1664 on the demise of Guru Harkrishan was to go against the wishes of Aurangzeb. Therefore, his assumption of the office of Guruship, undoubtedly an affront to Aurangzeb, was an act of courage.

In its historical context, this decision was indeed a momentous one. Guru Nanak and his four successors had made the Sikh Panth a kind of state within the Mughal empire. Every Sikh had virtually two loyalties: one to the Guru and the Panth and the other to the Mughal state. So long as the Sikhs did not have to choose between them there was no difficulty, but after the execution of Guru Arjan in 1606, Guru Hargobind obliged the Sikhs to make their choice by openly defying the government. Most Sikhs chose to side with him in this new positon, but not all. Furthermore, Dhir Mal, who did not accept Guru Har Rai as the Guru and put forth his own claims to be the successor of Guru Hargobind, was not disposed to offend the rulers in any way. Similarly, when Guru Har Rai nominated Harkrishan as his successor, Ram Rai felt encouraged to put forth his rival claims.

Ram Rai was patronized by Aurangzeb. Both Dhir Mal and Ram Rai, supported by some *masands*, were surely 'pro-establishment' in their attitude. This precisely was the posture adopted by the followers of Prithi Chand and his son Miharban. Thus, in 1664 there was no one to emulate the independence of Guru Hargobind. By assuming the *gaddi* of Guruship, Tegh Bahadur imposed this task upon himself.

With this background, the leadership of Guru Tegh Bahadur acquires a new dimension. He was opposed at Bakala by Dhir Mal and abandoned Bakala. At Ramdaspur he was not welcome to Harji and his followers. Travelling through the Majha and Malwa regions, he reached Kiratpur in the summer of 1665, where the descendants of Guru Hargobind were perhaps unwilling to accommodate him. He decided to found Makhowal. A few months later he was travelling towards the eastern Sikh Sangats. From 1666 to 1670 he stayed outside the Punjab, visiting places like Prayag, Benares, Buddh Gaya, Patna, Monghyr, Malda, Dacca and Dhubri (in Assam).

During 1673 and 1674 Guru Tegh Bahadur undertook intensive work in Malwa, inspiring people with confidence and encouraging them to face all odds and difficulties. This was a silent but sure protest against Aurangzeb's aggressive policy of persecution. In 1675 he received some Brahmans who had come to represent the plight of their co-religionists against the high-handed policy of Aurangzeb. The effect of Aurangzeb's persecution was felt in several parts of the empire. Guru Tegh Bahadur decided to defend the freedom of conscience which the emperor was denying on principle as well as in practice. Before he could meet the emperor, he was arrested and taken to Delhi. There he was kept in confinement for a few months. As proof of his nearness to God he was asked to perform a miracle. He refused to admit even the propriety of such an attempt. Alternatively, he was asked to embrace Islam. He refused. The result was his execution in Chandni Chowk in November 1675.

Guru Tegh Bahadur's martyrdom is recorded in the *Bachittar Nātak* in the following words:

> Without a murmur he gave up his life for the sake of holy men. For the sake of *dharm* he gave up his head. He did not divulge the secret of his

nearness to God. The true devotees of God shun the magical tricks of a miracle. Guru Tegh Bahadur did what none else could do. He defied the ruler of Delhi to the point of sacrificing his life.

Guru Gobind Singh was deeply influenced by the unqualified commitment and unflinching courage of his father and predecessor. Ratan Singh Bhangu, whose *Panth Prakāsh* testifies to the martyrdom of Guru Tegh Bahadur as a source of inspiration for the succeeding generations of Sikhs, attributed the fall of the Mughal empire to the martyrdom of Guru Tegh Bahadur. 'Henceforth the empire of Delhi began to shrink and the power of the Mughals began to lose its lustre.'[4] Guru Tegh Bahadur's martyrdom symbolizes the spirit of supreme sacrifice for the ideal of the freedom of conscience.

NOTES

1. For the Persian texts and their English translation, J.S. Grewal, *Guru Tegh Bahadur and the Persian Chroniclers*, Amritsar: Guru Nanak Dev University, 1976.
2. Gurbachan Singh Talib, *Guru Tegh Bahadur: Martyr and Teacher*, Patiala: Punjabi University, 1975.
3. Fauja Singh (ed.), *Guru Tegh Bahadur, Martyr and Teacher*, Patiala: Punjabi University, 1978.
4. Ratan Singh Bhangu, *Prāchīn Panth Prakāsh*, ed. Bhai Vir Singh, Amritsar: Khalsa Samachar, 1972 (rpt.), p. 39.

10

Bachittar Nātak: Proclamation of a Mission

The autobiographical *Bachittar Nātak* may or may not be the work of Guru Gobind Singh, but there is no doubt about its historical significance. It contains the most important clue to the institution of the Khalsa. Most modern historians have looked at the events of his life from the outside; consequently, they have missed the essential psychological background to the most momentous event of his life. It must not be forgotten that the *Bachittar Nātak* was composed only a couple of years before the institution of the Khalsa and, among other things, it embodies the conception of a mission which was sought to be clothed in the Khalsa.

The *Bachittar Nātak* opens with an invocation to God. But this is no ordinary invocation: 'I bow to the Holy Sword, with love and devotion'.[1] Without God's support there is no refuge and there is no other who is the protector of the meek. The comfort of *sants* and *sādhs* is His comfort and their misery is His misery. God cherishes the poor and the good and He can turn a blade of grass into a rock. The 'Holy Sword' refers to divine power as the destroyer of the wicked. The *Bachittar Nātak* presents a world-view in which God intervenes in the affairs of His creation from time to time to establish true worship. The agencies chosen for the purpose make use of physical force to overwhelm the forces of evil. Whenever God manifests His power in this way, there is no escape from it for the wicked.

No failure on the part of God's creatures is greater than their forgetfulness of God. He alone should command their devotion and worship. Agents like Krishna and Rama and gods like Vishnu, Brahma, and Shiva cannot be equated with the Creator. Indeed, the *raison d'être* of the universe is the worship of the One True Lord by all his creatures, and none should interpose himself between God and man. But God's creatures in the past had not honoured this moral commitment. God says:

> When I first created the universe, I made the demons who became evil and oppressive; they became intoxicated with the strength of their arms, and they ceased to worship the Supreme Being.

They were destroyed by God, and then:

> In their place I created the gods; but they too became entangled in power and self-worship; they started calling themselves supreme beings.[2]

Brahma, Vishnu, and Mahadev were as much to be blamed for this as the others. This was applicable to the earthly leaders as well as to heavenly creatures. Those who are specifically mentioned in this connection in the *Bachittar Nātak* are the Siddhs and Sādhs and Rikhīs in general and Datatariya, Gorakh, Ramanand, and Muhammad in particular. Their followers worshipped them rather than the Supreme Being. In fact, whoever could, established a *panth* of his own and, instead of discovering the True Lord, increased useless strife in the world.

Guru Nanak established true *dharm* in the Kaliyuga. God removed all suffering and sin from those who embraced the religion of Guru Nanak and they attained to liberation. The truth revealed by Guru Nanak was cherished by his successors who must all be regarded as one with Baba Nanak. Once it was recognized that they were all one, Guru Gobind Singh himself could be seen as the true successor of Guru Nanak.

Guru Gobind Singh was ordained by God to spread true religion among men and to bring them to their sense of duty towards God. He had come to fulfil God's purpose, without enmity towards anyone and without fear of anyone. He was a divine agent upholding the righteous against the wicked. God's servant, not God, he was nevertheless sent by the Master for the sake of *dharm,* to extend the true faith everywhere and to destroy the wicked and the sinful. Guru Gobind Singh's mission, therefore, was essentially to raise the saints and to root out the wicked as the enemies of God. The Sikhs were included among the saints, if not actually equated with them.

From the account of Guru Gobind Singh's battles in the *Bachittar Nātak* it is evident that he was convinced of his legitimate position as the true successor of Guru Nanak and of God's support to him in his arduous mission. Everywhere he attributes his success to God and thinks of himself and his Sikhs as under divine protection. It was incumbent upon the Sikhs in particular to realize that the cause of their Guru was the right cause. Nowhere does Guru Gobind Singh betray any bitterness against those who were opposed to him on the battlefield; but he is anxious to warn those of his followers or allies who had either betrayed him or had shown indifference to his cause. The successors of Babur and the successors of Baba Nanak exercised temporal and spiritual power through divine dispensation. The temporal authorities plundered those who had not delivered the Guru's money. Those who sought safety away from the Guru had come to grief at the hands of his opponents. Guru Gobind Singh was safe as his only refuge was God. 'What can the wretched enemy do to him whom the Friend preserves?' His devoted servants are preserved by God even 'as the tongue is preserved among the teeth'.

Guru Gobind Singh had no compassion for those who had left him and abandoned his cause, whether from self-interest or through fear of suffering. In fact, if any moral is to be drawn on this point from the *Bachittar Nātak,* it would be precisely this: those who had abandoned the Guru's cause were much worse than those who had opposed him openly in the field of battle.

> They who turn away from their Guru, their homes will be demolished in the next world, as in this. They shall be laughed at here and shall have no dwelling-place hereafter; they shall remain debarred from all hope. Nothing that they do shall succeed in this world, and they shall fall eventually into the pit of hell. They who turn away from the Guru's path shall have their faces blackened in this world and the next.[3]

We can see that in Guru Gobind Singh's view of the cosmic drama, the creator of the universe intervened from time to time to reinforce good in its struggle against evil and, depending upon the gravity of the situation, the divinely appointed instruments of good were entitled to a legitimate use of physical force against the wicked. But they who had been appointed for that task in the past had failed to establish His unqualified worship. Therefore all previous dispensations had been superseded by the *dharm* instituted by Guru Nanak; it was left for Guru Gobind Singh to defend the claims of that *dharm* by using physical force against the enemies of this divine dispensation. His Sikhs should be prepared for such a struggle in the cause of righteousness.

Guru Gobind Singh had got rid of the defaulters either by inflicting punishment on them or by disclaiming them as his Sikhs. In order to succeed in his *dharmyuddh,* he needed only those who were prepared to consecrate their lives to the great cause. This was the immediate background to his instituting the Order of the Khalsa. Its relevance for the Baisakhi of 1699 is quite obvious.

NOTES

1. *Sri Dasam Granth Sāhib,* ed. Ratan Singh Jaggi and Gursharan Kaur Jaggi, New Delhi: Gobind Sadan, vol. 1, pp. 104-5.
2. Ibid., pp. 146-7.
3. Ibid., pp. 176-7.

11

Zafarnāma: Declaration of Moral Victory

In his *Gursobhā* Sainapat refers to a letter sent by Guru Gobind Singh to Aurangzeb through Daya Singh and his five companions. He further relates how, marching through several important cities of India, Daya Singh reached Ahmadnagar and succeeded in getting that letter delivered into the hands of Aurangzeb after considerable difficulty. As a result, a *farmān* was issued by the emperor to the effect that Guru Gobind Singh could move about in safety. Sainapat briefly gives the contents of the letter written by the Guru, indicating first that all the wonderful things related in the letter could not but impress the emperor. Aurangzeb expressed the wish that the Guru should see him. But since the officials of the emperor had not honoured their pledged word, the ultimate responsibility for this perfidy lay with Aurangzeb, and if he wished that Guru Gobind Singh should meet him, all hostilities which were unjustified in any case must cease. Thus was established peace to the satisfaction of Guru Gobind Singh.[1]

Guru Gobind Singh's letter to Aurangzeb, known as the *Zafarnāma*, is included in the *Dasam Granth*. It is in Persian verse. Nearly all the known copies of the *Dasam Granth* contain this letter in either Gurmukhi or Persian script. It has been published by Ganda Singh after careful collation as an important source of Sikh history.[2]

The *Zafarnāma* contains references to some of the happenings in Guru Gobind Singh's life. The earliest in point of time is perhaps Guru Gobind Singh's armed conflict with the hill chiefs who are presented as idol-worshippers in contrast with the Guru who broke idols (metaphorically, being a monotheist). Then, there is a reference to some promises made by the Mughal officials, probably before the evacuation of Anandpur by Guru Gobind Singh who had resisted them for a considerable length of time. These promises were not kept; Guru Gobind Singh was obliged to fight the battle of Chamkaur in which he was overwhelmed by a disproportionately large number of Mughal troops and in which he lost nearly all his followers and two of his sons. Written and verbal messages were sent by Aurangzeb to Guru Gobind Singh, probably asking the Guru to present himself before the Emperor. Guru Gobind Singh's reply was composed at Kangar at a time when he had come to know about the execution of his other two sons at Sirhind. Guru Gobind Singh was not unwilling to meet the Emperor provided there was some tangible proof of the Emperor's good intentions. The urgency of the whole matter is underlined in the *Zafarnāma*.

These references are indeed valuable in themselves, particularly because of their autobiographical character. But they must be viewed in the context of the whole document and in conjunction with other contemporary or near-contemporary evidence. Guru Gobind Singh's writings are full of denunciation of the kind of religious opinion and practice that was prevalent among his contemporaries in the Punjab hills, and it may be conceded that his conflict with the hill chiefs arose largely, though indirectly, from these differences of religious beliefs and practices. The reference to this conflict in the *Zafarnāma*, besides assuming these differences, points out the justness of Guru Gobind Singh's monotheistic faith and the ironic injustice of the support given to the hill chiefs by Aurangzeb who prided himself on being an idol breaker. It is also significant that Guru Gobind Singh takes a stand on moral grounds.

The authenticity of the references to historical incidents is generally borne out by some of the available contemporary evidence. It is well known that the initial conflict of Guru Gobind Singh was with the hill chiefs, that Mughal contingents were sent to their aid with the approval of Aurangzeb, and that the Emperor was kept informed of the events (which included the death of the Guru's two sons in the battle of Chamkaur and the capture of his mother and the other two sons after the evacuation of Anandpur).

In one of the news items in the *Akhbārāt-i Darbār-i Mu'allā* (Jaipur), it is stated that Aurangzeb had ordered Guru Gobind Singh to present himself before the Emperor. A *farmān* in Mirza Inayat Ullah Khan's *Akhām-i-'Ālamgīrī* refers to a letter received from Guru Gobind Singh in which he had expressed his wish to meet Aurangzeb.[3] This evidence appears to support some of the things said in the *Zafarnāma.* A few other *farmāns* in the *Akhām-i-'Ālamgīrī* support Sainapat in his statement that a kind of peace was established between the Guru and the Emperor after he received Guru Gobind Singh's letter. In fact, Aurangzeb deputed a *gurz-bardār* and a *mansabdār,* Muhammad Beg and Shaikh Yar Muhammad, to approach Guru Gobind Singh through Mun'im Khan, the Governor of Lahore, and use all diplomacy in persuading him to meet the emperor. If Guru Gobind Singh wanted to march through the territory of Sirhind, his safety was to be guaranteed, and if he needed money for his travel, it was to be supplied from the booty seized from Anandpur.[4] Considering, then, that the historical incidents referred to in the *Zafarnāma* are on the whole authentic, the reference to promises broken by the Mughal officials may also be true, particularly because there is nothing improbable about the besieging commandants luring the besieged out of their entrenched positions by giving them all sorts of false promises.

It does not follow, however, that every detail of the *Zafarnāma* is to be accepted as literally true. It must not be forgotten that the text is in verse, a medium that imposes limitations of its own in spite of an author's honesty of purpose. The statement that through God's grace a single person can kill ten lakhs is to be taken only as an indication of faith in the power of God. At another place it is stated that forty starving men could not possibly face ten lakhs on the field of battle. It is generally believed that exactly forty followers were present with Guru Gobind Singh at Chamkaur. The number of the Khalsa at Chamkaur might have been forty, but this statement in the *Zafarnāma* can hardly be regarded as a valid evidence on the point.

The significance of the *Zafarnāma* lies more in its ideas and its general argument than in the factual information it contains. It opens with an invocation to God and the attributes of God mentioned here can be found in the other compositions of Guru

Gobind Singh. His God is merciful particularly to those who follow the way of truth and trust. Those who serve Him with devotion are protected by God against all enemies, and no harm can ever come to them. The only refuge of Guru Gobind Singh is Yazdān-Akāl (the Deathless One who embodied all goodness). The fact that Guru Gobind Singh had been protected by God was ample proof of the justness of his cause which was no other than the worship of the One True Lord.

Though Guru Gobind Singh had no quarrel with the government as such, he had to defend his cause with the force of arms if a quarrel was forced on him on account of his faith. The use of arms was his last resort in this situation. Indeed it was lawful to resort to arms when all other alternatives had failed.[5] It did not matter if his four sons had been killed, the Khalsa were still behind him.

Guru Gobind Singh took his essential stand on moral grounds, which lends unity to the seemingly slipshod *Zafarnāma*. The officials of Aurangzeb had forced an unjust war on him and had broken their oaths on the *Qur'ān*. If all this was done with the Emperor's approval, then the Emperor could not boast of being a Believer. He should have remembered the True Lord if in the life hereafter he wished God to remember him. By ignoring the question of justice, Aurangzeb had shown himself to be a stranger to statesmanship. In possession of immense power, he should not have forgotten that power was entrusted to the ruler for protecting innocent people and not for spilling their blood. The *Zafarnāma* thus became 'the epistle of moral victory' in the eyes of the Khalsa of Guru Gobind Singh.

NOTES

1. Sainapat, *Shri Gurū Sobhā*, ed. Shamsher Singh Ashok, Amritsar: Shiromani Gurdwara Prabandhak Committee, 1967, pp. 95, 97, 98, 99, 100, 101, 102.
2. Ganda Singh (ed.), *Mākhaz-i Tawārīkh Sikhān*, Amritsar: Sikh History Society, 1949, pp. 64-71.
3. Ibid., p. 73. J.S. Grewal and Irfan Habib (eds.), *Sikh History From Persian Sources*, New Delhi: Tulika/Indian History Congress, 2001, p. 98.
4. Ibid., pp. 98-9, Ganda Singh (ed.), *Mākhaz-i Tawārīkh Sikhān*.

5. The couplet that is often quoted on the point reads:
Chū kār az hama hīlat-i darguzasht
Halāl ast burdan b' shamshīr dast
'When there is no other way of dealing with the situation it is legitimate to take up the sword.' Note that this statement refers to a specific situation, the attack on Guru Gobind Singh by Mughal troops. He had no choice but to fight. To take this couplet as the basis of Guru Gobind Singh's general philosophy is misleading. Guru Gobind Singh's grandfather had taken up the sword and he himself had fought several battles even before the institution of the Khalsa. The legitimacy of the use of physical force in a righteous war has been underlined in the *Bachitter Nātak.*

12

Insistence on Justice

William Irvine was the first modern historian of Mughal India to pay serious attention to the relations of Bahadur Shah with Guru Gobind Singh. Basing himself on the statements of some early chroniclers like Warid, Irvine concluded that Guru Gobind Singh 'must have received some rank' from the Emperor. This conclusion has been rarely questioned by the modern historians of Mughal India. It appears satisfactorily to explain Guru Gobind Singh's presence at or near the court and camp of Bahadur Shah for over a year. The statements of some of the earliest chroniclers that Guru Gobind Singh had accepted service with the Emperor have lent a strong support to this view. It is interesting to note, however, that there are explicit and implicit statements in near-contemporary chronicles which mention only the presence of Guru Gobind Singh near the court and camp of Bahadur Shah. This evidence is generally ignored, presumably because no other reason of Guru Gobind Singh's presence with Bahadur Shah appears to be convincing. In fact no serious alternative to this explanation has been offered by the modern historians of Mughal India.

To some modern historians of the Sikhs, however, the explanation of Guru Gobind Singh's presence with the Mughal Emperor in 1707-8 does not mean an unqualified submission. The acceptance of a *mansab* in particular appears to be in flagrant contradiction with Guru Gobind Singh's character and earlier career. Indubhusan Banerjee, for instance, has argued at length against the service theory in his *Evolution of the Khalsa.* Unlike Irvine, Banerjee rejects the assertions of Persian chroniclers that Guru Gobind Singh accepted an official position in the army of Bahadur Shah on the grounds that the statements about the mere presence of the Guru with the emperor are more in consonance with the known character of Guru Gobind Singh. Indeed, though Banerjee does not say so, if Warid's whole account of Guru Gobind Singh is carefully examined in the light of what is now known of Guru Gobind Singh, Warid appears to be not only hostile to Guru Gobind Singh but also a very superficial and 'distant' observer of the events of his life. The literal acceptance of an isolated statement from Warid is extremely difficult to justify in the absence of supporting evidence.

Nevertheless, rejection of the service theory obliges the historian to offer a better explanation of Guru Gobind Singh's presence near the imperial camp for more than a year before his death in October 1708. Banerjee was quite alive to this obligation and he suggests that Guru Gobind Singh had met Bahadur Shah to seek redress against certain Mughal officials, notably Wazir Khan, the *faujdār* of Sirhind, who had inflicted heavy losses on Guru Gobind Singh. Curiously enough, the idea of revenge on Wazir Khan had suggested itself to Muhammad Qasim Lahauri.[1] Bhakt Mal goes to the extent of saying that Wazir Khan himself was so afraid of Guru Gobind Singh's success with Bahadur Shah that he hired an assassin to kill the Guru. Indeed, the fact that the two young sons of Guru Gobind Singh were executed at Sirhind on Wazir Khan's orders obliges one to believe that Guru Gobind Singh must have been actuated by a feeling of revenge against Wazir Khan. But there is no tangible evidence for this. In fact arguments from circumstantial evidence in favour of this view are convincing only if we assume a desire for revenge on the part of Guru Gobind Singh.[2]

The crucial point still to be determined is the purpose of the meeting with Bahadur Shah. The background of events must be taken into account. Guru Gobind Singh had instituted the Khalsa in 1699 and, soon afterwards, the chief of Kahlur was obliged to take notice of the growing numbers and activities of the Khalsa who appeared to threaten not only the jealously guarded authority of the chief, but also the integrity of his not very large dominions. His aim was to expel Guru Gobind Singh and the Khalsa from Anandpur on the plea that they lived within his territories without acknowledging his authority. But he soon realized that his own limited resources were not enough for achieving that aim. In fact, he failed to take the well-fortified Anandpur even with the aid of neighbouring chiefs. The only alternative left for him was to request his suzerain, Emperor Aurangzeb, for help. It was with the aid of the Mughal *faujdār* of Sirhind that Bhim Chand, the chief of Kahlur, succeeded in taking Anandpur finally in 1704. Their suçcess cost Guru Gobind Singh the lives of his chosen Khalsa, of all his four sons, and of his mother.

In 1705 Guru Gobind Singh negotiated with Aurangzeb. Sainapat's account of Guru Gobind Singh's life and mission gives briefly the contents of a letter he wrote to the Emperor. Guru Gobind Singh refers to the perjury of Mughal officials and underlines the moral obligation of the Emperor to pay immediate attention to this matter. He was willing to see the Emperor to discuss his case in person. That his letter had the desired effect on Aurangzeb is evident from one of his *farmāns* in which Mun'im Khan at Lahore is asked to make a reconciliation.[3] Before the end of 1706, Guru Gobind Singh had decided to see the Emperor. But Aurangzeb died while Guru Gobind Singh was on his way to Ahmadnagar, and the latter decided to see Bahadur Shah instead.

Guru Gobind Singh was given a reception by Bahadur Shah at Agra in July 1707. He went fully armed into the royal presence and was given a costly present along with a *khil'at*.[4] His appreciation of what passed between himself and the Emperor was soon conveyed to the Khalsa in the Punjab. This letter is most significant for its allusion to the purpose of the meeting. After mentioning the jewelled medallion and the *khil'at* presented to him, Guru Gobind Singh expresses his satisfaction with 'other matters'. He then informs the Khalsa that he would return to them in a few days. He asks the Khalsa to maintain friendly association, and to come fully armed to the Guru's presence on his return to Kahlur.[5] It is evident that Anandpur was very much in his mind, now as before. This is what a careful study of Guru Gobind Singh's whole career would lead one to expect. Anandpur, which had remained the cause of a protracted dispute between Bhim Chand and Guru Gobind Singh, was always regarded by Guru Gobind Singh as his ancestral inheritance and his 'home'. He had been unwilling to pay rent to the chief of Kahlur because no rent had ever been paid to him in the past. Guru Gobind

Singh's argument with the Mughal Emperor was basically a moral argument: in the initial conflict of the Guru with the hill chief, the Mughal officials had interfered on behalf of the party that had been in the wrong.

Guru Gobind Singh was not destined to return to Anandpur. His presence with or near the imperial court suited Bahadur Shah's purpose. As Prince Mu'azzam, Bahadur Shah had been sent towards the Punjab in 1696 and later appointed to the governorship of Kabul. Mun'im Khan was his deputy in Lahore. Thus, Bahadur Shaah had gained experience of the north-western parts of the empire. He was aware of the political situation in the Punjab. If the hill chiefs could be a source of trouble to the local *faujdārs*, the popularity of Guru Gobind Singh with his Sikhs scattered nearly all over the Punjab made him equally important from a political point of view. At one time, Bahadur Shah had been ordered by Aurangzeb to expel all the Sikhs from his territories, and thousands of Sikhs had been killed on their way to the Barakzais.[6] Bahadur Shah also knew that Aurangzeb had eventually decided upon reconciliation. In 1707, with the issue of succession to the Mughal throne not yet finally settled, it was in Bahadur Shah's interest to secure peace and order in the north-west; for his part it was highly politic to offend neither the hill chiefs nor Guru Gobind Singh: peace and order in the Punjab was indispensable to his success, and Guru Gobind Singh's awkward presence near the court was preferable to his dangerous freedom in the Punjab. The Emperor's gestures of good will and kindness were expected to keep the Guru in good humour and hopeful suspense.

In November 1707, when Bahadur Shah started on his campaign in Rajasthan, Guru Gobind Singh accompanied the imperial army and remained near the camp for ten more months. His continued presence with or near the camp could easily be interpreted by distant or superficial observers as his acceptance of service with Bahadur Shah, especially because Guru Gobind Singh and his Khalsa used to carry arms wherever they went. To many a contemporary and near contemporary chronicler, however, Guru Gobind Singh's presence with Bahadur Shah meant no more than mere presence.[7] On several occasions, Guru Gobind Singh left the camp to spend his time elsewhere in his own way. He continued preaching to all kinds of people. Little knowing that Bahadur Shah would be obliged to go from Rajputana to the Deccan to fight Kam Bakhsh, Guru Gobind Singh remained with the Emperor without participating in any of his campaigns. When Bahadur Shah moved towards Haidarabad, Guru Gobind Singh moved with him; he was probably encouraged to hope that the Emperor would soon be free to attend to the Punjab affairs. But Guru Gobind Singh died while Bahadur Shah was on his way to Haidarabad.

Within two years of Guru Gobind Singh's death, Bahadur Shah was obliged to move against the Khalsa in the Punjab as Guru Gobind Singh's followers had repudiated the government which had denied justice to him. They declared their sovereign rule, which in all probability, had been conceived by Guru Gobind Singh.[8]

On Guru Gobind Singh's death, it was represented to Bahadur Shah that the Guru's property should be considered for escheat. This has been regarded as proof of his having accepted service with the Mughals. This however is no proof. In the first place, Bahadur Shah ordered that this property was not to be touched as it was the property of a *darvesh*.[9] Second, the question of escheat could have come up because Guru Gobind Singh had died without an heir.[10]

NOTES

1. Muhammad Qasim Lahauri, '*Ibratnāma*, Amritsar Khalsa College, MS 1270. Irfan Habib, 'Guru Nanak, Guru Gobind Singh, and the Revolt under Banda Bahadur 1709-10 and 1713-16, from Muhammad Qasim "*Ibrat*", *Ibratnama*', in *Sikh History from Persian Sources*, eds. J.S. Grewal and Irfan Habib, New Delhi: Tulika/Indian History Congress, 2001, p. 115.
2. Khushwaqt Rai, *Tawārīkh-i Sikhān*, MS 1274. Sikh History Research Department of Khalsa College, Amritsar, p. 38. As an example of interpreting circumstantial evidence on the assumption that Guru Gobind Singh was thinking of avenging himself on Wazir Khan and that, consequently, Wazir Khan hired an assassin to murder him: Kirpal Singh, 'Facts about Guru Gobind Singh's Martyrdom', *The Sikh Review*, September-October, 1957, pp. 68-73.
3. Ganda Singh (ed.), *Mākhaz-i Tawārīkh Sikhān*, Amritsar: Sikh History

Society, 1949, p. 75. J.S. Grewal and Irfan Habib (eds.), *Sikh History from Persian Sources,* pp. 98-99.

4. Ganda Singh, *Makhaz,* p. 82. J.S. Grewal and Irfan Habib, *Sikh History from Persian Sources,* p. 106.
5. *Hukamnāme Guru Sāhibān, Mātā Sāhibān, Banda Singh ate Khālsā jī de,* ed. Ganda Singh, Patiala: Punjabi University, 1967, pp. 186-9.
6. Sri Ram Sharma, *The Religious Policy of the Mughal Emperors,* Bombay: Asia Publishing House, 1962, pp. 41-2.
7. For instance, Khafi Khan, *Muntakhab al-Lubāb,* Calcutta: 1984, pp. 651-2.
8. Banda Bahadur was sent towards the Punjab by Guru Gobind Singh shortly before his death. With the support of the Khalsa, he was expected to establish their rule. His early targets were the enemies of Guru Gobind Singh and his predecessors, which gives the impression that the purpose was revenge.
9. *Sikh History from Persian Sources,* p. 107.
10. The *Nairang-i Zamāna* and a report from the court of Bahadur Shah refer to a son of Guru Gobind Singh in 1708: *Sikh History from Persian Sources,* pp. 101-3, 107. The *Gursobhā* refers to Zorawar Singh, the son of Guru Gobind Singh in 1708: *Shri Gurū Sobhā,* ed. Shamsher Singh Ashok, Amritsar: Shiromani Gurdwara Prabandhak Committee, 1967, pp. 123-6. In the *Zafarnāma,* however, Guru Gobind Singh refers to the death of all his four sons : *Mākhaz-i Tawārīkh-Sikhān,* p. 1949. The *Chahār Gulshan* refers to Ajit Singh as the adopted son of Guru Gobind Singh, which clarifies the position: *Sikh History from Persian Sources,* p. 166.

13

Gursobhā: In Praise of the Khalsa

Sainapat enjoys the reputation of being one of the fifty-two bards patronized by Guru Gobind Singh. He has left to posterity a vivid account of the events of his patron's life in a work which was meant to glorify his achievement.[1] Sainapat's *Gursobhā* has been rightly regarded as one of the most valuable sources of Sikh history. In fact, it has been used as the basic source for what is often called the post-Khalsa phase of Guru Gobind Singh's life.[2] Our present purpose is not to examine the nature of evidence which the *Gursobhā* as a whole presents on the life of Guru Gobind Singh, but only to form an idea of the nature of his mission as presented by Sainapat.

Amidst frank admiration of all that was said or done by Guru Gobind Singh, Sainapat's preference for the creation of the Khalsa as the epitome of Sikhism and the *raison d'être* of Guru Gobind Singh's life comes into high relief. He accepts the account of the Guru's mission given in the *Bachittar Nātak.* Though in line with the true Gurus of the pure Panth, Guru Gobind Singh was sent by God to fulfil a specific divine purpose: to enable mankind to worship the true Lord, and to remove all obstacles from the path of this pursuit. To defend the claims of conscience against external interference, the purified Sikh followers of Guru Gobind Singh – the Khalsa – were to side with good against evil. As the vanguard of righteousness, they were secure in their eternal foundation in the image of the Guru himself; they were not to remain concealed or to suffer decrease; they were to be ever on the increase. This was how, according to Sainapat, the mission was conceived by Guru Gobind Singh.

Sainapat leaves the reader in no doubt that an important feature of the institution of the Khalsa was action against the *masands* who had been the mediating agency between a large number of Sikhs and the Guru. In fact the 'purification of the world' is equated by Sainapat with the 'removal of the *masands*'. The Sikhs were vital to the Guru as direct disciples and the Guru was indispensable to the Khalsa as water is to the fish. The link now forged between the Khalsa and the Guru was more important than any other human relationship. He was both father and mother. Through a vague but suggestive identification of God with Gobind and of Gobind with God, the Khalsa belonged to God through Gobind.[3]

The enunciation of the mission by Guru Gobind Singh on a certain Baisakhi made that day the most auspicious event in the life of the Guru. It was on that day that the chastening baptism (*khande kī pahul*) was administered to the true Sikhs who took upon themselves, consciously and deliberately, to dedicate their entire lives to the cause of righteousness. The baptized Sikhs became 'Singhs', an appellation which symbolized the courage of the Khalsa. They were asked to keep their *kesh* uncut, like their Guru and thus, even in external appearance they were cast in the image of their master. They were required to avoid all social intercourse with the *masands* and those who did not keep their *kesh* uncut. A baptized Sikh was not to smoke; he was not to observe the customary ceremony of *bhaddar.*[4]

The injunctions of Guru Gobind Singh regarding the observances (*rahit*) for the Khalsa were not acceptable to all Sikhs. Even on the day of initiation at Anandpur, only a part of the unusually large gathering accepted the purificatory baptism or the *rahit* of the Khalsa. The Khatris and Brahmans in particular were opposed to the new and radical injunctions, for they could not hope to maintain their status in the social order if they abandoned their age-old customs. Some of the Sikhs who had not gone to Anandpur for the Baisakhi refused to believe that the Guru had given any such instruction; some of them demanded a written order of the Guru; but some others did accept the *pahul* and the *rahit*. This situation led at places to dissensions among the Sikhs, leading to intervention by the Mughal officials. Some of the cautious, but nonetheless zealous, Sikhs went to the Guru himself for *pahul*.

Convinced of the divine sanction for Guru Gobind Singh's mission, Sainapat felt unhappy about its not being accepted by all the Sikhs in the first place. His explanation is significant: only the fortunate ones felt inclined to become the Khalsa. At places, he gives the impression as if it was preordained that some men would and others would not be fortunate enough to taste the baptism of the double-edged sword. Nevertheless, God could show the right path to whomever He was kind. Two kinds of people were marked for denunciation. Those who turned away from the Guru: they would never find release from the wheel of death-and-rebirth; and those who talked ill of the Khalsa: they would go to hell.[5]

Without minimizing the importance of the *rahit* in any way, Sainapat puts an equal, if not greater, emphasis on the worship of the one true Lord in the company of the devout (*sangat*). According to him it was through association with true Sikhs in a *sangat* that one could receive the grace of inclination towards the right path. The way to liberation, thus, lay through the *sangat*. The sanctity of the collective body of the Khalsa imparted to it an authority which the individual Sikh could not afford to ignore if he wished to remain a true Sikh. His faults and lapses could be forgiven by the *sangat*. In this respect there was no difference between the Guru and the *sangat*. Indeed, Sainapat makes it rather explicit that the true Guru and the *sangat* are one and the same. With the vague identification of the Guru with God on the one hand, and a clear identification of the *sangat* with the Guru on the other, Sainapat attributes almost a divine character to the collective body of the Khalsa which becomes sacrosanct and authoritative for the individual member. This idea gets linked with the statement of Guru Gobind Singh only a day before his death that the Khalsa represented his visible form (*rūp*). The office of Guruship was vested in the Khalsa. At the same time Guruship was vested in the *shabad-bāṇī* or the scripture.

NOTES

1. Two editions of the text have been published: *Shri Gurū Sobhā,* ed. Shamsher Singh Ashok, Amritsar: Shiromani Gurdwara Prabandhak Committee, 1967 and *Sri Gurū Sobhā,* ed. Ganda Singh, Patiala: Punjabi University, 1967.
2. Indubhusan Banerjee, *Evolution of the Khalsa,* Calcutta: A Mukherjee & Co., 1963, vol. II, pp.192-3; also, pp. 168-9.
3. *Sri Gurū Sobhā,* ed. Ganda Singh, pp. 168-9.
4. Ibid., pp. 22-5.
5. Ibid., pp. 26-7.

14

Celebrating Freedom: the *Vār* of Gurdas

The author of the forty-first *Vār* in the *Vārān Bhāī Gurdās* refers to himself as 'Gurdas'. He is generally referred to as 'Bhai Gurdas, the third', or 'Bhai Gurdas Singh'. There is a reference in his *Vār* to the end of Aurangzeb's family and the end of the twelfth century of the Hijra era. This indicates that the *Vār* was composed during the period of Sikh rule, probably towards the end of the eighteenth century. The title given to this *Vār* is *Rāmkalī Vār Pātshāhī Dasvīn kī*. However, the author refers to it as *Vār Bhagautī* in his work. The editor mentions an alternative title given to it: *Vār Sri Bhagautī jī kī Pātshāhī 10*. Probably the author was fascinated by Guru Gobind Singh's idea of *bhagauti* – the sword as the symbol of divine power employed in a righteous cause.[1]

The *Vār* was not a piece of secular literature for its author. Its reading could lead to liberation (*amrapad*), remove all sorrows and bestow bliss (*anand*). One could see God within oneself and all one's wishes could be fulfilled. He who recites the *Vār* to others will attain *muktī*. All his sins would be washed away and Dharmraj (Jamdharm) would not ask him to account for his deeds. At the end, the *Vār* is called '*mahā punit*'. It washes away all sins by generating trust (*partīt*). He who loves this *Vār* would have all his wishes fulfilled. All his sorrows are removed, and he enjoys peace and happiness. He who recites the *Vār* day and night would go to the divine court (Har Darbar).[2]

The use of two refrains divides this *Vār* formally into two unequal parts. In the first part of twenty *pauṛīs* the refrain used is *Wāh wāh Gobind Singh āpe gurchelā*. And in the second part of eight *pauṛīs* it is *Eion kar hai Gurdās pukārā, hae satgur muhe lehu ubārā.* The first six *pauṛīs* of the first part celebrate the Panth. In the eight *pauṛīs* that follow, praises of God are sung. The last six *pauṛīs* of this part celebrate the triumph of the Khalsa. The last eight lines of the twentieth *pauṛī* relate to the author's view of his *Vār* already noticed. Similarly, the last *pauṛī* of the *Vār* is about the *Vār* itself. Of the remaining seven *pauṛīs* of the second part, three relate to the Gurus and four to God. Thus the author dwells on three major themes: God, the Gurus, and the Sangat or the Panth.

When we read the *pauṛīs* relating to God we come upon epithets depicting his essential attributes. God himself is *onkār* and *ākār* (transcendent and immanent), who is and shall be. He can destroy and create in a trice without fear. The whole world is his sport (*khel*). He is the ocean of virtues. He is the Primal Being (*ād purkh*), the fearless (*anbhai*) and the boundless preceptor (*guru*) whose limits cannot be known. His depth cannot be fathomed. He is everlasting, gives without asking, and his is the true name (*sat-nām*). He is indestructible (*abnāsī*), has appeared in many forms, and is within everyone. He destroys sin (*aghnāsī*). He cannot be deceived. The incomprehensible, immortal, unchangeable God can be known through the *shabad* of the Guru. He is omnipresent (*sarab-biāpī*) and yet detached (*alep*). *Māyā* does not affect him.[3] We can see that this conception of God is characteristically Sikh.

Indeed, God is formless (*nirankār*). He is devoid of enmity (*nirvair*). He is the destroyer of sorrow (*dukh-dalan, dukh-bhanjan*). He is the kind master who bestows all kinds of gifts. He is perfect (*pūran*), the supreme God (*parmeshar*), the remover of sins (*patit-pāwan*), and the knower of innermost thoughts (*antar-jātā*). He is all-wise (*dānā*) and all-seeing (*bīnā*). He is the forgiver (*bakhsind*), himself the father and the mother. He is the destroyer of fear (*bhai-bhanjan, bhai-nāshan*), beautiful in form. He is the bestower of liberation (*mukand*). He himself is the one who leads to union (*jogī, sanjogī*). He is the protector (*rakhwālā*). Whatever he wills comes to pass. He is the true merchant (who takes accounts from his agents). He is merciful (*rahīm*). He himself is the male and the female. He is the king (*pātshāh*) who looks after all (his subjects). He is ever-present (*sadā hajūrā*).[4] It is clear that the attributes of God are coming from Gurbāṇī, including the compositions of Guru Gobind Singh.

God is the only object of worship for Gurdas. By serving him in the present age (*kalīkāl*), all sorrows are removed. By serving the True Master (*sachchā sāhib*), all one's wishes are fulfilled. Meditation on the Name is the most efficacious path to liberation. Birth as a human being is the precious opportunity to attain to liberation. One should worship God, the destroyer of fear (*bhai taras nās*). Liberation depends on God's grace. In the second part of the *Vār* Gurdas offers a fervent prayer to God. The refrain itself is indicative of the mood: 'Lead me to liberation O True Guru!' Even Brahma, Vishnu and Shiva cannot know God (without his grace). 'We are full of lust, anger, and falsehood. You are the forgiver and the redeemer'. There is no one else who can lead us to liberation. Your *hukam* covers the earth and the waters. 'One can swim across only by worshipping you'. The only way to liberation (*muktī*) is the worship of the only True Lord. 'The humble Gurdas is your devotee. His life has become easy by reciting your Name. Forgive all his sins and omissions and accept him as your slave'.[5]

All the ideas associated with divine self-revelation find mention in this *Vār*: Truth, Guru, Name, Shabad, Hukam, and Nadar. God is the truth (*sachch*). His throne is true (*sachchā*). He is the true master (*sachchā sāhib*). He is the true merchant (*sachchā vapārī*). The worldly occupations are all false by contrast. God is the true Guru (*satgur, satgur sachchā*). He is the Guru who commands praise (*wāhgurū*). Devotion is to be addressed to the Guru. Gur-bhagtī here is the synonym for Har-bhagtī. The True and priceless Name (*satnām*) is bestowed by God. The Name is the name of God (Har-nām). As we noticed earlier, God is known through the *shabad* of the Guru. This statement can refer to God's revelation as *shabad* and also to the *shabad* of the Gurus, or Gurbāṇī. In any case there is a direct reference to the *shabad* contained in the Granth. The word *nadar* is not used, but the idea of God's grace is emphasized by the attribute of *rahīm*. The word *kirpā* (kindness, mercy) is used explicitly in connection with the attainment of liberation.[6]

The idea of grace is closely allied with God's *hukam.* Since God is all powerful and nothing happens without His will, the way to liberation lies in his grace alone. In other words, grace is an expression of God's will. Gurdas emphasizes the importance of *hukam* as comprehending grace. In the twenty-seventh *pauṛī* of his *Vār* he dwells on both *kirpā* and *hukam.* It was God's *hukam* that through his grace Gurdas should write his *Vār.* Without God's *hukam* not even a leaf can move. Only that happens which he commands. All creation is subject to his *hukam.* Only he who recognizes his *hukam* can attain liberation. Not only the sun and the moon, but also Brahma, Vishnu and Mahesh are subject to God's *hukam.* All cherish the dust of his feet. The earth and the sky are subject to God's *hukam,* and so is each breath and every morsel. Without his *hukam* no one is born and no one dies. He who recognizes his *hukam* acquires stability. 'That is why Gurdas prays aloud: save me O True Guru'.[7] In the *Vār,* thus, we find the same theology as in the compositions of the Gurus from Guru Nanak to Guru Gobind Singh.

Gurdas refers to Guru Nanak at several places in the *Vār.* In one place he is simply Nanak. In another, he is Guru Nanak. He does not stand alone. He is at the head of a line of ten Gurus, the first *mahal.* He is not God, but is closely allied with divinity. His position as the true Guru on earth assimilates him to the True Guru, that is, God. A new dispensation was initiated by 'Har Satgur Nanak'. He meditated on the Name and worshipped the Creator. By promulgating the path of 'devotion to god' (Har-bhagtī) he saved the earth, and the whole of mankind, in accordance with the command of the ineffable (*alakh*) and the infinite (*apārā*). All things come to a happy end by serving Guru Nanak. He enabled Guru Angad to recognize God. The second *mahal,* Guru Angad, sang the praises of God. The third *mahal,* Guru Amar Das, realized God within himself by serving the true Guru (Angad). The fourth manifestation (*pargāsā*), Guru Ram Das, dedicated himself to God. The fifth, Guru Arjan, compiled a Granth of authenticated *shabad.* The recitation of this Granth was made current so that the whole world was redeemed by reciting the Name day and night.[8]

The sixth *avtār,* Guru Hargobind, held the sword and vanquished many a foe. He gave anxious moments to the Mughals who had started oppressing the devotees of God. The seventh *mahal,* Guru Har Rai, practised deep and long meditations so as to gather all power unto himself, but without revealing the fact to others. He strengthened the godly side. Guru Harkrishan reached Delhi to give up his life. He adopted the form of a boy to highlight the injustice of the Mughals: his death brought great discredit to them. He was received with honour in the divine court. Aurangzeb, who had shown hostility towards the Guru, ensured the end of his own family; incurring sins, they all went to hell. Guru Tegh Bahadur gave his head to stabilize the world. He did not reveal his power and the Mughals were deceived. He reached the divine court in accordance with God's will. The Mughals incurred blame, which became the cause of their downfall. Thus, the nine *mahals* adopted the way of devotion to defy and defeat the Mughals. The shouts of victory were heard by the whole world.[9]

Guru Gobind Singh, the tenth *avtār,* instituted the Khalsa to annihilate the Turks and to make the whole earth a garden of flowers (*gulzār*). None could withstand the Singh warriors, whose victory removed all sorrow and made worship of Immortal God secure. The followers of the path of devotion started by Guru Nanak were free to pursue it without hindrance.[10] We can see that Gurdas makes no distinction between Guru Nanak and his successors. The unity of the Gurus is reinforced by using *mahal, pargās,* and *avtār* as synonyms. Each carried forward the work of Guru Nanak. The tenth *avtār* enabled the followers of his predecessors to safeguard their cherished tradition against oppression and external interference. Gurdas does not see any difference between the followers of Guru Nanak and Guru Gobind Singh, between the Sikh and the Singh.

The first six *pauṛīs* of the *Vār* should be read in this perspective. The true congregation (*sat-sangat melā*) was established by God through Guru Nanak. The members of this congregation were invited by Guru Gobind Singh to taste the baptism of the double-edged sword. In this way 'Gur-sangat' was made Khalsa. 'Praise be to Gobind Singh who himself is the Guru and the disciple'.

His true injunction must be heard by all who are dear to the Guru; join the true congregation (*sat-sangat*). They who forget the master find no place in this *sangat*. They who turn to the Guru, their foreheads shine when they reach the true court. Remember 'Har-Gur-Gobind' in the ambrosial hours. The five adversaries (*kām, krodh, lobh, moh, hankār*) are subdued in the *sangat*. Only the self-centred (*manmukh*) remain in misery and sorrow.[11]

Gurdas contrasts the *manmukh* with the Gurmukh, as it is done in Gurbāṇī. It is important to remember, however, that the Gurmukh of the *Vār* is the Khalsa. All creation suffers from *haumai* but they who are enabled to recognize God's *hukam* become Gurmukh. Others are misled to remain affiliated to other than God. The gift of the Name is bestowed by God through his grace. The recipients of his grace are Gurmukhs, whose lives comes to fruition while the *manmukh* suffers the sorrow of rebirth. Only the fortunate ones turn to Gurbāṇī. They are Gurmukh. They are comparable with the woman who has a good husband. The *manmukh* is like an abandoned woman, the Gurmukh is a bright swan and the *manmukh*, a crow. The Gurmukh meets God and the *manmukh* wanders in transmigration. True is the Master, true his command, and true is Gurbāṇī. They who serve the True Guru receive peace and bliss. The *manmukh* suffers in the divine court, like sesame seeds in the oil-press. The Gurmukh is found in the true congregation (*sat-sangat*) where the praises of God are sung and truth is disbursed. He stands distinguished from the *manmukh* in the true court where true justice is dispensed.[12] The refrain of these *pauṛīs* reinforces the impression that whatever was true of the Sikh-Sangat is true the Khalsa-Sangat.

Guru Gobind Singh became manifest (*pragtio*) as the tenth *avtār*. He worshipped God and started the Khalsa Panth. With the *kesh* on their heads and the sword in their hands the Khalsa vanquished the enemy. They wore the *kachh* of sexual restraint and took up arms. They proclaimed the true victory (*fateh*) of the Guru and won the field. They annihilated the demon-like enemies. The worship of God was made manifest in the world. Thus rose the Singh warriors in their blue clothes. They proclaimed the Name (Har-nām) by destroying the wicked Turks. No one could withstand them; mighty leaders (*sardārs*) took to their heels; the rulers (*rāje, shāh*) and their nobles (*amīrs*) were reduced to dust.

The mountains trembled and the earth shook. People abandoned their homes and the world suffered misery in the clash. 'There is no one except the True Guru who puts an end to fear' (*bhai kātanhārā*). No one could stand against the might of the Khalsa. 'Praise be to Gobind Singh, at once the Guru and the disciple'.[13]

The Khalsa was instituted neither in response to any exegency nor with the idea of capturing political power as an end itself. In accordance with the *hukam* of Gurbar-Akal came intuitive understanding and the Khalsa was created in a perfect manly form. When the Singhs rose with a roar the world was frightened. They killed the *sultāns*, and the *pīrs* concealed themselves. The Turks and the Muslims, all things Islamic, lost their former dominance: the *Qur'ān* and the *sharī'at*; the mosque, the prayer, and the call to prayer; the *kalma* and the *sunnat* (circumcision); the *qāzīs* and the *mullās*; the *fātiha*, the *darūd* and the *zikr*; the *pīrs* and their *mazārs*. The religion and the *'ummat* of Mahammad were overshadowed by 'the third religion' (*tīsar mazhab*) and 'the third *panth*' of the Khalsa. The third *mazhab* and the third *panth* were different and distinct also from the Indic (*hindak*) tradition represented by the Vedas, Puranas, Shastras, temples and idols of stone, the *yagya* and the *hom*, the Brahman, Pandit, and Jotki. The *hukam* of Akal was made manifest in the world. The sword taken up by the Khalsa in accordance with the command of Guru Gobind Singh was meant to establish the worship of Akal on a secure footing by eliminating its enemy; the 'victory of the Guru' was meant to make the truth prevail.[14]

The larger purpose of the Khalsa sanctified Sikh rule in the eyes of Gurdas. Misery and sorrow yielded place to peace and bliss. The Khalsa wielded power without fear but with true justice. The things associated with Satyayuga were made current in the Kaliyuga. The annihilation of the Turks, the *mlechh*, was a prelude to the spread of truth. True *dharm* was made manifest so that the praises of God could be freely sung. Falsehood and deceit vanished before truth when the victory of the Guru ushered light in the world. There was no persecution on the basis of religion. In fact, what was established firmly by the Khalsa was freedom of the conscience. The freedom which the Khalsa won for themselves was extended to others. It became possible now to perform *jagg* and *hom*. The world began to live in happiness. It was made resplendent by the *dharm* promulgated by the Gurus to remove darkness. Here Gurdas gives a longish comment to the effect that the Sikh faith, that is, the faith of the Khalsa, leads to liberation. He invites others to seek refuge in Guru Gobind Singh.[15]

Guru Gobind Singh commands praise as a disciple of the Primal Being (*mard kā chelā*) who wrought revolution through the Khalsa. They raised their standards over the earth and became its rulers. They took care of the world and promoted happiness. They triumphed over the self-centred. They established true rule, and made true *dharm* manifest in the world in accordance with the *hukam* of Akal. Their victory established true seats of power. The world was reassured and could worship God without fear. The devotees of God could now join the congregation of the Guru's followers (*gur-sangat melā*). The Sikhs of the Guru (Gursikh) could now promote the way of devotion shown by the Guru (Gur-bhagtī). He who appropriates the Name is acceptable to God. He is freed from *kām, krodh, lobh, moh* and *hankār,* and he is enabled to practise the inner discipline. Here Gurdas uses metaphors from Yoga to refer to the path of liberation, control of the breath, the six *chakras, sunn-smādh* and *ānand.*[16] He leaves no doubt, however, that he is talking of the path of Guru Nanak.

If we look only for factual information in the *Vār,* we are bound to be disappointed. But the work as a whole provides extremely useful information on the view of the Khalsa propagated by a popular Sikh writer in the last decade of the eighteenth century. Bhai Gurdas does not try to provide a description of the institution of the Khalsa. He is emphatic nonetheless about the importance of baptism by the double-edged sword. He takes it for granted that Guru Gobind Singh accepted *khandedhār-pahul* from the Khalsa. They who taste the *pahul* keep their *kesh* uncut, wear the sword, and adopt the name Singh. They also wear *kachh* as the symbol of sexual restraint. They are manly (*mardānā*) not simply because they are brave warriors but also because they keep flowing beards. They adopt '*Wāhegurū jī kī fateh*' as a form of greeting. They wear blue dress. The Khalsa does not represent a new order; they are a continuation of the Sikh Panth instituted by Guru Nanak and his successors. They believe in the unity of the ten Gurus, and in Guruship of the Granth and the Panth. Not to belong to the Khalsa Panth is to be a non-Sikh. The identification of the Sikh with the Singh is complete.

Bhai Gurdas celebrates the triumph of the Khalsa and provides justification for Sikh rule but not as an end in itself. Attained through martyrdom, Sikh rule is sanctified by freedom of belief and the dispensation of justice. The faith and ideology of the Khalsa is the same as that of the pre-Khalsa Panth. Both the Sikh faith and the Khalsa Panth had an identity that was different and distinct from that of Muslims and Hindus. The religious faith of the Khalsa is still more important than their politics. Gurdas himself does not pray for power, or seek patronage. He prays for the boon of the Name, association with the Sangat, eradication of *haumai*, acceptance of the *hukam*, and attainment of liberation. There is no earthly power now to stand in the way of this pursuit. Freedom of the conscience is ensured by political freedom. Gurdas sings of this liberation.

NOTES

1. *Vāran Bhāī Gurdās*, ed. Giani Hazara Singh, Amritsar: Khalsa Samachar, 1962 (4th edn.), Vār 41: pauṛīs 1, 19, 20, 28. The word *bhagautī* was used by Sainapat in the *Gursobhā* for the sword. It may be pointed out that the epithet 'Kalka' is used for the deity in pauṛī 1 of the Vār, but God is both male and female in pauṛī 13. What is far more important, the conception of God in this Vār is characteristically Sikh.
2. Ibid., pauṛīs 20, 28. Probably, the *Vār* was expected to be sung by *dhādīs*.
3. Ibid., pauṛīs 7, 8.
4. Ibid., pauṛīs 9, 10, 11, 12, 13.
5. Ibid., pauṛīs 8, 11, 12, 13, 25, 26.
6. Ibid., pauṛīs 1, 3, 5, 6, 7, 9, 12, 14, 15, 18, 20, 21, 23, 26, 28.
7. Ibid., pauṛī 27.
8. Ibid., pauṛīs 1, 21, 23, 24.
9. Ibid., pauṛīs 21, 22, 23.
10. Ibid., pauṛī 2, 4.
11. Ibid., pauṛī 1.
12. Ibid., pauṛīs 2, 3, 4, 5, 6.
13. Ibid., pauṛī 15.
14. Ibid., pauṛīs 16, 17.
15. Ibid., pauṛīs 17, 18.
16. Ibid., pauṛīs 19, 20.

15

In Persian Historiography

There is hardly a historian of the Sikhs who has not underlined the crucial importance of Guru Gobind Singh. This is true not only of the majority of modern historians but also of the late eighteenth-and early nineteenth-century Persian chroniclers who generally wrote for their British patrons. In the life of Guru Gobind Singh no other event is equated in importance with the institution of the Khalsa. This historiographic tradition of over two hundred years is the historian's tribute to Guru Gobind Singh.

Nevertheless, a true appreciation of the crucial role of Guru Gobind Singh in Sikh history demands a close attention. The chief difficulty of the historian arises from the paucity of contemporary or near-contemporary evidence. No doubt, there are Guru Gobind Singh's own valuable compositions in verse and his *hukamnāmas* in prose, some very useful reports and *farmāns*, an almost contemporary account of his life, and many near-contemporary references to some of the events of his life. However, only a small proportion of this evidence relates directly or indirectly to the Khalsa. It may be pointed out that even this evidence has not been used by all the modern historians of Guru Gobind Singh. They have generally depended upon later evidence.

Indeed, abundant material on the life and mission of Guru Gobind Singh both in Persian and Punjabi came into existence in the late eighteenth and early nineteenth centuries. But to interpret this later evidence is not an easy task. Most of the modern historians of Guru Gobind Singh have adopted the very simple method of selecting one and rejecting another detail from one or more of the chronicles. But once that selection is made, the isolated point or passage is treated as literally true. It is extremely difficult to find justification for this simple method of treating later evidence. It should be unwise to reject tradition merely because it is much later to the events. The later tradition can provide useful clues to past probabilities. However, it cannot be taken literally.

The point may be illustrated with a specific example. A favourite 'authority' on what happened on the Baisakhi of 1699 is the *Tawārīkh-i Panjāb* by Ghulam Muhiyuddin alias Bute Shah. One passage from this work is often quoted with approval.[1] Guru Gobind Singh is supposed to be addressing the great gathering at Anandpur as follows:

> Let all embrace one creed and obliterate difference of religion. Let the four Hindu castes who have different rules for their guidance abandon them all, adopt the one form of adoration, and become brothers. Let no one deem himself superior to another. Let none pay heed to the Ganga and other places of pilgrimage which are spoken of with reverence in the Shastras, or adore incarnations such as Ram, Krishan, Brahma, and Durga but believe in Guru Nanak and other Sikh Gurus. Let men of the four castes receive my baptism, eat of one dish, and feel no disgust or contempt for one another.

This exhortation is so detailed that some modern historians have believed it to be the report of some eye-witness.[2] But the authority of this passage rests on nothing more than its plausibility. In fact this passage becomes plausible only when it is taken out of its context. The speech which Ghulam Muhiyuddin ascribes to Guru Gobind Singh begins with a significant statement.

> You should remember that the Musalmans have maltreated us. They have killed our ancestors and, having been uprooted from our homes, we have taken refuge from their tyranny in these mountains. Now, in accordance with the mandatory wish of my father, Guru Tegh Bahadur, I cherish the desire of avenging myself upon my father's murderers.[3]

This statement is significant because, in Ghulam Muhiyuddin's considered view, the one consuming passion of Guru Gobind Singh was vengeance: 'So long as I live', he is made to say earlier, 'I shall meditate revenge, to the point of risking my life in pursuit of this purpose.'[4] It was for this purpose that, according to Ghulam Muhiyuddin, Guru Gobind Singh had taken an irrevocable decision to muster armies and conquer territories, and it was for this very purpose that he created the Khalsa. [5]

Ghulam Muhiyuddin attributes this motive to Guru Gobind Singh on an obvious assumption about human psychology: a son would naturally think of vengeance upon his father's murderer. Ghulam Muhiyuddin's extremely faulty chronology could lend further support to his assumption. The creation of the Khalsa is placed by him soon after the execution of Guru Tegh Bahadur in 1675; all the battles of Guru Gobind Singh follow upon the creation of the Khalsa.

If Ghulam Muhiyuddin's whole account of Guru Gobind Singh is analysed, it becomes possible to see that he was basing himself either on the tradition which had developed during the past hundred years rather than on any early evidence. This is evident from his treatment, for instance, of the episode of the Goddess, the forecast about the end of the *masands* in the future, the wanderings of Guru Gobind Singh after the battle of Chamkaur, the composition of the *Dasam Granth* at Talwandi Sabo, the cause and circumstances of Guru Gobind Singh's death. In fact, Ghulam Muhiyuddin does not betray any anxiety about early evidence, and we may be sure that the speech which he attributes to Guru Gobind Singh on the day of creating the Khalsa is purely an imaginative feat. Direct speech was a stylistic feature with the author of many a chronicle, and the *Tawārīkh-i Panjāb* is quite full of it. Thus, it may be safely stated that this particular passage deserves no special credence.

If we analyse the chronicles of Buddh Singh, Bakht Mal, Khushwaqt Rai, Ahmad Shah of Batala, Ganesh Das, Sohan Lal Suri, and Aliuddin, we find that the character of their work is not essentially different from that of Ghulam Muhiyuddin's *Tawārīkh*. One finds them depending occasionally on earlier chronicles for one small detail or another, but in their presentation the creation of the Khalsa is invariably related to the feeling of revenge and the episode of the Goddess. Indubhusan Banerjee had argued at length against the alleged worship of Durga by Guru Gobind Singh on the eve of instituting the Khalsa. His argument is grounded on a two-fold principle: confrontation of later tradition with contemporary evidence and the possibility of later addition becoming current under changed historical circumstances.[6]

Much of the later tradition has been discarded by modern historians. The general consensus is confined to a few prominent articles: a large gathering at Anandpur on the Baisakhi of 1699, the awesome call for the laying down of life for the Guru, the offer of their heads by 'the cherished five' (*panj piārās*), their initiation into the Khalsa through baptism by the double-edged sword (*khande kī pahul*), the acceptance of the *pahul* by Guru Gobind Singh from 'the cherished five', Guru Gobind Singh's address to the gathering, the acceptance of the *pahul* by thousands of persons and its rejection by Brahmans and Khatris, the injunctions regarding the essential *rahit* of the five k's (*kesh, kirpān, kaṛā, kanghā and kachhā*), the adoption of the appellation 'Singh' by the Khalsa, injunctions regarding abstinence from tobacco and other intoxicants, the enunciation of a distinct way of life for the Khalsa, and the vesting of Guruship in the Khalsa Panth and the *Ādi Granth.*

If we turn to contemporary and near-contemporary evidence, much of this detail gets confirmed. That a considerable number of Sikhs used to visit Anandpur at the time of Baisakhi and that on the Baisakhi of 1699 many Sikhs were especially asked to come, that *khande kī pahul* was administered to those who were willing to become the Guru's Khalsa (though no exact figures are mentioned anywhere), that a considerable number of people present did not take the *pahul*, that the Khalsa were required to wear *kesh* and arms, that they were required not to smoke, that the appellation of 'Singh' came to be adopted by a large number of the Khalsa – all this is there in the earliest evidence. However, the call for the laying down of life for the Guru, his request to 'the cherished five' to administer *pahul* to him, and the formulation of '5Ks' are not to be found in the available contemporary evidence. Though the formulation is not mentioned in pre-colonial sources, there is enough evidence for the use of each of the 5 Ks from the very beginning. In other words, the debate can be about 'formulation' and not the substantive items. On the other two items, we find near contemporary evidence.

If we go to the writings of Guru Gobind Singh, we find him

preoccupied with the nature of religious missions in general and of his own mission in particular under the trying circumstances of internal stress in the Panth and external interference by the contemporary rulers, both Rajput and Mughal. After long and deep reflection on his heritage as well as his own situation he had come to regard himself as the divinely appointed saviour of *dharm*, which for him meant primarily the faith enunciated by Guru Nanak. He was acutely conscious that the distinct path promulgated by Guru Nanak had been cherished and defended by his successors. It was Guru Gobind Singh's duty to conscientiously promote this dispensation. His primary concern was with the claims of conscience which he decided to defend with the use of physical force.

In order to achieve this objective, Guru Gobind Singh had first to consolidate the Panth. There is enough evidence to suggest that the inconvenient mediacy of the *masands* was removed. Rival claimants to Guruship and their followers were excommunicated. The initiation into the Khalsa through baptism by the double-edged sword and the adoption of *rahit* sharpened the social identity of the Khalsa who already belonged to a distinct socio-religious fraternity. The decision to wear arms and to fight made the Khalsa a political community, with the aspiration to sovereign rule.

After 1699, the Sikhs were identified with the Khalsa, though the Khalsa as yet was not identified with the Singh. The delegated authority, which had formerly belonged to the *masands*, came now to be vested in the Khalsa Sangat. Collectively, they succeeded the Guru. In the course of the eighteenth century, the Khalsa was identified with the Singh. Thus, both in his life and after his death, Guru Gobind Singh made himself master of the imagination of his followers.

NOTES

1. M.A. Macauliffe, *The Sikh Religion*, London: 1909, vol. V, pp. 93-4. For the original passage, Bute Shah, *Tawārīkh-i Punjāb*, Amritsar: Khalsa College, MS 1128.
2. Indubhusan Banerjee, *Evolution of the Khalsa*, Calcutta: A. Mukherjee & Co., 1963, vol. II, p. 115. Lakshman Singh, *Guru Gobind Singh*, Lahore:

1909, pp. 51-2. Kapur Singh, *Parasharprasna or the Baisakhi of Guru Gobind Singh,* Jalandhar: 1959, pp. 4-5.

3. Bute Shah, *Tawārīkh-i-Punjāb,* f. 405.
4. Ibid., f. 397.
5. Ibid., f. 400.
6. Indubhusan Banerjee, *Evolution of the Khalsa,* vol. II, pp. 97-108.

16

The Sikh Tradition of Martyrdom

Sikh history, observes Hew McLeod, is one of martyrdom from the death of Guru Arjan to the present day. He tends to link this aspect of the Sikh tradition with the heroic tradition of the Punjab. The village bards (*dhādīs*) who used to sing of courage and sacrifice began to praise the Sikh martyrs in the eighteenth century. The bards, apparently, did not make any distinction between the pre-Sikh or non-Sikh heroic tradition and that of the Sikhs. McLeod himself adds that martyrdom appears to be the culmination of heroism. Themes of heroism and martyrdom can be witnessed in the Central Sikh Museum in the precincts of the Harmandir Sahib in Amritsar and Baba Baghel Singh Museum adjoining Bangla Sahib Gurdwara in New Delhi, where paintings and weapons are displayed together. In popular posters too, heroism and martyrdom are as much emphasized as the doctrine of the divine Name.[1]

Talking about 'the joining of Heaven and Earth, and the role, in this joining of dead human beings' in the Christian tradition, Peter Brown argues in *The Cult of the Sants* that the analogy of 'the cult of the hero' with 'the Christian cult of the martyrs' breaks down because of the crucial distinction that the Christian martyrs 'enjoyed close intimacy with god'. 'This was the *sine qua non* of their ability to intercede for and, so, to protect their fellow mortals'. The martyr was an intercessor in a way in which 'the hero could never have been'. Furthermore, the heroism of the martyr had always been strictly dissociated from normal human courage, and the death of the martyr was vibrant with a miraculous 'suppression of suffering'. The celebration of the memory of the matyrs was a reassurance that 'good power' overcomes 'evil power'.[2] Martyrdom in the Christian tradition, thus, stands linked with ideology, metaphysics, and social function.

Bhai Jodh Singh looks upon Sikh martyrdom as grounded firmly in Sikh ideology. The Sikh conception of love (*prem*) involves the willing acceptance of God's will (*bhāṇā*). Guru Nanak says: 'If you aspire to play the game of love, bring your head on the palm of your hand when you come to me. When you tread the path of love, give up your head without hesitation'. This conception of love is reiterated by Guru Arjan: if love could be purchased with gold then Ravan (master of the golden Lanka) would not have given his head (to Shiva). The gift of love cannot be obtained without self-sacrifice. This is the meaning of Guru Gobind Singh's verse: *jin prem kiyo tin hī prabh pāyo.* When Guru Gobind Singh resolved to institute the Khalsa he invoked the principle of sacrifice in love, and gave the call: ' Is there anyone who loves the Guru so much that he is ready to give his head for the sake of *dharm.*'[3] Bhai Jodh Singh links the martyrdom of Guru Arjan and the institution of the Khalsa with Guru Nanak's conception of sacrifice in love, equating martyrdom with dying for the cause of faith.

Guru Nanak emphasizes the difficulty of the path of loving devotion by using the metaphor of the double-edged sword. To tread the straight path was to walk on the edge of a double-edged sword (*khandedhār galī ati bhīṛī*). Guru Amar Das uses the words *khanniyon tikhkhī, vālon nikkī* for the faith promulgated by Guru Nanak. Bhai Gurdas uses the mataphor of the double-edged sword to underline the sacrifice involved in following in the path Guru Nanak. Significantly, however, Bhai Gurdas uses this metaphor after the martyrdom of Guru Arjan. The fact of martyrdom imparts a somewhat literal character to the metaphor. Guru Hargobind, following in the footsteps of his father and predecessor, is leading the Sikhs on the Gurmukh-mārg which is as sharp as the edge of a double-edged sword (*khandedhār*).[4] The edge of the sword as a metaphor begins to border on reality.

It is not generally realized that the martyrdom of Guru Arjan weighs heavily with Bhai Gurdas and looms large in his mind. When the crisis comes Guru Arjan does not lose his equanimity. Absorbed in the remembrance of God he mingles with His light.[5] Guru Hargobind 'bears the unbearable'. His martial interests and activities provide the hedge of hardy trees for the orchard of Sikh faith. He is the king of the temporal as well as the spiritual realm and he assumes the responsibility of leading his followers in both. He has assumed a different role but only in appearance; essentially, there is no difference, as his true devotees know.[6] The total justification which Bhai Gurdas offers for whatever Guru Hargobind does is a measure of his appreciation for the sacrifice that Guru Arjan calmly made in 'the game of love'.

The martyrdom of Guru Tegh Bahadur was a deliberate and conscious act. Accounts of his martyrdom indicate first that he was asked to perform a miracle as proof of his nearness to God, but he rejected the notion that miracles proved the veracity of faith. It is equally clear that Guru Tegh Bahadur gave his head deliberately in confrontation with the ruler of Delhi for the cause of truth (*dharm*) and for the sake of the pious (*sādhs*). The religious import is obvious.[7]

The author of the *Gursobhā* mentions *tilak* and *janjū*, *karm-dharm*, *dharmsāla*, and *sarb-dharm* as protected by Guru Tegh Bahadur. We know that Guru Tegh Bahadur is generally called *hind dī chādar* (the protector of Hind) and the saviour of 'Hinduism'. But Sainapat calls him *jagg chādar* (the protector of the world).[8] 'Hind' is not excluded from 'the world' and 'Hinduism' is not excluded from *sarb-dharm*. Guru Tegh Bahadur may thus be seen as defending with his life the principle of the freedom of conscience. This principle was implied in Guru Nanak's denunciation of the discrimination practised by the state which taxed gods and their temples.[9] Aurangzeb was using political power to promote the interests of Sunni Islam at the cost of others. The conflict between the practice of coercion and the principle of freedom was inevitable.

The *Gursobhā* is significant in another way too. Its author does not refer to the call given by Guru Gobind Singh for sacrifice in the cause of *dharm* – he takes the call for granted. At one level the Khalsa represents direct affiliation with Guru Gobind Singh. But this affiliation is sealed by the baptism of the double-edged sword. The symbolic significance that *khandā* had acquired in Sikh tradition has to be kept in mind. The *khandedhār pahul* symbolizes the determination to lay down one's life in a righteous cause. After the first evacuation of Anandpur, when Guru Gobind

Singh and his Khalsa were attacked at Nirmoh, a number of them died fighting in the field. The author of the *Gursobhā* says that they were 'fortunate' to be able to prove themselves to be the Khalsa by sacrificing their life. When Sahibzada Ajit Singh dies fighting in the battle of Chamkaur, Guru Gobind Singh himself remarks, 'Today he has become the Khalsa in the court of the True Guru.' This amplifies the import of the phrase *Wāhegurū jī kā khālsā* used by the author of the *Gursobhā.* Martyrdom was thus an in-built feature of the institution of the Khalsa. As Sainapat puts it, what was concealed earlier was made manifest now.[10]

The word used for the Sikh martyr, as for the Muslim martyr, is *shahīd.* McLeod observes that this Arabic word was originally introduced into Punjabi to express an important feature of Islamic culture.[11] Does the use of the word *shahīd* imply that martyrdom in the Sikh tradition had something to do with this feature of Islamic culture? The answer to this question lies in the Sikh attitude towards the Muslim *shahīd.* The word *shahīd* and its plural *shuhda* are found in a composition of Guru Nanak:

> Baba! Allah is inscrutable and boundless. His names are holy, His abode is holy, and He is the true sustainer. His will (*hukam*) cannot be comprehended; none can describe it. Not even a hundred poets together can describe its smallest fraction. None knows His worth though all hear and talk about Him. There are *pīrs, paighambars, sāliks, sādiqs, shuhda, shahīd, shaikhs, mashāikh, qāzīs, mullās* and adept *darveshes.* They read *prayers* (*darūd*) in the hope of His grace. He consults none to make or unmake, to give or take away. He alone knows His *qudrat* and He alone does whatever is done. He watches everyone and bestows His grace on whomever He pleases.[12]

This stanza shows Guru Nanak's familiarity with the categories of persons who were believed to hold a religious or spiritual status in Muslim society. Among them were *shahīds* who were the object of popular worship in the time of Guru Nanak (like Sakhī Sarvar and Mas'ūd Sālār). They were important enough to be taken notice of. But they had no sanctity in the eyes of Guru Nanak. It is absolutely clear that the *shahīd* of Islamic culture is noticed by Guru Nanak only contextually and not appreciatively. There was no validity of any claim of his nearness to God. Bhai Gurdas reveals a similar attitude towards the *shahīd* of the Islamic culture in one of his Vars.[13]

The use of the word *shahīd* for the Sikh martyr does not carry any significance in terms of 'influence'. The word came into currency much later than the 'events' of martyrdom in Sikh history. If anything, the Sikh martyr presents a parallel and an alternative to the *shahīd* of Islamic tradition within the ideological and metaphysical parameters of the Sikh tradition. This was symbolized by the erection of Gurdwaras at the places of martyrdom. In fact, whereas the *shahīd* of Islamic tradition could, and did, become an object of popular worship, the Sikh martyr remains squarely within the 'orthodox' Sikh tradition. In other words, martyrdom is more central to the Sikh than to the Islamic tradition.

The ideal of martyrdom, according to McLeod, involves triumphant glory for the Khalsa. For justice and for the Panth, the Sikhs are taught to undergo suffering to the point of martyrdom. This message received 'a force and a coherence' from the Singh Sabha Movement absent in the pre-colonial period of Sikh history.[14] Harjot Oberoi spells out the role of the Singh Sabha protagonists in making martyrdom more central to the Sikh faith. The Tat Khalsa during the Singh Sabha Movement were keen to establish 'Khalsa' identity as the only Sikh identity, and for this purpose they encouraged 'the rewriting of history'. One kind of text through which they could do this was 'histories of martyrs'. Sikh heroic figures from the eighteenth century were shown to have been 'punished, tortured, or killed for desiring to retain cultural markers'. The meaning attached to the tales of martyrdom was martial bravery but underneath their bloody surface lay 'a corpus of multivocal *signata*'. Oberoi refers to Bhagat Lakshman Singh's book on Sikh martyrs to show how he attaches great importance to *kesh* as the emblem of the lofty ideals of the Khalsa.[15]

We may turn to two major works written before the advent of the Singh Sabha Movement in order to see whether or not there is any support for the views put forth by McLeod and Oberoi. The first of these two is the *Chaupa Singh Rahitnāma*, translated by McLeod himself. It says: 'Regard that spot as *shahīdganj* where Sikhs have given their heads for the sake of their faith'. Even more significant are the two words added to this injunction 'Light a lamp there'.[16] The word *shahīd* for the Sikh martyr has made its appearance here along with the sanctity of the place of martyrdom, and its veneration.

The *Rahitnāma* of Chaupa Singh is important for a few related points as well. Its author talks of two categories of Sikhs, the *keshdhārī* and the *sahajdhārī*. But even the latter are told not to observe the rites of *bhaddan* or ritual shaving of the head and the Brahmanical rites associated with it. Furthermore, even a *sahajdhārī* should not observe traditional mourning; he should arrange reading of the *Guru Granth*, ending with *kīrtan, bhog,* and *ardās*. The countenance should remain sightworthy. To keep the *kesh* without taking the *pahul* is to act like a buffoon (*bhand*) and a dancing boy (*bhagtiā*). Clearly, thus, *kesh* and *khandedhār pahul* go together.[17]

The sanctity of the *kesh* is underlined in a number of ways. The Sikh of the Guru should take good care of his *kesh*, comb it twice a day, and wash it with curd. He should not touch the *kesh* with unclean hands and stay free of lice. He should neither pluck out grey hair nor dye it. He should not insult another Sikh by grasping his *kesh*, beard, or turban. Ten more injunctions regarding the *kesh* make it absolutely clear how important it is for Sikhs. *Kesh* is the outward symbol of the inner faith of the Sikh. Through the Guru's grace *kesh* symbolizes *sikhkhī*. The Sikhs of the Guru will preserve *sikhkhī* till the end of their life. The Sikh Panth is nothing if not the *panth* of *dharm*. The *muktā* Sikhs sacrifice their life in battles against the 'Turks' and preserve their *sikhkhī*. Thus, the *pahul*, the *kesh*, and martyrdom go together. No wonder, then, that the removal of hair is equated with incest.[18]

Furthermore, the *kesh* serves as the marker of a distinct Sikh identity. Just as Guru Arjan prepared a scripture distinct from all others, so did Guru Gobind Singh create a Panth distinct from all others. The *keshdhārī* Sikhs are like a mote in the eyes of Hindus and Musalmans: it cannot be removed, it does not dissolve; it is a constant source of irritation. The Khalsa were given such a marker that even a single Sikh should stand out in a crowd of Hindus and Musalmans. Indeed, with the *kesh*, turban, and flowing beard how could he be concealed?[19] Thus the *pahul*, the *kesh*, and martyrdom go together to serve as the markers of Sikh identity.

Turning to Ratan Singh Bhangu, our second writer, we find that martyrdom for him is the core of the Sikh tradition. He expected his *Guru Panth Prakāsh* to make the reader, the reciter, and the listener firm in faith. They who listen to it go to battle and never turn their back; they die on the field of battle and mingle with the *shahīds* as water mingles with water.[20] Bhangu talks of the martyrdom of Guru Tegh Bahadur, the *sāhibzādas*, Bhai Tara Singh, Bhai Mani Singh, Bhai Bota Singh, Bhai Matab Singh, Bhai Taru Singh, Bhai Sukha Singh and Nihang Gurbakhsh Singh, among others. In the process he reveals his own ideology of martyrdom.

Guru Tegh Bahadur gave his head for the sake of others (*parsuārth*): he saved the *dharm-karm* of the Hindus. The Brahmans of Kashmir and other Hindus were being forcibly converted to Islam. Fear spread everywhere and Brahmans from several places came to Guru Tegh Bahadur for help. It was decided that the 'Turks' should be asked to convert the Guru first. He went to the 'Turks' on his own initiative. They asked him to perform a miracle (*karāmāt*), or accept Islam. Guru Tegh Bahadur asserted that *karāmāt* invited God's displeasure (*qahr*). Eventually, however, to save his *dharm-karm*, he said that he would show a miracle: they would not be able to cut off his head. They were taken in. He was beheaded. This was how he gave his head for the sake of others. There was a metaphysical dimension to the moral drama being enacted on the earth. The *pīrs* and *paigambhars* of the 'Turks' were removed by the True Lord from His True Abode (*sach-khand*). This, in turn affected earthly affairs: 'from that moment the *pātshāhī* of Delhi began to decline, from that moment the power of the Turks began to diminish'.[21]

The Sāhibzādas and the other Khalsa who died fighting after the final evacuation of Anandpur are presented as *shahīds*. The idea of *parsuārth* is reiterated and martyrdom diminishes the power of the 'Turks'.[22] Where did the status of *shahīd* come from? Guru Gobind Singh tested his Sikhs: 'Is there any Sikh who can give his head?', he asked the congregation. Sikhs who thought of Bhai Gurdas's reference to the 'Guru's *sāṇg*' offered themselves. The Guru slaughtered goats instead. For their readiness to lay down their lives, the five volunteers were given the status of *shahīd* (*shahīdī pad*).[23]

Bhai Tara Singh 'used to carry his head on his palm', standing for justice and defying the 'Turks'. He believed that martyrdom led to *pātshāhī*. This invited attack from the Mughal administrators. With other like-minded Sikhs he faced the enemy undaunted, refusing to take the chance to escape. He courted martyrdom, living up to the words of the Guru: 'Give your head but never give up your resolve.'[24]

Bhai Mani Singh changed the order of the contents of the *Guru Granth*, the visible body of the Guru, and the *sangat* made the comment that his body too would be cut into pieces. Believing that this would come true, Bhai Mani Singh approached the *sangat*, which is no different from the Guru, to pray that his body may be cut into pieces but his faith (*sikhkhī*) may remain intact. Years later, Bhai Mani Singh was hacked limb by limb but his head remained one with its *kesh*, and thus, his *sikhkhī* was saved. After his martyrdom Bhai Mani Singh becomes the *deoṛīdār* of the Sāhibzādas. No one else is his equal for the way in which he lived and died as a Gursikh.[25]

Bota Singh sacrificed his head to protect the honour of 'Singhs'. When the 'Singhs' were virtually eliminated by the Mughal administrators someone saw him and remarked, 'How is this Singh still alive?' Others commented that he could be an imposter, or a coward. 'The Khalsa fights in the van, unafraid of death. The Khalsa defies the state to stake his head'. As if stung by a scorpion, Bota Singh resolved to defy the Mughals, to give his head, prove his Khalsahood and justify the Khalsa's claim to *pātshāhī*. He began to collect duty at one *anna* a cart and one *paisa* a donkey. He was joined by a Ranghreta Singh. Troops were sent against them, and they were asked to surrender in the face of an overwhelming force. They refused to submit, they fought stubbornly with simple weapons to their last breath, and attained to martyrdom. They joined the *derā* of *shahīds* who were holding the *pīrs* and *paighambars* (of the Turks) under a siege.[26]

Even more emphatically than the martyrdom of Bhai Mani Singh, the martyrdom of Bhai Taru Singh underscores the sanctity of the *kesh*. His scalp was removed with his hair intact while he was alive. As a true Sikh, Bhai Taru Singh had supported the Khalsa with his modest means and without giving offence to the administration. For the sake of the Panth, and to expose the

'Turks', he bore all kinds of hardship. He told the Sikhs gathered around him that 'the true Guru had given his head for the sake of the Sikhs. As a Sikh of that Guru, how could he save his head'?[27] Taru Singh and Subeg Singh saved the honour of the Panth as true Sikhs by courting martyrdom.[28] Matab Singh did not wish to lag behind in giving his head to weaken the 'Turks'. This was his way of being faithful to *dharm* and to *sikhkhī*. Not to lose faith and not to forget the Guru while giving one's head was his ideal too. How else could one attain to the status of a *shahīd*? Offering himself voluntarily to be broken on the wheel, he attained martyrdom. Bhangu narrates the story of the martyrdom of Mitt Singh to explain how a *shahīdganj* was raised and the wishes of those who made offerings there were fulfilled.[29]

When Zain Khan, the Afghan governor of Sirhind, was defeated and killed and the fort of Sirhind was occupied by the Khalsa in 1764, they decided to build a *dehurā* at the spot where the two younger Sāhibzādas were beheaded. The aged men of the place were consulted to identity the exact location. The Khalsa resolved to erect a *darbār* there, with standards and a drum (*nagārā*). Some Sikhs were appointed for worship (*pūjā*). On the following morning the Panth held a *dīwān* and constructed a platform. Five weapons were placed at this *takht*, as a form of the Guru (*Gur-sarūp*). A Singh was appointed as the custodian (*mukhtiār*) of this place. A *rabābī* was appointed for reciting *shabads*. Jāgīrs were assigned for the maintenance of this *dehurā*. Offerings were made there by many who circumambulated the place and recited *bāṇī*. All their wishes were fulfilled.[30]

A *shahīdganj* was raised at the spot where Nihang Gurbakhsh Singh was cremated along with other martyrs just behind the Akal Bunga in Amritsar. Prayers made there found a sure response and many Sikhs distributed *kaṛhā parshād* there for their wishes having been fulfilled. Nihang Gurbakhsh Singh had always led the Khalsa in battle. Now he was the leader of the Singhs who died fighting a huge force of Afghans to defend the Harmandir Sahib. They had resolved not to leave the place and offered the prayer (*ardās*) that they may preserve *sikhkhī* with the *kesh* on their heads. Gurbakhsh Singh was exultant like a bridegroom and observed all the rites of marriage (with death). As members of 'the marriage party' all his companions resolved to die with him. 'May I attain to martyrdom' was their constant prayer, and they were determined not to show their back. On his martyrdom Nihang Gurbakhsh Singh was taken to the presence of the True Guru by Bhai Mani Singh and Bhai Taru Singh. He was later born as Ranjit Singh with the Guru's blessing that his authority would be recognized by the entire Khalsa.[31]

There is hardly any doubt that martyrdom for Ratan Singh Bhangu was the core of 'the Sikh tradition'. It was linked with *parsuārth* or selfless sacrifice, whether for the Panth or for others. Commitment to the Sikh faith and concern for its visible emblem, the *kesh*, was common to all Sikh martyrs. Martyrdom was closely linked with the idea of the sovereignty of the Panth. In this connection Bhangu presents a metaphysics of martyrdom and the efficacy of prayer offered to the martyrs. Logically, monuments called *shahīdgani* were raised and maintained as sacred spaces.

In the Sikh *ardās*, among other things, the Khalsa are reminded to turn their thoughts to the Cherished Five, the Four Sāhibzādas, the Forty Muktās, the loyal members of the Khalsa who gave their heads for their faith, who were hacked limb from limb, scalped, broken on the wheel or sawn asunder, never forsaking their faith, and who were steadfast in their loyalty to the uncut hair of the true Sikh. This part of the *ardās* enshrines the tradition of martyrdom celebrated by Ratan Singh Bhangu.

Bhai Kahn Singh Nabha, a great protagonist of the Singh Sabha Movement, defines *shahīd* as a person who sacrificed his life in *dharmyudh*, and *shahīdī* as the act of laying down one's life for the sake of *dharm*. Shahidganj is the place of martyrdom. The best known of these places were at Lahore, Amritsar, Fatehgarh, and Muktsar. Among the *shahīds* venerated at these places were the younger Sāhibzādas, the Forty Muktās, Bhai Mani Singh, Bhai Taru Singh, Nihang Gurbakhsh Singh, and a large number of unnamed *shahīds*. They all belonged to the seventeenth and eighteenth centuries. Like the *ardās*, Bhai Kahn Singh's entries in the *Mahan Kosh* make a historical statement, a statement about an essential feature of the past Sikh tradition. It is obvious that the protagonists of the Singh Sabha Movement cherished this feature of the Sikh tradition, and they tried to make it familiar to a large number of Sikhs. But they could not possibly make it more central to the Sikh tradition than Ratan Singh Bhangu.

They were not the first to link martyrdom with the Sikh faith, or the Sikh faith with the *kesh*, or the *kesh* with the *khandedhār pahul*, and all of these with Sikh identity. This had been done already in the two works we have noticed. We can see that the role of the Singh Sabha Movement in popularizing martyrdom as an essential feature of the Sikh tradition has been misunderstood and exaggerated by McLeod, and even more so by Oberoi.

NOTES

1. Hew McLeod, *Sikhism*, London: Penguin Books, 1997, pp. 129, 130-1.
2. Peter Brown, *The Cult of the Saints: Its Rise and Function in Latin Christianity*, Chicago: The University of Chicago Press, 1981, pp. 1, 5-6, 79-80, 101.
3. Bhai Jodh Singh, '*Jin Prem Kiyo Tin Hī Prabhu Pāyo*', *Ek Murit Anek Darshan*, ed. S.S. Amol, Jalandhar: Khalsa College, 1967, pp. 44-5.
4. Bhai Gurdas, *Vārān Bhāī Gurdās* ed., Giani Hazara Singh, Amritsar: Khalsa Samachar, 1962, Vār 24: pauṛī 21.
5. Ibid., Vār 24: pauṛī 23. 'As the black bee remains enrapt in the petals of flowers to enjoy fragrance, the Guru also spent the night of suffering by joyfully keeping his concentration on the feet of Lord. The Guru like a rainbird spoke to his disciples that the teachings of the Guru should not be forgotten'. Jodh Singh, *Varan Bhai Gurdas: Text, Transliteration and Translation*, Patiala: Vision and Venture, 1998, vol. II, p. 85.
6. Bhai Gurdas, *Vārān Bhāī Gurdās*, Vār 24: pauṛīs 21, 22, 23, 24, 25, 26; Vār 39: pauṛī 3.
7. McLeod refers to the 'alternative Sikh tradition' in *The Chaupa Singh Rahit-Nāma*. This work refers to the first arrest of Guru Tegh Bahadur on account of complaints by close relatives (*sanbandhī sāk*). The 'Turks' called him for the second time but the master did not go. His idea was to expose their falsehoods. The Turks were to be uprooted because they listened to evil men and failed to give justice. Deliberately, the master managed to get himself arrested. He gave his head in Delhi after two months of 'questions and answers'. W.H. McLeod, *The Chaupa Singh Rahit-Nāma*, Dunedin: University of Otago Press, 1987, pp. 79-80, 167-8. There is no reference to Brahmans here. But does this 'tradition' contradict the tradition about Brahmans? In any case the language of the *Rahit-Nāma* leaves no doubt about the injustice of the state and Guru Tegh Bahadur's commitment to the truth.
8. Sainapat, *Shri Gurū Sobhā*, ed. Shamsher Singh Ashok, Amritsar: Shiromani Gurdwara Prabandhak Committee, 1967, pp. 10-11, 15.
9. J.S. Grewal, *Guru Nanak in History*, Chandigarh: Panjab University, 1969, pp. 157-8.

10. Sainapat, *Shri Gurū Sobhā*, pp. 29, 30, 33, 40, 41, 42, 64, 90.
11. Hew McLeod, *Sikhism*, p. 130.
12. *Ādi Sri Gurū Granth Sāhib Jī* (Sri Damdami Bir, various printed editions, standard pagination), p. 15. Cf. Manmohan Singh (tr.), *Sri Guru Granth Sahib*, vol. I, Amritsar: Shiromani Gurdwara Prabandhak Committee, 1964, pp. 180-81.
13. Bhai Gurdas, *Vārān Bhāī Gurdās*, Vār 8: pauṛī 8.
14. Hew McLeod, *Sikhism*, p. 129.
15. Harjot Oberoi, *Construction of Religious Boundaries, Culture, Identity* and *Diversity in the Sikh Tradition*, New Delhi: Oxford University Press, 1994, pp. 330-1. Oberoi goes on to add that the drive for a standard Sikh identity can be traced to the need of the new elites for a sub-culture that would suit their changed surroundings. They were impelled to rewrite the social grammar of their society by the political, economic, and cultural environment of the colonial rule.
16. McLeod, *The Chaupa Singh Rahit-Nāma*, p. 110.
17. Ibid., pp. 63, 64, 68, 83. The alternative use of the phrase '*kesān dī pahul*' leaves no doubt about the inevitable link.
18. Ibid., pp. 65, 68, 77, 88-9, 112, 120, 133.
19. Ibid., pp. 80, 134.
20. Ratan Singh Bhangu, *Prachīn Panth Prakāsh*, ed., Bhai Vir Singh, New Delhi: Bhai Vir Singh Sahit Sadan, 1993 (rpt.), pp. 470-1.
21. Ibid., pp. 34-9.
22. Ibid., pp. 55-9, 61-4.
23. Ibid., pp. 176-8.
24. Ibid., pp. 187-98.
25. Ibid., pp. 223-8. There were other Sikhs who were broken on the wheel in the horse market in Lahore.
26. Ibid., pp. 243-6.
27. Ibid., pp. 268-72, 289-92.
28. Ibid., p. 301.
29. Ibid., pp. 287-8.
30. Ibid., pp. 352-3.
31. Ibid., pp. 408-10.

17

Rāj Taregā Khālsā

After the Sikh congregational prayer on all occasions of personal or social importance, the *rāj karegā khālsā* anthem is recited aloud in unison by all present before the *Granth Sahib*. Rendered into English, the anthem reads:

1. Verily through the order of God, the Immortal, was instituted the Panth. Incumbent upon all the Sikhs is to regard the Granth as the Guru.
2. Regard the Granth as the Guru, the manifest body of the Gurus. He whose mind is pure can find the Guru in the *shabad*.
3. The Khalsa shall rule and none will remain obdurate. All shall come into the fold after much humiliation; only they who take refuge (in the Panth) shall be safe.
4. The Divine Name is the ship to cross the ocean of mortality. They who devoutly reflect upon it are ferried across by the Guru.
5. He who wields the double-edged sword and wears the emblem of royalty, the crowned lord of the universe, gives us protection.

The ideas embodied in this anthem relate to two basic themes: the Panth and the Granth. The first line of the opening couplet is logically connected with the third and the fifth couplet; the second line of the opening couplet is logically connected with the second and the fourth couplet. In fact, the anthem may be re-arranged for the purpose of analysis. The ideas related to the Panth are:

Verily through the order of God, the Immortal, was instituted the Panth. The Khalsa shall rule and none will remain obdurate. All shall come into the fold, after much humiliation; only those who take refuge (in the Panth) shall be safe. He who wields the double-edged sword and wears the emblem of royalty, the crowned lord of the universe, gives us protection.

The ideas related to the Granth are:

Incumbent upon all the Sikhs is to regard the Granth as the Guru. Regard the Granth as the Guru, the manifest body of the Gurus. He whose mind is pure can find the Guru in the *shabad*. The Divine Name is the ship to cross the ocean of mortality. They who devoutly reflect upon it are ferried across by the Guru.

To take up the first theme, in the *Bachittar Nātak* composed a couple of years before Guru Gobind Singh instituted the Khalsa in 1699, his mission is presented as directly ordained by God; to institute a Panth which may not only protect the pious but also extirpate the wicked. The *Bachittar Nātak* was familiar to all Sikh writers from Sainapat in 1711 to Ratan Singh Bhangu in 1841. They all invoke the *Bachittar Nātak* to underline the divine sanction behind the institution of the Khalsa Panth. 'Verily through the order of God, the Immortal, was instituted the Panth' is an unmistakable echo of the *Bachittar Nātak*.

The idea that the Khalsa were to rule may be expected to appear, obviously, after the institution of the Khalsa. Sainapat closes his *Gursobhā* on a confident note: Guru Gobind Singh, 'the king of kings' (*shāh-i shāhān*), shall establish righteousness upon earth through the Khalsa. Further, 'the rulers of the world shall tremble before him and relinquish their territories'.[1] Koer Singh and Sarup Das Bhalla, writing in the third quarter of the eighteenth century, project the idea that sovereign rule had been potentially bestowed upon the Khalsa by Guru Gobind Singh.[2] The author of the *Prem Sumārg*, who attributes his work to Guru Gobind Singh, prophesies the establishment of Sikh rule.[3]

The idea of protection was only a logical corollary to the idea of divine sanction behind the Khalsa and the establishment of their rule. The protector wields the sword and wears the emblem of royalty. Sainapat dwells on the majestic appearance of Guru Gobind Singh wearing the sword and other arms, the emblem of royalty on his head, and 'victory of God' (*Wāhegurū jī kī fateh*) on his lips.[4] We may be sure that the 'protector' of the last couplet, 'who wields the double-edged sword and wears the emblem of royalty', is no other than Guru Gobind Singh who is referred to as the master of the world. Also, the protection in question is assured in the context of an armed struggle for sovereignty.[5]

Turning to the second theme, the writers of the eighteenth century project the idea that Guruship after Guru Gobind Singh was vested in the Granth. Sainapat refers to the eternal *bāṇī* as the Guru.[6] Koer Singh says that there is no Guru equal to the *Guru Granth*, and that he who reads the Granth finds the Guru. At several places he makes the explicit statement that the Granth is to be regarded as the Guru.[7] The author of the *Mahimā Prakāsh* is also explicit on this point: after the ten Gurus, the *Granth Sahib* became the Guru of the Sikhs and those who wished to speak to Guru Gobind Singh henceforth should read the *Ādi Granth*.[8] Kesar Singh Chhibber says that Guru Gobind Singh vested Guruship in the *Granth Sahib*; therefore, 'our Guru is the *Granth Sahib*'; those who do not regard the *Granth Sahib* as their Guru are not Sikhs of the Guru. Kesar Singh exhorts the Sikhs to believe in the truth of what is there in the Granth and in *dasven pātshāh de vāk*. However, he attributes the decision to Guru Gobind Singh that only the *Ādi Granth* was to be regarded as the Guru; the *bāṇī* of Guru Gobind Singh himself was not to be bound with it.[9] The author of the *Prem Sumārg* refers to the *Pothi-Granth* containing the *bāṇī* of the Gurus from Guru Nanak to Guru Tegh Bahadur, and states explicitly that Sabad-Bāṇī was to be regarded as the Guru. According to him, anyone who wished to converse with the Guru could do so by reading the *bāṇī*.[10]

The doctrine of Guru Granth may be seen as logically springing from Guru Nanak's equation of the *shabad* with the Guru. The *shabad* was soon equated with *bāṇī*, as in fact in the very phrase Sabad-Bāṇī, and the *bāṇī* was collected in the Granth. Therefore, the Granth was the Guru. Also, the Guru according to Sikh belief was indispensable for liberation. The metaphors of 'ladder' and 'boat' are used to convey this idea. The Name was expressed through the *shabad*. Therefore, the *Guru Granth* was the ship to cross the ocean of mortality.

From the foregoing paragraphs it is evident that the ideas contained in the *rāj karegā khālsā* anthem were current between 1696 and 1776, from the time of the composition of the *Bachittar Nātak* to that of the *Mahimā Prakāsh*. Before 1696, Guru Gobind Singh had participated in two battles, one against the hill chiefs and the other in support of the hill chiefs against the Mughal *faujdārs* and their allies. A few unsuccessful expeditions had been sent against Guru Gobind Singh himself by the Mughals. With this background, the *Bachittar Nātak* was addressed primarily to the Sikhs to convey the idea that Guru Nanak's dispensation was meant to transcend all previous ones, that Guru Gobind Singh was a legitimate successor of Guru Nanak, and, therefore, also the defender and promoter of that dispensation.

Through the institution of the Khalsa in 1699 Guru Gobind Singh sought to ensure that only those individuals were recognized as Sikhs who gave their allegiance directly to the Guru, without the mediacy of the *masands* and without recognizing the claims of rival groups like the Minas, the Dhir Mallias and the Ram Raiyas, that the Khalsa of Guru Gobind Singh bore arms, and that they followed the tenets and practices promulgated by Guru Nanak. The institution of the Khalsa brought Guru Gobind Singh into conflict with the hill chiefs first and then with the Mughal *faujdārs*, and this conflict remained unresolved until the Guru's death. Within two years, his followers established sovereign Sikh rule in the Sutlej-Jamuna Divide and the Bist Jalandhar and Bari Doabs of the Punjab. Their success, however, was shortlived; their leader, Banda Bahadur was captured in 1715 and executed in 1716. Then, from 1716 to 1752, the Khalsa of Guru Gobind Singh suffered severe persecution at the hands of the Mughal governors of Lahore, but survived. In fact, they increased their strength and striking power so as to triumph over Ahmad Shah Abdali between 1752 and 1773. Already in 1765 the Khalsa had struck coins in Lahore as a formal declaration of sovereignty. By 1776 surely, their rule over the Punjab was firmly established.

However, before coming to any conclusions about the period of crystallization for the *rāj karegā khālsā* anthem we may consider another idea which came into currency in connection with the Panth during the eighteenth century. Sainapat talks of the form (*rūp*) of the Khalsa as the very form of the Guru, and he also talks of the *jāmā* which the Guru bequeathed to the Khalsa.[11] Forty years later, Koer Singh talks of the Guru remaining amidst the Khalsa all the time, and the *sarab-sangat* being the Guru's *rūp*.[12] Kesar Singh Chhibber, writing in 1769, says that the Guru is Khalsa and the Khalsa Guru.[13]

It came to be generally believed in the eighteenth century that personal Guruship had ended with the death of Guru Gobind

Singh and was henceforth vested in the Khalsa. The author of the *Prem Sumārg* emphatically asserts that the members of the Khalsa Panth were not to believe in any personal Guru after Guru Gobind Singh. Instead, if anyone wanted to see the Guru, he should go to an assembly of the Khalsa and look upon it, in faith and respect, to see in it the Guru himself.[14]

However, the idea of Guru Panth is not adequately represented in the anthem. This omission is all the more significant for the fact that after the establishment of Sikh rule the idea of the Guru Panth was being relegated to the background while the idea of the Guru Granth was coming into higher relief. Therefore, it may be suggested that whereas the ideas of the anthem came into currency after the institution of the Khalsa and before the establishment of Sikh rule, the anthem itself assumed its crystallized form after the establishment of Sikh rule. Once crystallized, the ideas acquired a momentum and sanctity of their own to survive into the nineteenth century. Even if they were on the brink of oblivion under British rule for some time the protagonists of the Singh Sabha and the Akali movement revived them and, consequently, the anthem has come down to the present day with the doctrine of Guru Granth as the more important idea.

However, the third couplet, with *rāj karegā khālsā,* has in all probability come down from the days of Guru Gobind Singh. This couplet occurs in a manuscript of 1718-19 which contains the *Nasīhatnāma.* It is not the original *Nasīhatnāma* but a copy. Obviously, therefore, the *Nasīhatnāma* was composed earlier than 1718-19. W.H. McLeod places it close to, but after, the *Gursobhā.* He does not give any reason. He is simply reluctant to entertain the idea of a *rahitnāma* of the time of Guru Gobind Singh. Karamjit Malhotra has argued that the *Nasīhatnāma* could be earlier than 1708. There is nothing in the contents of this work to suggest that it was composed after 1708. Indeed, there is no reference to the Granth as the Guru, and there is no reference to the Panth or the Khalsa as the Guru.[15] These two ideas occur in the *Gursobha*: it is explicitly stated that Guru Gobind Singh enunciated them only a day before his death.

NOTES

1. Sainapat, *Shri Gurū Sobhā,* ed. Shamsher Singh Ashok, Amritsar: Shiromani Gurdwara Prabandhak Committee, 1967, pp. 136-8.
2. Koer Singh *Gurbilās, Pātshāhī 10,* ed. Shamsher Singh Ashok, Patiala: Punjabi University, 1968, pp. 131, 134, 135, 139.
   Sarup Das Bhalla, *Mahimā Parkāsh,* ed. Shamsher Singh Ashok and Gobind Singh Lamba, Patiala: Punjab Languages Department, 1970, vol II, p. 828.
3. Randhir Singh (ed.), *Prem Sumārg,* Amritsar: Sikh History Society,1953, p. 94.
   The *Prem Sumārg* is placed by W.H. McLeod in the 1820s: *Sikhs of the Khalsa: A History of Khalsa Rahit,* New Delhi: Oxford University Press, 2003, p. 150. In his recent translation of the *Prem Sumārg,* McLeod is inclined to place it late in the eighteenth century. In any case, the *Prem Sumārg* contains material of the eighteenth century. The statement made by its author remains relevant for our present purpose.
4. Sainapat, *Shri Gurū Sobhā,* pp. 104-5.
5. *Sri Dasam Granth Sahib,* eds. Ratan Singh Jaggi and Gursharan Kaur Jaggi, New Delhi: Gobind Sadan, 1999, pp. 188, 189.
6. Sainapat, *Shri Gurū Sobhā,* p. 132.
7. Koer Singh, *Gurbilās Pātshāhī 10,* pp. 283, 284, 286.
8. Sarup Das Bhalla, *Mahimā Prakāsh,* p. 892.
9. Kesar Singh Chhibber, *Bansāvalīnāma Dasān Pātshāhiān kā,* ed. Ratan Singh Jaggi, Chandigarh: Punjab University, 1972 (vol. II, *Parkh*), pp. 136, 163, 198, 215, 221, 222.
10. Randhir Singh (ed.), *Prem Sumārg,* pp. 4, 6, 7.
11. Sainapat, *Shri Gurū Sobhā,* pp. 132.
12. Koer Singh, *Gurbilās Pātshāhī 10,* pp. 138, 139.
13. Kesar Singh Chhibber, *Bānsavalīnāma Dasān Pātshāhiān kā,* p. 164.
14. Randhir Singh (ed.), *Prem Sumārg,* p. 18.
15. Karamjit K. Malhotra, 'The Earliest Manual on the Sikh Way of life', in *Five Centuries of Sikh Tradition: Ideology, Society, Polity and Culture,* eds. Reeta Grewal and Sheena Pall, New Delhi: Manohar, 2005, pp. 55-81.

Part 3

SIKH POLITY

18

Ahmad Shah of Batala on the Misl

Ahmad Shah of Batala was the first writer to use the term *misl* in the history of the Sikhs.[1] Since the late eighteenth century is generally looked upon as the '*misl* period', we may examine Ahmad Shah's conception of the *misl* as a description of the eighteenth-century Sikh polity.

The first half of Ahmad Shah's account of the Sikhs falls into three significant parts: one dealing with Guru Nanak and his eight successors; the second covering the time of Guru Gobind Singh and Banda Bahadur; and the third marking the activity of the Singhs for half a century after Banda's death. Ahmad Shah does not see any essential connection between these three phases. In fact he makes a sharp distinction between a Sikh and a Singh, which impels him to look upon the first phase of his account as quite distinct from the two later phases. In the first phase, there was no hostility between the Mughal emperors and the Gurus. The followers of Guru Nanak were peaceful holy men and they were generally respected by their contemporaries. Out of regard and veneration, Akbar granted revenue-free land to Guru Ram Das at Amritsar. Depending largely upon what he had heard from some of the respectable Sikhs of his own time, Ahmad Shah traces the tortures undergone by Guru Arjan to Chandu Shah's enmity and does not attribute the Guru's death directly to those tortures. He notices Guru Hargobind's armed activity, but does not attach much importance to it. He attributes Guru Tegh Bahadur's execution on Aurangzeb's order to Ram Rai's rivalry with the Guru. Ahmad Shah believes in fact that there was no opposition or conflict between the Mughal emperors and the Sikh Gurus before the time of Guru Gobind Singh. In any case, the Sikhs had never thought seriously of opposing the government.[2]

Guru Gobind Singh's immediate reaction to the execution of his father was to take revenge. He instituted a new order for that purpose. Among the religious and social obligations of the members of this new order were to wear arms all the time almost as a matter of duty to wage war against their enemies. Guru Gobind Singh took *pahul* from 'the cherished five' whom he had initiated into the new order and, consequently, the Khalsa became the Guru and the Guru became the Khalsa. They were knit by the bond of mutual dependence. As a result of Guru Gobind Singh's conflict with the hill chiefs, he occupied about a hundred miles of territory around Anandpur. He was bent upon creating a dominion for himself and his Singhs. But Aurangzeb's intervention on behalf of the hill chiefs foiled all his designs, and Guru Gobind Singh suffered much in his conflict with the government. In despair, he wrote a conciliatory letter to Aurangzeb, took service with Bahadur Shah and, finally, invited his own death by inciting the sons of an Afghan who had been killed by Guru Gobind Singh to avenge themselves upon their father's murderer. At the same time he deputed Banda to take revenge for the death of his own sons and ancestors. Consequently, Banda launched the Singhs on a career of conquest. On Banda's fall, however, the mission of Guru Gobind Singh as conceived by Ahmad Shah ended in failure.[3]

It is not difficult to see that Ahmad Shah's account of the Guru's mission does not possess much historiographic validity. But what is more relevant at the moment is to note that he does not see any connection between the second and the third phase of his account, just as he does not see much connection between the first and the second.

Ahmad Shah does not attribute the political success of the warlike Singhs to any religious or ideological factor. Due to the heedlessness of Muhammad Shah, the *zamīndārs* and *qānūngos* in the time of Zakariya Khan began oppressing the peasants, obliging many of them to join the Singhs in practising robbery. The sympathetic villagers afforded refuge to the lawless Singhs, while Lakhpat Rai and Jaspat Rai kept Zakariya Khan in the dark about their depredations. The first serious warning about ignoring the lawlessness of the Singhs came to Zakariya Khan from Nadir Shah. It came rather late. At any rate, during the invasions of Ahmad Shah Abdali, the Singhs started plundering the towns, and they built their own fortresses. Soon they came to feel strong enough to oppose Ahmad Shah Abdali. The defeat of his commander Jahan Khan served as a signal for the Singhs to occupy territories. The inability of Taimur Shah to pay any attention to the Punjab enabled them to establish their rule from Saharanpur to Attock and from the borders of Sind to the Shivaliks.[4]

It was to narrate the history of Sikh rule in the Punjab before the establishment of Ranjit Singh's state that Ahmad Shah decided to give an account of the most important *misls*, one by one. It is obvious that the *misl* was the most meaningful unit of Sikh polity for Ahmad Shah. His evidence on the immediate past in particular becomes important. His strongest point appears to consist in his honest intention of giving what he regarded as factual information.

Ahmad Shah makes no comment on the term *misl*, perhaps assuming that its meaning was clear to his contemporaries. He indicates, however, that it was a sort of association or grouping. There were more than four or five hundred *sardārs* among the Singhs but pre-eminent for their armies, followers, and territories were only a few groups. The most important of these, from Ahmad Shah's standpoint, were the Bhangis, the Faizullapurias, the Nakkais, the Kanhiyas, the Ramgarhias, the Ahluwalias and of course the Sukarchakias. The *misl* was normally headed by a single chief and acted as a unit for the purpose of war. But it could also have branches with separate armies and administration. This brief statement about the *misls* may be examined in the light of Ahmad Shah's own evidence.

The association of the Singhs with their leaders was voluntary, and succession to leadership was not necessarily determined by kinship. For example, Bhuma Singh, Natha Singh, and Jagat Singh became the willing associates of Chhajja Singh Bhangi and, on his death, Bhuma Singh became the leader. It is rather interesting to note that the association did not remain a single unit. On

Bhuma Singh's death, leadership went to his associate Hari Singh, while Natha Singh and Jagat Singh founded a *derā* of their own. Though Hari Singh was acknowledged as the chief leader of the *misl*, Natha Singh and Jagat Singh were succeeded by Jhanda Singh and Ganda Singh. It is this kind of division or branch which Ahmad Shah appears to have had in mind when he refers to the *misls* having branches with separate armies and (later on) administration. Ahmad Shah notices the occasions of territorial occupation in most cases. Among the Bhangis, for instance, Hari Singh was the first to start *mulk-gīrī*. The various leaders of the *misls*, and presumably the leaders of separate branches, occupied territories independently of one another. The three successors of Kapur Singh Faizullapuria, for instance, started *mulk-gīrī* at about the same time as Hari Singh but quite separately from him and from one another.[5]

Ahmad Shah does not say so, but it is valid to infer from his evidence that territories were occupied largely on the *misl* basis. This is not to suggest that there was no cooperation between the leaders of one *misl* and another during the phase of territorial occupation. In fact, Ahmad Shah explicitly states that sometimes territories were occupied jointly by members of two or more *misls*. The example he knew best was that of the Kanhiyas and the Ramgarhias who occupied the territories around his hometown, Batala. They divided its revenue equally amongst themselves, but there were other modes of sharing the revenue between members belonging to different *misls*.[6] Nevertheless, territories were generally occupied separately by the *misls*. The nearness or actual contiguity between the territories of members of one and the same *misl* or the branch of a *misl* would support this inference.

The character of the *misl* changed considerably after the territorial occupation had been effected. It may be relevant in this connection to note that the name borne by a *misl* was not always connected with its founder. The name Kanhiya, for instance, embodies a tribute to the eminence of Jai Singh among the associates of Amar Singh, the original founder of the *derā*. At no stage did the members of this association all belong to Jai Singh's village Kanha Kachha. The name Ramgarhia was acquired by its bearers through a gallant action in one desperate situation. This commemoration of an individual's prowess in war on the eve of territorial occupation is not without significance. Whereas in the second quarter of the eighteenth century the aim of the Singhs had been to paralyse the administration, at the beginning of the third quarter it was to establish their own government. The qualities of leadership in war came to be prized more than ever before. The large number of associates or followers who joined the most reputed leaders increased their striking power which, in turn, was reflected in the extent of territories occupied by the various *misls*. Within the *misl* itself, the chief was likely to acquire larger territories than any other member of the *misl* and thus, the pre-eminence which he had enjoyed as a commander was consolidated through this acquisition of larger resources. He would naturally expect his associates to continue acknowledging his superior status. Defection from one *misl* to another against the wishes of the chief was discouraged by him. For instance, Nand Singh, who was an associate of Jhanda Singh Bhangi, had occupied Pathankot and when he transferred it to his son-in-law Tara Singh Kanhiya, Ganda Singh Bhangi attempted to wrest it from the Kanhiya *sardār*.[7] It is not clear, however, whether or not the rights claimed by the chief over his associates were justified by the original, albeit informal, terms of association.

Apparently, the chief of the *misl* did not exercise strict control over his associates. Their obligation according to Ahmad Shah was limited to active cooperation with the chief only in those situations which called for armed action. For the rest, they were virtually independent. They exercised full authority in the territory under their control. It is relevant to note in this connection that the three *sardārs* who occupied Lahore did not all belong to the same *misl*, and even the two who did, established separate administration in the respective shares of the city and its suburbs. Indeed, in a very real sense the associate was as autonomous as the chief. The principle of hereditary succession, which came to be established in all the *misls*, was adopted as much by the associates as by the chiefs themselves.[8]

With the acceptance of the principle of hereditary succession, the character of the *misl* was radically changed. For all practical purposes the qualitative difference between the chief and the associate was first minimized and then obliterated. In the last quarter of the eighteenth century there were, strictly speaking, no chiefs-and-associates but only so many *sardārs* of major or minor consequence. Given their conflicting interests and ambitions, the events of this last phase become easily explicable. The *sardārs* of different *misls* could fight against the *sardārs* of some other *misls*, and the *sardārs* of more than one *misl* could fight against the opposing *sardārs* forming alliances with non-Sikh chiefs.[9] All this characterizes the politics of the late eighteenth-century Sikh world.

Within their own administration the *sardārs* acted without constraint. Ahmad Shah mentions a few instances of high-handedness. Mala Singh, Jassa Singh Ramgarhia's brother, for example, made many a fair damsel of Batala the victim of his profligacy. But then, his own subjects turned against him and invited the Kanhiyas to dislodge him from Batala. Sayyid Ghulam Ghaus was imprisoned and ill-treated by the Kanhiyas and he was obliged to leave the country; but on his way to Khurasan he was persuaded by Mahan Singh not to leave his native place. According to Ahmad Shah, Haqiqat Singh Kanhiya was harsh towards his Muslim subjects; but Haqiqat Singh's son, Jaimal Singh, was extremely kind and considerate to them.[10] Ahmad Shah notices that nearly all the *sardārs* bestowed cash and revenue-free villages upon the Akalis.[11] It may be added that in the late eighteenth century revenue-free grants were by no means confined to the Sikhs.[12]

On the basis of this brief analysis of Ahmad Shah's evidence on the eighteenth-century Sikh polity it may be suggested that the nature and function of the *misl* underwent a considerable change from the second to the last quarter of the century and, consequently, no simple definition of the *misl* is easily possible. Nevertheless, it is useful to make a distinction between what may be called the pre-territorial and territorial phases of the *misl*. The members of a *misl* united to fight and conquer and divided to rule. The voluntary association of Singhs, irrespective of their local or family affiliations, with a leader chosen for his recognized merit and willingly followed, appears to characterize the first phase. The proliferation of *misls* and the growing political aspirations of the leaders led to the occupation of territories, largely on the *misl* basis, which in due course transformed the character of the *misl*. In spite of the differences in resources, the differences between all the chiefs came to be minimized until they all became equally autonomous *sardārs*. Consequently, before the close of the eighteenth century, the relationships earlier established by the *misl* vanished almost completely. Some of the conquerors of territory had not associated with any chief from the very beginning.

NOTES

1. The section entitled 'Zikr-i Guruān wa Ibtidā-i Singhān wa Mazhab-i Īshān' of Ahmad Shah's *Tārīkh-i Hind* was appended to a lithographed edition of Sohan Lal Suri's *Umdat ut-Tawārīkh*. All the references here are to this appendix. Sohan Lal Suri, *Umdat ut-Tawārīkh*, 5 Daftars, Lahore: New Imperial Press, 1888-89.
2. Ibid., pp. 2, 3, 4, 5.
3. Ibid., pp. 5-6, 7, 8-9, 10-11, 12.
4. Ibid., pp. 12-14.
5. Ibid., pp. 15, 18.
6. Ibid., p. 14.
7. Ibid., pp. 16, 18-19, 21.
8. Ibid., p. 14. For instance, Haqiqat Singh was an associate of Amar Singh, the founder of the *misl* which came to be called Kanhiya; when Jai Singh became the chief of the *misl*, Haqiqat Singh was his associate and obtained his share of territories as a 'Kanhiya'. On Haqiqat Singh's death, his only son Jaimal Singh succeeded to his estates and 'ruled' for several years. Ahmad Shah, *Tārīkh-i Hind*, MS 1291, Sikh History Research Department, Khalsa College, Amritsar.
9. Ahmad Shah's brief account contains several instances of such conflicts. Ahmad Shah, *Tārīkh-i Hind*, pp. 16, 17, 18, 23, 24, 25.
10. Ibid., pp. 20, 23.
11. Ibid., p. 14.
12. Indu Banga, *Agrarian System of the Sikhs: Late Eighteenth and Early Nineteenth Century*, New Delhi: Manohar, 1978, p. 161 and n 67. Veena Sachdeva, *Polity and Economy of the Punjab During the Late Eighteenth Century*, New Delhi: Manohar, 1993, pp. 123-4. The reference on these pages is to the Akal Bunga; income of the Akal Bunga was shared by the Akalis.

19

Ganesh Das on the Secular Aspirations of the Khalsa

A general analysis of the *Chār Bāgh-i Panjāb* reveals that its author, Ganesh Das, was essentially concerned with the acquisition and maintenance of political power in the past.[1] He is, moreover, one of the very few to supply substantial information on Sikh polity. This information is all the more useful for being unconsciously supplied for the most part.

A Khatri of the Badhera subcaste, Ganesh Das introduces himself as the *qānūngo* of the *pargana* of Gujrat and a *zamīndār* of that town in the Punjab. Many of his ancestors had served the government of their times. He mentions one Bhawani Das as the *ra'is* of Gujrat to whom Nadir Shah addressed a *farmān* which is reproduced in the *Chār Bāgh.* It is quite likely that this *ra'īs* was Ganesh Das's grandfather Bhawani Das. At any rate, his father Shiv Dayal was the '*āmil* and *nāzim* of Fatehgarh in the *pargana* of Gujrat.[2] His own position as the *qānūngo* and *zamīndār* of the town of Gujrat was much of a piece with the long tradition of his family.

Ganesh Das was fairly well qualified to write a history of the Punjab. From his familiarity with the popular *āyāt* and Persian classics, and his command over Persian, it is evident that he had received a good education according to the standards of his time. In the course of his work he reveals his familiarity also with many a historical work of medieval India. Before writing the *Chār Bāgh* he had attempted a short history of the Sikhs. His *Rājdarshinī* has survived as a valuable source for the history of Jammu. His flair for the details of administration may be attributed to his professional experience. His family connections enabled him to collect more varied information than what would have been accessible through personal effort and experience.[3]

The bulk of the *Chār Bāgh* is devoted to the history of the Sikhs and a large proportion of Sikh history is given to the house of Ranjit Singh. In fact the portion dealing with the first 250 years of Sikh history is little more than a background to the rise of the Sikhs into political power. But it is a significant background. Ganesh Das sees an intimate connection between the activity of Guru Gobind Singh and Banda and the Sikh struggle for independence. He does not treat Banda as a mere rebel; he underlines the fact of his having established an independent government and administration.[4] From this to the re-establishment of Sikh power was a long but inevitable step. At any rate Ahmad Shah was the last Mughal ruler of the Punjab and, in Ganesh Das's view, the power established by the Sikhs was as legitimate as that of the Marathas or Ahmad Shah Abdali, or even the Mughal rulers.[5]

Ganesh Das refers to the ruling Khalsa as the Sikhs of Guru Gobind Singh and traces the origin of their power to the time of Guru Hargobind. Nanak Shah Darvesh, the founder of the order (*silsilah*) of the Sikhs, had been completely free from any sectarian prejudice and used to have friendly associations with both Hindus and Musalmans. Obviously, the Sikhs had no conflict with the government in the beginning. In fact Akbar had great regard for Guru Arjan, paid him a visit, and conversed with him for his own edification. However, Jahangir pronounced capital punishment upon Guru Arjan for his benediction upon the rebel prince Khusrau and the grief-stricken Sikhs began to feel resentment and animosity. Consequently, the son and the successor of Guru Arjan adopted a soldierly life and, in due course, came into armed conflict with the functionaries of Shah Jahan. This was obviously an unequal contest and Guru Hargobind retired to Kiratpur into the territory of a refractory hill raja. Thirty years after the demise of Guru Hargobind, Aurangzeb Alamgir was actuated by strong sectarian prejudices to order the execution of his son Guru Tegh Bahadur, and a large number of people felt outraged enough to attach themselves to Guru Tegh Bahadur's son and successor Guru Gobind Singh.[6]

Ganesh Das attributes political motives to Guru Gobind Singh himself and looks on Banda's activity as almost an overflow from the pent up feelings of revenge and retaliation. Guru Gobind Singh decided to avenge himself on the persecutors of his predecessors. He was confirmed in this decision by the overbearing and persecuting spirit of the fanatical section among the Muslims who accentuated the conflict between him and the Emperor. Guru Gobind Singh instituted the Khalsa as much through a divine command as through his own decision to establish a dominion independent of the Mughal Emperor. Initiating five of his most devoted followers into the order of the Khalsa he himself took *pahul* from them and declared that 'the Guru is the Khalsa and the Khalsa is the Guru'. The Khalsa started bearing arms with a determination to wage war against the 'Muslims' as an essential part of their obligations. They started demanding *kharāj* from the emperor's subjects as a matter of right. Guru Gobind Singh suffered much in this conflict. The news of his death through a wound inflicted by an Afghan was received by the Khalsa, and the Hindus, with dismay, resentment, and anger. They rose up in arms under the leadership of Banda, whom Guru Gobind Singh had nominated as his deputy. Banda declared his rule over the country around Anandpur and demanded submission from the *zamīndārs* and the peasantry in that region. Banda's dominion was however short lived; yet when he and his followers were being executed at Delhi, none of them recanted and all of them declared that they would be born again in accordance with the will of Immortal God to settle the score with their enemies.[7]

Though Ganesh Das occasionally notices undercurrents in the beliefs of the Khalsa, he emphasizes the political aspect of Guru Gobind Singh's mission and connects his aim of political ascendancy with his personal feeling of revenge. By ignoring the religious dimension Ganesh Das tends to give primacy to the idea of retaliation among the Khalsa.

In his treatment of the Sikh struggle for independence, however, Ganesh Das gives primacy to the political ambition of the Khalsa and not so much to their spirit of retaliation and revenge. After Banda's death the Khalsa took to a roving life in order to avenge themselves upon the 'Muslims' and the agents of the Mughal government and, in spite of elaborate and consistent measures of repression and persecution adopted by the Mughal governors of Lahore, they did not give up their claim to independence and dominion. Even Ahmad Shah Abdali failed to put a stop to their aggrandizement. Ganesh Das notices Amritsar as a place for congregations of the Khalsa and the presence of the Akalis there.[8] He notices also the Khalsa's firm belief in the use of arms as a religious duty. But he does not look upon the faith of the Khalsa as relevant for political activity. He does not discern any mystical entity in the collective body of the Khalsa. For him the Khalsa were merely an aggregate of individual Singhs who were politically active.

Consequently, though he presents some of the Sikh leaders as acting in concert, Ganesh Das does not invoke the sanction of any *gurmatā* for this. Though he assumes that there was some sort of grouping among them, he does not attach much importance to the institution called the *misl*.[9] Lahore was occupied and partitioned not through a collective decision of the entire Khalsa then present at Amritsar, but by three Sikh leaders – Lehna Singh, Gujjar Singh, and Sobha Singh. Charhat Singh tried to cement his informal political alliance with Gujjar Singh by a matrimonial tie between his daughter and the latter's son. It was on the sagacious advice of Jassa Singh and the Bhangi leaders that coins declaring the sovereignty of the Khalsa were struck at Lahore. The minting of this coin was not confined to Lahore, for every *sardār* established his own mint in the districts under his control. This manifesto of the Khalsa sovereignty was at the same time the declaration of many an individual *sardār's* sovereign status. It is not without significance, therefore, that Ganesh Das uses the term *bādshāh* for Jassa Singh, Chanda Singh, Ganda Singh and Hari Singh.[10]

Indeed, whatever the sanction behind the authority of the individual *sardār*, he acted as an autonomous ruler strictly in accordance with the dictates of practical good sense and his interests. This is evident first from the manner in which the territorial occupation was effected: each leader and each individual established his government wherever he could in the Punjab. Each of these new rulers established his own administration, using his personal discretion. For example,

Charhat Singh and Gujjar Singh led a joint expedition into the Sindh Sagar Doab and, on its successful conclusion, partitioned the conquered territories amongst themselves. Charhat Singh appointed Dharam Singh to guard Miani and Pind Dadan Khan, made Tehal Singh Chhachhi the *thānedār* of Dalaur to look after the salt mines, appointed Sehaj Singh to the *faujdārī* of Dhan, and made Dal Singh Gill the *nāzim* of Ahmadabad, assigning him a *jāgīr* in the Rachna Doab. Gujjar Singh gave Rawalpindi in *jāgīr* to Milkha Singh, appointed Ram Singh as the *tappadār* of Sarai Kala, and Jodh Singh Atariwala as the *tahsīldār* of Pothohar, while the *tappa* of Tarali and the fortress of Rotala were conferred upon his own brother, Chet Singh. Ganesh Das states that the other *sardārs* acted in a similar manner.[11]

Ranjit Singh was distinguished from his contemporary Sikh rulers chiefly because of a more successful pursuit of his political aims and ambition.[12] Ganesh Das does not notice any other significant difference.[13] Already in the 1780s, Hari Singh and Karam Singh had struck a new coin at Amritsar with an inscription different from the one on the coin struck earlier at Lahore. Ranjit Singh continued to use both these inscriptions on his coins, though he closed all mints other than those of Lahore and Amritsar.[14] Even if these inscriptions are taken to signify divine sanction for the sovereignty and authority of the Sikh rulers, there was no difference between the position of Ranjit Singh and that of an eighteenth-century Sikh ruler.[15] They were all alike in concentrating political power into their own hands. It is interesting to note in this connection that Ganesh Das uses the title Singh Sahib for individual *sardārs* like Gujjar Singh, Mahan Singh, and Sahib Singh, and refers to the Bhangis as 'the royal house of Bhanga Singh Bahadur'.[16] Ranjit Singh's administration differed from that of his predecessors in degree rather than kind. The offices of the *sipasālār*, the *dīwān*, the *subadār*, the *nāzim*, the *faujdār*, the *thānadār*, and the *'āmil* were not unknown in the late eighteenth century. The *qānūngo*, the *tahsīldār*, and the *kārdār* were as familiar to the subjects of the late eighteenth century Sikh rulers as to the subjects of Ranjit Singh. The conferment of *jāgīrs* by Ranjit Singh was only an extension of the practice of his predecessors.[17] Ganesh Das does notice a few minor modifications introduced by Ranjit Singh as, for instance, the abolition of some oppressive and irregular cesses.[18] Nevertheless, Ranjit Singh's administration in its main outline was not essentially different from that the other Sikh rulers.

With his primary interest in the acquisition and maintenance of power through the instrumentality of force and finance, Ganesh Das does not pay much attention to the use to which their power was put by the Sikh rulers. He does not concern himself with the effects of their policies on the life or fortunes of the various sections of the contemporary society.[19] He does not notice any social or economic change accompanying the political revolution brought about by the Khalsa.[20] He notices in fact that under Sikh rule, as under the Mughal, the Khatris held a large number of subordinate posts and at times a few important ones.[21] It is quite evident from some of the cases incidentally mentioned by Ganesh Das that by employing non-Sikhs (both Hindu and Muslim) in the service of the state Ranjit Singh was following the practice of his predecessors. According to Ganesh Das, the importance of the Khatris increased in the administration of Ranjit Singh.[22] But that again was a difference of degree and not of kind.

Ganesh Das appears to minimize the importance of religious faith and feelings of the Khalsa in motivating their politics and giving them a sense of solidarity and cohesion. By ignoring religious undercurrents he brings into higher relief the more mundane aspects of the activity of the Khalsa. Ganesh Das does not see any incompatibility between the religious beliefs and political aspirations of the Khalsa and the ambition of a single individual to concentrate power in his hands without any institutional check upon the use of his power. His assumption that Ranjit Singh did not materially depart from the administrative principles and practices of his Sikh predecessors becomes important when we know that Ganesh Das's strongest point was his experience of Sikh administration.

NOTES

1. J.S. Grewal, 'Ganesh Das's Chār Bāgh-i Punjāb'. *Proceedings of the Indian History Congress,* Patiala: 1967.
2. Ganesh Das, *Chār Bāgh-i Panjāb,* ed. Kirpal Singh, Amritsar: Khalsa College, 1965, pp.1, 81, 170.
3. Ibid., pp. 221, 247. The ancestors of Ganesh Das's father-in-law, a Puri

Khatri of the village Kharat in the *pargana* of Gujrat, had served as *faujdārs* in the Chahar Mahal during the time of Muhammad Shah and Ahmad Shah Abdali. It was through such family connections that Ganesh Das could get information from records of Muhammad Shah's reign at Sialkot.

4. This is evident from Ganesh Das's use of the phrases like *mumālik rā mutasarrif shudah* (p. 67) and *mulk-i maftūh rā mutqābiz shudah* (p. 119) and his reference to the appointment of Nar Singh to the *subadārī* of Sirhind.
5. Ibid., pp. 78, 79, 101. Ganesh Das specifically states that Ahmad Shah Abdali had the *bādshāhī* of the Punjab for ten years and the Marathas ruled over it for more than a year. The legitimacy of Sikh rule in the Punjab is taken for granted. It started in 1765, with the occupation of Lahore.
6. Ibid., pp. 105, 108-9, 110-11.
7. Ibid., p. 115, 118, 123.
8. Ibid., pp. 124–6.
9. Ganesh Das uses the word *misldārān* once (p. 144); but he uses the term *mutwassil* also for the same individual (p. 147); it is interesting to note that they shift their allegiance from Sahib Singh Bhangi to Ranjit Singh. Significantly, the holders of *misls* (*misldārān*) are not the heads but constituents of a larger unit under a chief or *sardār.* See also note 12, below.
10. Ibid., pp. 127, 128, 130, 131, 132, 133.
11. Ibid., pp. 131-2. When Charhat Singh conquered the territory around the fortress of Kunjah, he gave it in *jāgīr* to Mal Singh and bestowed Kalara and Kuthala upon Himmat Singh (p. 130). When Ganda Singh and Jhanda Singh conquered Multan, they appointed Diwan Singh to its *sūbadārī* (p. 132).
12. Ganesh Das attributes political ambition (*bu-i riyāsat*) to Charhat Singh in the very beginning of his active career (p. 135). This is true of almost every *sardār,* even some of those who are designated as *misldārs,* like Nar Singh Chamiariwala, Bagh Singh Hallowalia and others, who are mentioned as *misldārs* of the Bhangis (p. 144). They claimed independent sway (p. 146). The conflict between Mahan Singh and Bhangi *sardārs* was essentially due to the former's anxiety to extend his dominions (*mulk-gīrī*) at the cost of those of the others (p. 135).
13. Some differences no doubt existed. The title *sarkār-i a'lā* or *sarkār-i wālā,* which Ganesh Das uses for Ranjit Singh, is not used by him for any of the late eighteenth century Sikh rulers. Though the title *madār al-mahām* is used for a few of the officials of the late eighteenth century Sikh rulers, it was more customary with Ranjit Singh to confer titles on his officials. Ganesh Das uses the epithet *makhdūmah-i jahān* only for a widow of Ranjit Singh. The office of *wazārat* too is mentioned only in

connection with Ranjit Singh's government, and so is the court of justice. All this would suggest no doubt a definite movement towards the establishment of a full-fledged monarchy under Ranjit Singh. This was, however, a culmination of earlier tendencies.

14. Ganesh Das, *Chār Bāgh-i Punjāb*, pp. 132-3.
15. These inscriptions are well known to the students of Sikh history and historians have generally inferred from their use that the coins were meant to declare the sovereignty of the Khalsa as a collective entity in the name of God through the grace of Guru Nanak and Guru Gobind Singh. These inscriptions were originally used in the time of Banda on a seal and coins. Just as Ranjit Singh was adopting the practice of the late eighteenth-century Sikh rulers, so too they had been following the example of Banda.
16. Ganesh Das, *Chār Bāgh-i Panjāb*, pp. 133, 136, 139, 152.
17. There are frequent references to these offices in the late eighteenth century as well as in the early nineteenth century. Ibid., pp. 132, 136, 137, 145, 146, 148-9, 151, 226, 250, 254, 262, 298, 304, 308, 309, 322, 336, 377, 381, 399.
18. Ibid., pp. 130, 134, 136, 141, 147-8, 162, 169, 211, 219, 249, 250, 296, 297, 299, 300, 301, 306, 317, 319, 321, 324, 330, 334, 343, 399.
19. Ganesh Das mentions at places some of the measures adopted by the Sikh rulers as much in the interest of their subjects as their own, in particular the re-peopling of the towns and the settlement of the countryside. He also mentions a few cases of the grant of revenue-free lands. On the whole, however, he is concerned with the fortunes of the ruling class. It is interesting to note in this connection that Ganesh Das was very much wedded to the idea of a social organization based on distinctions between its various constituents. In fact his ideal society consisted of an hierarchy of four basic sections: the rulers, the courtiers, and the army are compared by him with fire; the learned are associated with water; the merchants and traders, with air; the *zamīndārs*, with earth. Ganesh Das believed that in the best interests of the society as a whole all these four elements should remain in their proper and determined order.
20. This is not insignificant because Ganesh Das was very much aware of the political revolution brought about by the Khalsa. In fact he noticed that in purely political terms the Jatt had outstripped the Khatri.
21. Ganesh Das's preoccupation with the Khatris becomes evident from the fact that he devotes ten consecutive pages to them at one place (pp. 283-93) and refers to them at several other places in the *Chār Bāgh-i Panjāb*.
22. Ganesh Das, *Chār Bāgh-i Panjāb*, p. 284. The indispensability of the Khatris for the *diwani* in particular had dawned upon the Sikh rulers soon after the establishment of their rule.

20

Eighteenth-Century Sikh Polity

Historians of Mughal India have seen very little connection between the faith of the Khalsa and their polity. Jadunath Sarkar, for instance, congratulates the Mughal government for successfully breaking up Guru Gobind Singh's power and for having robbed the Sikhs of a common leader and a rallying centre. 'Thereafter the Sikhs continued to disturb public peace, but only in isolated bands. They were no longer an army fighting under one chief, with a definite political aim, but merely moving bodies of brigands, extremely brave, enthusiastic, and hardy, but essentially plunderers uninspired by any ambition to build up organized Government in the land. If Ranjit Singh had not risen, there would have been no large and united State under Sikh dominion, but a number of petty principalities in the Punjab with a ruling aristocracy of Sikh soldiers, sending their organized marauders every year to raid and lay the country waste'.[1] Not only were the politics of the Sikhs unconnected with their religion on this view, there was hardly a Sikh polity worth the name.

Many historians of the Sikhs, on the other hand, have postulated a close connection between the political organization of the Khalsa and their faith. John Malcolm, for example, attributed the institution of *gurmatā* to Guru Gobind Singh himself and regarded 'the spirit of equality' as the vital principle of the Sikh Commonwealth.[2] Horace Hayman Wilson thought of the eighteenth century Sikh polity as 'a sort of theocracy'.[3] For J.D. Cunningham, the Commonwealth of the Khalsa was theocratic: 'God was their helper and only judge, community of faith or object was their moving principle'.[4] Lepel Griffin saw an intimate connection between Sikh polity and the 'democratic nature' of Sikhism.[5] Many other historians have seen Sikh polity sprouting from the Sikh religion.[6]

However, the assumption of a direct relationship between the political organization of the Khalsa and their religion has landed the historians, albeit unconsciously, into considerable difficulties. Malcolm, for instance, in spite of his emphasis on the importance of the Akalis as the authoritative guardians of the *gurmatā*, did not see any principle of cohesion among the Sikhs and thought of their apparently theocratic constitution as in reality 'an oligarchy'.[7] Cunningham, who propounded the concept of 'theocratic confederate feudalism' in relation to Sikh polity, found it nonetheless idle to call an 'ever-changing' state of alliance and dependence by the name of a constitution'. He suggested therefore that we must look for an outline of the Sikh political system 'rather in the dictates of our common nature, than in the enactments of the assemblies, or in the injunctions of their religious guides'.[8] The clue to an understanding of Sikh polity thus lies rather in the practical demands of their historical circumstance than in the ideals and institutions of Sikhism. Examples of unsatisfactory formulation can be multiplied. [9]

In a discussion of eighteenth-century Sikh polity, Banda Bahadur provides the starting point, though not the easiest point to start with. After he had defeated the Mughal *faujdār* of Sirhind, sovereign rule was established in the conquered territories. This political success was attributed to the grace of Guru Nanak and Guru Gobind Singh, and power was thought to have been derived ultimately from God.[10] At the same time, in the formal choice of a capital, the striking of a new coin, the use of a new seal, the adoption of a new calendar marking the conquest of Sirhind, and in the displacement of Mughal officials by Sikh governors and other subordinate officers, one can see an attempt to supplant the existing government in its major detail.[11] Banda came to assume what Ganda Singh significantly, though probably incidentally, calls a 'regal state'.[12] However, Banda did not assume kingship for himself, and for some of his most important associates[13] he was not a Guru. Banda, thus, occupied an indeterminate position.

During the third quarter of the eighteenth century, the position of a few Sikh rulers is not difficult to characterize. In the Sutlej-Jamuna Divide after Banda's death, a petty *zamīndār* from a powerful Jatt clan was quietly increasing his power, away from the main currents of Punjab politics. In 1723 he possessed only 30 villages as a collector of revenues on behalf of the Mughal state. At times he sought the help of the fugitive Majha Sikhs, his co-religionists, against the neighbouring Muslim *zamīndārs*, but he stood neutral between his brother-Sikhs and their over-mighty enemies. He used his influence with the Mughal *faujdār* of Sirhind, to whom he rendered at least a nominal submission, for crushing the power of a dangerous Muslim rival, but he wrested several villages from the *faujdār*. He provisioned the Mughal emperor in distress, but also occupied some of the Mughal territory. He provided food and fodder to the Marathas at Panipat, but received from them a huge sum of money in return. He plundered the Afghan troops on their march back to Afghanistan, but also became a tributary to the Shah of Afghanistan. This was Ala Singh.[14] The guiding principle in his life seems to have been the acquisition of power and the establishment of effective rule. In 1761, he was in control of 726 villages and towns. Before his death in 1765, the year in which some of the Sikh leaders of the central Punjab declared their sovereignty at Lahore, Ala Singh founded a Sikh kingdom which legally, though nominally, derived its authority not from God but from Ahmad Shah Abdali.[15] Thus, within half a century of Banda's death was founded a monarchy which even in theory was not based on any religious assumptions. For Ala Singh, there was no incompatibility between the Sikh religious ideals as he understood them and the monarchial form of government which he established.[16] Incidentally, he cannot be treated as a member of any *misl*. To talk of Phulkian *misl* is to talk of a non-entity.

The only significant difference in the position of Ala Singh and that of Ranjit Singh was that the latter attributed his power to the grace of God by continuing to use the coins with the inscriptions originally used by Banda and subsequently by late eighteenth-century Sikh chiefs.[17] Theoretical derivation of power from God did not affect the nature of his sovereign rule in territories inherited or conquered by him. In fact, Cunningham's statement on the theocratic character of the political constitution of the Sikhs, that God was their helper and only judge, would establish rather the complete independence of each Sikh chief in his own dominions than a theocracy in the territories subjugated by the Sikhs as a whole. In his submission to God the Sikh chief denied allegiance to an earthly sovereign.

Indeed, if we turn to the politics and government of the Sikh leaders of the central Punjab, we find them informally behaving like kings in their own little kingdoms. Charhat Singh, the eldest son of Naudh Singh, for instance, established his *de facto* rule, even before the declaration of Sikh sovereignty at Lahore, over a solid block of territory in the Rachna Doab where in the early 1750s he had established his *rākhī* or protection around villages inherited from his father.[18] In 1761, he maintained his independence against the Afghan governor of Lahore and then rebuilt and fortified Gujranwala as his capital. In 1764, when he conquered the district of Gujrat, he constructed forts and appointed his own commandants and *faujdārs* in these as in other conquered territories. In 1765 we find him appointing his own governor at Wazirabad, giving a *jāgīr* worth four thousand rupees a year to a commandant, granting villages to some of his old servants, and asserting his superior rights over Rai Jalal in the southern Rawalpindi district. By 1774 he was helping a Rajput prince against his father's Sikh overlord, Jhanda Singh Bhangi. Before his death during this conflict, Charhat Singh not only enjoyed complete autonomy in his own principality but could also freely enter into political alliances with both Sikh and non-Sikh chiefs. Here was a small state with its power vested primarily in the person of Charhat Singh. It was bequeathed on his death to his son Mahan Singh. If we look to the general pattern of politics and government of the Sikh principalities at this time, Charhat Singh was by no means an exception.[19]

Thus, if we are looking for the existence of Sikh theocracy in any sense other than the theoretical derivation of a Sikh chief's autonomous power from God, we must look for it in the central Punjab between the death of Banda in 1716 and the declaration of Sikh sovereignty at Lahore in 1765. This much is implied indeed in the view that the 'democratic' institutions of the Sikhs had become a mere farce in the last three decades of the eighteenth century. Here it may be pointed out first that the Sikh leaders did not occupy any considerable territories before 1750. However, from about 1745 the Sikhs had adopted some sort of organization; there was a close co-operation among a large number of Sikh leaders; they acted at times more or less as a single body. The two most important institutions of the Sikhs, the Gurmatā and the Dal Khalsa, which are generally treated as both theocratic and democratic, are believed to have been evolved by the Sikhs during this phase of their history. It is necessary therefore to grasp the proper significance of developments during this phase.

The clue to an understanding of both the Gurmatā and the Dal Khalsa, which were closely connected with each other, lies in the importance which the Khalsa had come to attach to Amritsar. This place was in no way associated with Guru Gobind Singh, but its importance to the Khalsa was real. After Banda's death, his supporters were divided into two camps: the Bandais who regarded Banda as the Guru, and the Tat Khalsa who refused to believe in any personal Guru after the death of Guru Gobind Singh. At this time there were several other 'divisions' among the Sikhs and a few individuals had attempted to assume Guruship.[20] In the absence of a generally recognized leader, and with the question of Guruship still somewhat indeterminate, to control the places of Sikh pilgrimage was *inter alia* to control and influence Sikh opinion. Hence the Bandais and the Tat Khalsa contested the control of Amritsar which, since the days of Guru Arjan, was the most central if not the most frequented place of Sikh pilgrimage.[21]

In one of the gatherings at Amritsar, the Sikh leaders decided to organize their striking power. According to Hari Ram Gupta, they did this 'to defend their person and property against a tyrannical Government. In order to popularize their faith, the needs of the individuals who were daily joining them had to be attended to. Their relations and friends leading peaceful lives in villages had to be protected, and those who opposed them had to be silenced. To follow a systematized course of plunder a plan of action has to be prepared, weapons and provisions had to be got ready. In a word organization was needed.' Thus, it was to meet the practical demands of their historical situation that the Sikh leaders decided to form *jathās* or groups for self-defence and for the acquisition of the means to political power. With an increase in their striking power increased the risk of their becoming a more conspicuous target of their enemies, and the Sikh leaders were live to the increasing need of unity among them. 'The odds were so heavily against them that uniting and acting in one body and on one principle was with them a law of necessity. Being surrounded with danger their only hope of success lay in unity, as this was the sole means of their preservation'.[22] Unity of action was achieved through the Dal Khalsa or the combined fighting units of a large number of Sikh leaders. They acted as one body, particularly when they were to face a powerful opponent.

The limited scope of Gurmatā and the limited function of Dal Khalsa are underlined: 'whenever there was no emergency each division acted independently, or in concert, as necessity or inclination suggested'.[23] The decisions which the Sikh leaders at Amritsar took from time to time were ad hoc deliberations of voluntary gatherings and their scope was confined to matters concerning the preservation or augmentation of striking power; they stopped short of territorial occupation and rule.[24] Quite intelligible in terms of the historical circumstance, they appear to be the expression of a sense of unity among a considerable number of Sikh leaders at a most critical period of their history.

This is not to suggest, however, that the religious faith of the Khalsa had no relevance for their politics. The perseverance with which they suffered all kinds of hardship and the tenacity with which they pursued power were inspired by their firm belief in the mission of Guru Gobind Singh as they understood it. They were hopefully convinced of their destiny to rule as the elect of God through their acceptance of the *pahul*. This belief in their common destiny, coupled with a sense of communal kinship, gave them a solidarity which was strengthened by the external circumstance. The doctrines of Guru Panth and Guru Granth symbolized the unity of the entire body of the Khalsa, and imparted sanctity to *gurmatās*. However, to look upon their religious faith as a motive force in their politics is not the same thing as to postulate the translation of their religious ideals into their polity.

The phase in which Rākhī, Misl, Dal Khalsa and Gurmatā

played a crucial role in the history of the Sikhs began around 1745 and ended around 1765. This was the phase in which Sikh rule was established over a large part of the Punjab. The bearing of these 'institutions' on the acquisition of power and acquisition of territories was quite close.

Rākhī was not a phase preceding territorial occupation, though the area brought under 'protection' (*rākhī*) was generally occupied at a later stage by the same leader who brought it under his 'protection'. Thus a leader of the Khalsa could establish his control over one area and extend his protection to another at the same time. What was involved in Rākhī was really a concession, indeed a large concession, in the rate of assessment, and a surety that no one else would be allowed to interfere with the cultivators who accepted the Rākhī of a Khalsa leader. The cultivator had to pay only a fifth of the produce from land, instead of the usual one-half or nearly one-half. The Rākhī became more and more extensive as the Khalsa leaders became more and more effective in redeeming the promise of protection. The Rākhī thus became the source of finance and an instrument of extending political influence, and eventually of territorial occupation.

The fighting units, called *derās* or *jathās*, were formed in the 1730s. These units multiplied in the 1750s for the purpose of effective action and occupation of territories. At a later stage, the epithet *misl* came to be applied to such units. They were never static, uniform, or formal. In one case the entire unit could consist of one leader and his followers; in another, it could be a combination of several small units accepting the leadership of one person for a specific purpose or campaign. The booty could sometimes be divided on the unit basis but the territories occupied were generally divided on the individual basis. Those who formed one such unit were likely to remain combined for offensive and defensive action, but it was not obligatory for an individual member to remain under the same leader. During the crucial phase of 1745–65, shifts were rather uncommon, which gives the impression as if the combinations formed for a limited purpose were permanent units of Sikh polity. In almost every case the meaning of the *misl* as a fighting unit was lost when territories were occupied.

The term Dal Khalsa was used for a combination of the forces of several units. The strength and composition of the Dal Khalsa thus changed from one major compaign to another. The purpose of this combination was the same, a united action. During the phase from 1745 to 1765 the different units combined to take united action more often than ever before or after, and this gives the impression that the Dal Khalsa was a kind of standing army of the Khalsa operating as a single unit.

Furthermore, before concerted action was taken it was necessary to meet, discuss, and resolve. The resolutions of a considerable number of leaders and their followers adopted at any given place or time were called Gurmatās. Since most of the important resolutions were adopted at Amritsar at the times of Baisakhi and Diwali, when a large number of the Khalsa used to be present, the Gurmatā came to be associated with Amritsar. During the phase from 1745 to 1765 most of the important Gurmatās were in fact adopted at Amritsar. A Gurmatā was not legally or constitutionally binding even on the members present; but it was morally binding even on those who were not personally present. This was because they all subscribed to the doctrine of Guru Panth and Guru Granth. A Gurmatā passed by the Khalsa in the presence of the *Granth Sahib* was like the command of the Guru and had to be obeyed.

The principle of equality built into the doctrine of Guru Panth entitled every individual member of the Khalsa to fight and conquer. That was why, from the very beginning, territories were generally occupied by individuals, and if they were occupied by more than one conqueror in combination they were soon divided. Ratan Singh Bhangu, who often talks in terms of Misls, the Buddha and Taruna Dals, and the Dal Khalsa, states explicitly that according to a resolution adopted at the Akal Takht in Amritsar whoever occupied a village first would remain its legitimate master. None was to be displaced from a place he occupied. That was why there was a tendency among the smaller leaders to occupy small places, while the bigger leaders occupied towns and cities. If the need arose, the entire unit came to the help of its member to ensure that he was not unjustly ousted.

Bute Shah's comment in connection with the occupation of territories by the Sikhs in the Sarkār of Sirhind in 1764 makes a lot of sense: 'Among them they have a custom that any place or village is deemed to belong to any one of the Singhs who appropriates it by throwing a piece of cloth or his whip or anything else. If such a person owns only one horse, even the master of an army does not raise any objection to his claims'. This process threw up a large number of Sikh rulers during the third quarter of the eighteenth century. Each one of them tended to act as a sovereign ruler, justifying the prophetic remark attributed to Guru Gobind Singh that every Singh in the saddle would acquire political power.[25]

NOTES

1. Jadunath Sarkar, *A Short History of Aurangzeb*, Calcutta: 1930, p. 168.
2. John Malcolm, *A Sketch of the Sikhs*, London: 1812, p. 145.
3. H.H. Wilson, 'Civil and Religious Institutions of the Sikhs', *The Sikh Religion: A Symposium*, Calcutta: Sushil Gupta Private Ltd., 1958, p. 61.
4. J.D. Cunningham, *A History of the Sikhs*, Delhi: S.Chand and Co., 1966 (rpt.), p. 94.
5. Lepel Griffin, *Chiefs and Families of Note in the Punjab*, Lahore: 1940.
6. A.C. Banerjee, for instance, looks upon the Sikh community as being governed by principles of 'equality and democracy'. For him, eighteenth-century Sikh polity was a 'confederacy which was democratic in composition and religious in its cohesive principle': *Anglo-Sikh Relations*, Calcutta: 1949, pp. lxiv, lxvii. For Teja Singh, the federal form of Sikh government in the late eighteenth century was derived directly from the democratic organization of the Khalsa: *Sikhism: Its Ideals and Institutions*, Delhi: Orient Longman, 1951. N.K. Sinha agrees with Cunningham that Sikh polity had in it 'an element of theocracy' and also that it was 'in its spirit undoubtedly a democracy': *Rise of Sikh Power*, Calcutta: A Mukherjee and Co., 1960 (3rd edn.), pp. 108, 110. Some of the historians who have treated the late eighteenth century as a background to the subjects of their study have, naturally, accepted and repeated these ideas. See, for example, G.L. Chopra, *The Panjab as a Sovereign State*, Hoshiarpur: Vishveshvaranand Vedic Research Institute, 1960 (2nd edn.), pp. 91-2; Fauja Singh Bajwa, *Military System of Sikhs (1799-1849)*, Delhi: Motilal Banarsidas, 1964, pp. 12, 13, 17 & n.
7. John Malcolm, *A Sketch of the Sikhs*, pp. 111-12, 119, 120, 121.
8. J.D. Cunningham, *A History of the Sikhs*, pp. 95-6.
9. For A.C. Banerjee, the Sikh confederacy (which on the same page is democratic in composition and religious in its cohesive principle) had arisen out of a desperate war and 'could not become an instrument of civil government': *Anglo-Sikh Relations*, pp. lxvii-viii. In N.K. Sinha's

view the dissolution of the *misl* organization was 'a historical certainty' because the Sikh chiefs (all of a sudden as it were) 'degenerated from self-sacrificing fighters for the national cause into self-seeking freebooting barons': *Rise of Sikh Power*, pp. 116–17. On this view, the theocratic confederate feudalism was a 'decayed institution' already within three years of the establishment of Sikh sovereignty, and it went on decaying from day to day till it degenerated into the military monarchy of Ranjit Singh. Similarly, for Teja Singh, the *misls* in the beginning 'had developed the Sikh character to a high degree and the noblest features of Sikh organization appeared in those days; but about the time of Ranjiṭ Singh they had lost their old efficacy and selfishness and internecine quarrels had reduced the democratic forms to a mere farce': *Sikhism: Its Ideals and Institutions*, p. 46.

10. This may be inferred from the inscriptions on the coin and the seal of Banda's time. Ganda Singh, *Banda Singh Bahadur*, Amritsar: Khalsa College, 1935, pp. 82, 83 and facs. opposite p. 153. Whereas success may be seen as being derived from God in the first, it is clearly derived in the second by Guru Gobind Singh from Guru Nanak. The inscriptions are:

    Sikka zadd bar har do 'ālam tegh-Nānak wāhib ast,
    Fateh Gobind Singh, shāh-i shāhān, fazl-i sachchā sāhib ast.

    and,

    Degh-o tegh-o fateh nusrat bedrang,
    Yāft az Nanak Guru Gobind Singh.

11. Ibid., pp. 40, 50, 72, 76, 82-4, 101, 112. The author suggests (ibid., 85) that 'no regular form' of government was established. Probably he has some specifically 'Sikh' government in mind. He mentions 'the total abolition of the Zamindari System' (pp. 85, 86, 87, 242), but unfortunately does not cite evidence for this important statement which is often repeated by other historians.
12. Khushwant Singh, *A History of the Sikhs*, Princeton: Princeton University Press, 1963, pp. vol. I, p. 107.
13. Teja Singh and Ganda Singh, *A Short History of the Sikhs*, Delhi: Orient Longman Ltd., 1950, p. 114.
14. For an outline of Ala Singh's political career, Kirpal Singh, *Life of Maharaja Ala Singh of Patiala and His Times*, Amritsar: Khalsa College, 1954; Hari Ram Gupta, *A History of the Sikhs*, Shimla: Minerva Book Shop, 1952, pp. 1, 137-43; N.K. Sinha, *Rise of Sikh Power* pp. 12, 37, 38, 40, 41, 43, 52. Lepel Griffin, *The Rajas of the Panjab*, London: 1873, pp. 1-29. Indu Banga, 'Alha Singh: The Founder of Patiala State', in *The Punjab Past and Present: Essays in Honour of Dr Ganda Singh*, eds. Harbans Singh and N. Gerald Barrier, Patiala: Punjabi University, 1976, pp. 150-60.

15. According to the contemporary author of the *Jangnāma*, Qazi Nur Muhammad, on whose evidence Gupta's statement is based, Ahmad Shah conferred upon Ala Singh 'a title, invested him with *khilat*, kettledrums and banners, and installed him in the independent chieftainship of Sarhind for an annual subsidy of three and half lakhs of rupees': *A History of the Sikhs*, vol. 1, p. 230. The coin struck at Patiala bears the inscription:

    Hukm shud az qādir-i-bechūn b'Ahmad Pādshāh,
    Sikka zann bar sīm-o zar az auj-i māhī tāb'māh.

16. The monarchical character of Ala Singh's government has never been questioned by the historians. It may be pointed out that the rule of the other Phulkian chiefs in this respect was not different from Ala Singh's. The use of the term *misl* for these chiefs means little more than the fact that they had descended from a common ancestor, Phul.
17. For the coins of the Sikhs, Surinder Singh, *Sikh Coinage: Symbol of Sovereignty*, New Delhi: Manohar, 2004.
18. It is useful to follow the individual chief in his whole career even in secondary works. For Charhat Singh, Hari Ram Gupta, *A History of the Sikhs*, vol. I, pp. 95, 99, 158-59, 160-61, 172, 196, 216, 218, 225, 232, 237, 241, 244, 247, 248, 263, 264; N.K. Sinha, *Rise of Sikh Power*, pp. 13, 15, 28, 30, 33, 40, 42, 58, 60, 64.
19. Talking of the 'absolute form of government of the Sikh Chiefs', H.R. Gupta observes that each Sikh chief was 'independent of others, and had direct dealings with the neighbouring independent states. Each sardar had some officers to register political correspondence, while the ecclesiastical affairs were administered by the Akalis who were in charge of the Temple and the Tank in Amritsar'. He is careful to add, however, that these Akalis did not interfere with the 'temporal authority of the Sikh chiefs': *History of the Sikhs*, vol. I, p. 327. The autonomy of each 'Bhangi' chief comes out clearly in Veena Sachdeva's M.Phil. dissertation, 'The Rule of the Bhangis (1765-1810)', Guru Nanak Dev University, Amritsar, 1981.
20. Teja Singh and Ganda Singh, *A Short History of the Sikhs*, pp. 109-16.
21. Khushwant Singh notices the anxiety of the followers of Banda and the Tat Khalsa to control Amritsar, but dismisses it as meaningless triviality: *A History of the Sikhs* vol.1, pp. 121-2. J.C. Archer was nearer the truth when he observed that the failure of the followers of Banda to secure for themselves the administrative contol of the shrine at Amritsar was 'more decisive in their fortunes than any idiosyncrasies of garb or diet or domestic arrangement'. *The Sikhs in Relation to Hindus, Muslims, Christians and Ahmadiyas: A Study in Comparative Religion*, Princeton: Princeton University Press, 1946, p. 223.
22. Hari Ram Gupta, *History of the Sikhs*, vol. 1, pp. 20-1, 48.

23. Ibid., p. 55.
24. It is often said, for instance, that the occupation of Lahore was decided upon in a Gurmatā, but only three chiefs occupied it and they too could agree only on its partition. It is worth noticing that Charhat Singh came later to demand a share and got at least the Zamzama gun.
25. The phrase used by Ratan Singh Bhangu for the emergence of such a situation was '*hanne hanne mīrī*'.

21

'Pātshāh of the Panth Jassa Singh Ahluwalia

One way of clarifying the issue of Sikh polity during the late eighteenth century is to concentrate on the career of a single leader. We may turn to Jassa Singh Ahluwalia for this purpose. He is generally regarded as the most eminent of the leaders of the Khalsa during the third quarter of the eighteenth century. He is also looked upon as the best representative of the Khalsa of Guru Gobind Singh. The court chronicler of his 'house', Ram Sukh Rao, refers to him as Maharaja Jassa Singh Bahadur and as 'the Master of the Panth'. But Ram Sukh Rao is not alone in praising Jassa Singh Ahluwalia. Ratan Singh Bhangu refers to him as the 'Pātshāh of the Panth', and among the Persian writers, Khushwaqt Rai recalls Jassa Singh as the 'Bādshāh of the Singhs' while Sohan Lal Suri refers to him as 'Sarkār Khālsā', an epithet generally believed to have been reserved for Ranjit Singh.[1]

Not much is known of the early career of Jassa Singh. He was born in 1718 in a family of Kalals in village Ahlu between Lahore and Qasur. Around 1730, he was baptized as a Singh by a well known Sikh leader, popularly called Nawab Kapur Singh. Soon after, Zakariya Khan decided to adopt a conciliatory policy towards the Singhs, offering to their leader a robe of honour (*khil'at*), a title (*khitāb*), and revenue-free land (*jāgīr*). They chose Kapur Singh to receive this honour, and he came to be known as Nawab Kapur Singh. The Singhs began to subsist on the revenues of twelve villages around Ramdaspur (Amritsar). At this time the duty of managing the stores of grain for the horses of the

Singhs was assigned by Kapur Singh to the young Jassa Singh. This situation did not last long because Zakariya Khan reverted to his earlier policy of repression. It was during this phase of persecution that Bhai Mani Singh was executed. The Singhs got some respite when Nadir Shah invaded the country. Nawab Kapur Singh had more than a thousand armed followers at this time, and Jassa Singh could have been among those who plundered the Persian troopers passing through the Punjab on their return from Delhi in 1739.

Jassa Singh emerged as a leader of some consequence before Ahmad Shah Abdali took over the Punjab from its Mughal rulers. In 1746 Jassa Singh led a band of Singhs into the Rachna Doab where he was attacked by the *faujdār*, Jaspat Rai, the younger brother of Lakhpat Rai who was the Diwan of Lahore under Yahiya Khan. Jaspat Rai was killed in an encounter near Eminabad, and the town was plundered by the Singhs. Diwan Lakhpat Rai vowed to avenge the death of his younger brother. He pursued the Singhs closely, obliging them to cross the Ravi into the Bari Doab first and then to cross the Beas into the Jalandhar Doab and eventually take refuge in the Malwa across the Sutlej. Thousands of Singhs were killed in this campaign, but Jassa Singh and his horsemen were among those who survived the holocaust. In 1748, Jassa Singh was among the leaders who defeated Salabat Khan, the *faujdār* at Amritsar. A year later he assisted Diwan Kaura Mal in his campaign against Shah Nawaz Khan of Multan on behalf of Muin al-Mulk as Governor of Lahore. Shah Nawaz was defeated and killed by the combined forces of Kaura Mal and Jassa Singh. Soon after the death of Nawab Kapur Singh and Muin al-Mulk in 1753, Jassa Singh occupied Khwaspur and conquered Fatehabad which was to serve as his headquarters for over twenty years.[2]

Between 1754 and 1765 Jassa Singh emerged as the most important leader of the Khalsa. In April 1754 he defeated Aziz Beg and Bakhshinda Beg, the commandants who had come to attack Amritsar. In 1757, he plundered Ahmad Shah's army when it passed through Goindval and Fatehabad on its return from Delhi. A few months later he fought in the battle of Mahilpur on Adina Beg Khan's side against the commandants sent by Ahmad Shah Abdali's son Taimur Shah as Governor of Lahore.

The Afghan commandant Buland Khan was killed in this battle, and the Afghan troops admitted defeat by leaving the field. Before the end of 1757, Jassa Singh defeated Sa'adat Khan whom Ahmad Shah Abdali had appointed at Jalandhar. 'From that moment', says the eyewitness Tahmas Khan, 'the peace and order that had been established in that country was disrupted and the Sikhs rose in revolt on all the four sides.' In the beginning of 1758 Ubaidulla Khan, the Afghan general, invaded the Jalandhar Doab but was defeated by Jassa Singh and other Sardars. Tahmas Khan's comment is again significant: 'After this, in whatever direction the army went, it was defeated. Eventually, even the environs of Lahore were not safe. Every night the Sikhs would come in thousands to attack the city. They devastated all the *muhallas* outside the city wall.'[3]

The uneasy alliance of the Singhs with the Marathas came to an end when the latter appointed Adina Beg Khan as their governor in the Punjab. He tried to suppress the Singh Sardārs. His commandants, Hira Mal and Gulsher Khan, were defeated and killed by the Singhs under the leadership of Jassa Singh. Adina Beg Khan died in September 1758. In March 1759, Siddiq Beg of Sirhind attacked Anandpur; Jassa Singh was wounded in this battle, but not vanquished. When Ahmad Shah Abdali marched into the Punjab towards the end of the year, Jassa Singh attacked his general, Jahan Khan, who was encamped near Lahore, and inflicted heavy losses on him. During 1760, while Ahmad Shah Abdali was staying in the Delhi region, there was no Afghan commandant in the Punjab who could withstand the combined forces of the Khalsa. After Ahmad Shah's return to Kabul in 1761, Ubaid Khan marched from Lahore against Charhat Singh at Gujranwala. Jassa Singh Ahluwalia reached there to defeat the Afghan governor. Under the leadership of Jassa Singh, the Khalsa attacked Lahore and occupied the city, while Ubaid Khan watched helplessly in the fort.

It was at this time that the controversial coin in the name of Jassa Singh was struck at Lahore. One view is that it was struck by the supporters of Jassa Singh, if not by Jassa Singh himself. Another view is that Jassa Singh did not strike such a coin, nor did he allow any one else to do so. The coin was said to bear the inscription:

Sikka zadd dar jahān b'fazl-i Akāl,
Mulk-i Ahmad girift Jassā Kalāl.

The omission of the epithet 'Singh' from this inscription, the mention of Jassa Singh as 'Kalal', and the implied claim that Jassa Singh alone was the ruler are the arguments used against the authenticity of this coin. Indeed, according to Ganesh Das, the bigoted *'ulamā* of the Punjab composed this inscription, struck it on a few rupees, and took them to Ahmad Shah Abdali at Kabul in order to provoke him.[4] The most significant aspect of this coin for our present purpose is that whoever struck it assumed Jassa Singh Ahluwalia to be the foremost leader of the Khalsa.

There is enough evidence in support of this inference. Early in 1762, Ahmad Shah Abdali struck a heavy blow on the Khalsa in the Malwa region when thousands of them were killed in a single action. The event is referred to as the Great Carnage (*waddhā ghallūghārā*). The majority of the leaders were involved in this action. In a long account of the action in Ratan Singh Bhangu's *Panth Prakāsh*, two leaders emerge as the most eminent: Charhat Singh and Jassa Singh Ahluwalia. At one place in the account, both are brought together to discuss the strategy of defence. Charhat Singh suggested a pitched battle by forming right and left wings around a centre. Jassa Singh suggested a ring around the non-combatants, so that they could move away while fighting the enemy, and it was this view that prevailed. He received over a score of wounds in this running fight.[5]

Nevertheless, three months later we find Jassa Singh Ahluwalia leading the Khalsa against Zain Khan, the Afghan governor of Sirhind, who was obliged to pay 50,000 rupees as *nazrāna.* Jassa Singh led the Khalsa against Ahmad Shah near Amritsar in October 1762. The Shah fought for a day and retreated to Lahore during the night. Early in 1764 Jassa Singh led the Khalsa against Zain Khan once again. Zain Khan was defeated and slain, and the entire Sarkār of Sirhind was occupied by the conquerors. Before the end of the year Ahmad Shah Abdali marched into the Punjab and went towards Delhi, but returned from Kunjpura. He was opposed by the Khalsa the moment he crossed the river Sutlej. Battles were fought on three successive days. The forces of the leaders of the Khalsa were divided into three large units:

the right, the left, and the centre. The 'mountain-like' Jassa Singh Ahluwalia was in the centre. Ahmad Shah Abdali was on the defensive throughout his return march, his authority was confined to his camp.[6] Before he reached Kabul, Lahore was occupied by the Khalsa and coin was struck as a formal declaration of sovereign status in 1765.

Towards the end of his reign, Jassa Singh Ahluwalia ousted the Ramgarhias from their territories in the Bari and Jalandhar Doab. Conflicts among the Sikh rulers were not uncommon in the 1770s, but Jassa Singh Ahluwalia alone went to the extent of sending an eminent Sikh chief into exile. Probably he alone was in a position to do so due to the influence and good will he commanded among his fellow rulers. Ratan Singh Bhangu's comment on this development is rather significant. He praises all the four Ramgarhia brothers for their invincible courage; none who fought against them ever saw their back. But they were themselves responsible for their ignominious fall: they laid hands on the 'Pātshāh of the Panth'.[7]

Around 1780, the year of Ranjit Singh's birth, Jassa Singh Ahluwalia was virtually a king, holding and exercising political power in a well defined territory without formal checks on the exercise of that power. His court was more formal than that of any other Sikh ruler of the time. The Diwān and the Bakhshī, the Musāhibs and Muqarrabs, Munshīs and Mutasaddīs, commandants of the army, attendants (*khidmatgārs*), mace-bearers (*chobdārs*) and heralds (*naqībs*), all came to the *darbār* in formal dress and sat or stood in accordance with rank and position. The civil matters were presented by the Diwān and the army matters by the Bakhshī; they stood up in front of Jassa Singh to present their cases and for his signature on files as a mark of his formal approval.

In a conquering career of over a quarter of a century, Jassa Singh had occupied many towns and villages. He left many a pocket of territory in the hands of *ījāradārs* and Chahārumī *zamīndārs*. The entire conquered territory, thus, was not directly administered by him. The largest chunk of his territory was in the Bari and Jalandhar Doabs, and in the Malwa region across the river Sutlej. Some of the easily identifiable places are Fatehabad, Goindval, Khadur, Vairowal, Sarhali, Sultanpur, Nadala, Begowal, Miani, Kapurthala, Nur Mahal, Bajwara, Urmar, Tanda, Makhu, Kot Isa Khan, and parts of Jagraon. In the Sirhind region there were Payal, Naraingarh, Bassi, Bharog, Salaudi and Kotla Nihangan.

Jassa Singh Ahluwalia established his political control over many other territories without taking over the responsibility of administration. Ram Sukh Rao talks of Jassa Singh Ahluwalia's claim to *nazrāna* or contingents from several rulers. His statement that he obtained tribute from Qasur, Jhang, Pakpattan, Multan, Mankera, and Dera Ghazi Khan, or from Bikaner, Jammu, and the hill chiefs in general, does make a lot of sense in the context. The petty chiefs or *zamīndārs* of Jandiala and Jodhanagari in the Mājhā were retained as tributaries for a number of years. In the Jalandhar Doab, the non-Sikh chiefs of Kapurthala, Talwan, Nakodar, and Phagwara had been paying tribute to Jassa Singh before these areas were annexed. The old principalities of Jaswan and Kutlehr and the new principality of Jalandhar were tributary to him. In the Malwa region, the chiefs of Malerkotla, Raikot, and Mani Majra paid regular tribute to Jassa Singh. He is said to have collected *nazrāna* from the Sikh chiefs of Kot Kapura, Kaithal, Jind, Nabha, and Patiala. On one occasion he asked Raja Ala Singh to send contingents for a campaign. Soon afterwards, the rulers of Patiala, Nabha, and Jind submitted to Jassa Singh that they were not in a position to pay the enhanced *nazrāna*. In the context of this relationship we can understand the help given by Jassa Singh to the rulers of Patiala against their Sikh and non-Sikh opponents.

The army of Jassa Singh Ahluwalia is estimated at 3,000 to 15,000 men. The strength of this army did not remain static thoughout the period of his rule. Furthermore, there were three categories of men at his disposal: the Khās Fauj, the troopers recruited and maintained by his *jāgīrdārs*, and the contingents provided by his vassals. Jassa Singh himself was the commander-in-chief of the army. For the Khās Fauj, however, he appointed a Bakhshī whose duties were limited to the keeping of muster rolls and the disbursement of pay as ordered by the chief. The Khās

Fauj was divided into *derās* under *sardārs* or *sarkardas*; each *derā* was further divided into *misls* or *jamā'ats* under *misldārs* and *jamādārs.* These units were not of uniform strength, but consisted of men belonging to the same clan or social background. They were recruited mostly from amongst the Jatts. The troopers were paid in cash and kind after every six months, but they were allowed to keep the spoils except guns and arrows. The *jāgīrdārī* troopers used to go home after a campaign and returned only when called. They had to procure their own horses, weapons, dress, food, and tents. Besides the sword and the dagger, the spear and the bow, the troopers of Jassa Singh used matchlocks which could be fired from long and short range. They were excellent marksmen. Cavalry was almost the only arm of Jassa Singh's army, and hence the great importance of horses which he always tried to procure either as *nazrāna,* or as part payments of revenues, or through purchase. In all important campaigns he led the army personally and fought, if necessary, at close quarters (*kotah hathiār*).

In the civil administration of Jassa Singh Ahluwalia, the Diwān was assisted by the *dārogha* of the treasury (*toshakhāna*). The dominions of Jassa Singh being scattered and rather small were not divided into provinces. The largest unit of civil administration was called *ta'alluqa* or *pargana,* and its size varied. Every *ta'alluqa* had a Kārdār for the purpose of land revenue, but not necessarily a Kārdār exclusively for itself. In certain places a *thānadār* collected the revenue and performed some judicial duties like the Kārdār. But the two offices were distinct. The old agency of *chaudharīs* and *muqaddams,* and other intermediary *zamīndārs,* was employed by Jassa Singh in the revenue administration of his dominions. Whereas in the army of Jassa Singh the Singhs were predominant, in the civil administration we find a considerable proportion of Khatris and Brahmans, and Muslim Rajputs and Jatts. Among the intermediaries too, we find a large number of non-Singhs who enabled the Kārdārs to collect the revenue mostly in kind through *batāī* or *kankūt,* and in some places in cash.[8]

Jassa Singh Ahluwalia made extensive use of the well known system of *jāgīrdārī.* He continued to pay the servants of the state in terms of revenue from land rather than in cash. The area from which a servant of the state was authorized to collect the revenue was called his *jāgīr* and in that capacity he became a *jāgīrdār* or the holder of a *jāgīr*. The *jāgīr* given to an individual was large or small, depending upon the kind of service he performed or the position he held. Charhat Singh of Talwan, for instance, was given a *jāgīr* worth 50,000 rupees a year for maintaining 150 horsemen. Those who served the state were sometimes given *jāgīrs* for subsistence, which was virtually a kind of pension. Mansukh Rai, a Khatri of Jalalabad, got 15 *ghumāons* worth 12 rupees a year in subsistence *jāgīr*. It may be added that, since the amount of revenue alienated in favour of an individual was to correspond to his pay or pension, it was not possible for Jassa Singh to run the *jāgīrdārī* system without maintaining adequate records.

Revenue from land was alienated in favour of individuals and institutions for serving the society in one way or another. Such individuals belonged to several categories, but the largest share of this patronage went to persons and institutions connected with religion. Jassa Singh Ahluwalia confirmed the old grants enjoyed by Muslim and Hindu grantees in his dominions, and gave new ones of his own. However, most of the new grants were given to establishments connected with the Sikh Gurus and their descendants. Jassa Singh gave revenue-free land to many persons of several other categories. He gave such grants to *dhādīs*, for example, and to those who were successful in extending cultivation. Mali Singh of Sathiala got revenue-free land worth 150 rupees a year for extension of agriculture. Muhammad Azim and Imam Bakhsh, two Muslim Jatts of Jalalabad, got 100 rupees each. Sabit Shah got two *ghumāons* and three *marlas* of land in the pargana of Tarn Taran for the upkeep of his *khānqah*.[9]

This brief outline of Jassa Singh Ahluwalia's career and his position as a ruler leaves no doubt that, in terms of Sikh polity, if there was a difference between him and Ranjit Singh, it was a difference only of degree and not of kind. The monarchical form of government was well established in the territories conquered by the Singhs much before Ranjit Singh appeared on the political scene.

NOTES

1. Khushwant Singh, *A History of the Sikhs*, New Delhi: Oxford University Press, 1999 (rpt.) vol. I, p. 201.
2. Much of the information on Jassa Singh has come from Ram Sukh Rao, *Fateh Singh Pratāp Prabhākar*, ed. Joginder Kaur, Patiala: 1980, and Ganda Singh, *Sardar Jassa Singh Ahluwalia*, Patiala: Punjabi University, 1990 (rpt.).
3. Tahmas Khan, *Tahmas Namah* in *Sikh History from Persian Sources*, eds. J.S. Grewal and Irfan Habib, New Delhi: Tulika/Indian History Congress, 2001, p. 176.
4. Ganesh Das, *Chār Bāgh i Panjāb*, ed., Kirpal Singh, Amritsar: Khalsa College, 1965, pp. 130-1. In the inscription given by Ganesh Das the word *takht* is used instead of *mulk* as the first word in the second line.
5. Ratan Singh Bhangu, *Prachīn Panth Prakāsh*, ed. Bhai Vir Singh, New Delhi: Bhai Vir Singh Sadan, 1993 (rpt.), pp. 366-7.
6. Ganda Singh, *Sardār Jassa Singh Ahluwalia*, pp. 149, 152 (based on the *Jangnāma* of Qazi Nur Muhammad)
7. Ratan Singh Bhangu, *Prachīn Panth Prakāsh*, p. 291.
8. This exposition of the polity and administration of Jassa Singh Ahluwalia is based almost entirely on the work of Ram Sukh Rao.
9. Ram Sukh Rao's work, combined with Indu Banga, *Agrarian System of the Sikhs: The Late Eighteenth and Early Nineteenth Century*, Delhi: Manohar 1978, pp. 139 n 84, 150.

22

'Sarkār Khālsā': Singh Sāhib Ranjit Singh

Khushwant Singh has popularized the view that Ranjit Singh ruled in the name of the Khalsa, using the term 'Sarkār Khālsā' for his government; neither his name nor effigy appears on the coins current in his dominions.[1]

Banda Bahadur had used one inscription on coins and another on his seal, both inscriptions implying that the power and authority of the rulers was derived from God and the Gurus. These legends were used by the Sikhs who established their rule in the late eighteenth century. One kind of coin was minted at Lahore and the other at Amritsar. Both these coins were current in the dominions of the Sikh rulers, including the territories of Charhat Singh and Mahan Singh, the predecessors of Ranjit Singh. It was natural for Ranjit Singh to continue with a well established tradition. Furthermore, there was no need to issue a personal coin as a declaration of sovereignty, precisely because the coins current in the Sikh dominions ensured the theoretical sovereignty of each ruler.[2]

The term 'Sarkār Khālsā' has been interpreted as the 'government of the Khalsa' on the assumption that it could not and it did not refer to an individual ruler. By now we know, however, that the term Sarkār Khālsā, like 'Singh Sāhib', was used in the late eighteenth century for the individual Singh or Khalsa ruler.[3] In any case, it is not a single phrase here or there which is important for Sikh polity. It is the character of the government and administration which has to be examined for an appreciation of Ranjit Singh's polity. We propose to do this with reference to the decade after the Treaty of Amritsar signed by Ranjit Singh with the British in 1809, on the basis of evidence contained in the work of his court historian, the *Umdat ut-Tawārīkh* of Sohan Lal Suri.[4]

The process of conquest which Ranjit Singh had started in 1799 by occupying Lahore assumed momentum after 1809. Before the conquest of Multan and Kashmir ten years later, he annexed a large number of forts, towns and villages belonging to a large number of Sikh, Hindu, and Muslim chiefs. The Sikh territories annexed by him included Hariana, Jalalpur, Manawar, Islamgarh, Bajwat, Gujrat, Chunian, Dipalpur, Satghara, Jethpur, Haveli, Muhiyuddinpur, Jalandhar, Patti, Fatehgarh, Sujanpur, Hajipur, Mukerian, Rawalpindi, Sri Hargobindpur, and Miani. By the end of the decade, several families of Sikh chiefs were subverted, including the Bhangis of Gujrat, the Nakkais, Buddh Singh Faizullapuria, the Kanhiyas excepting Sada Kaur, the Baggas, the Thehpurias and the Ramgarhias. Indeed, the only Sikh chief besides Sada Kaur to survive was Fateh Singh Ahluwalia, and both of them were subordinate to Ranjit Singh.

The territories of Rajput chiefs annexed by Ranjit Singh included Kangra, Sayyidgarh, Kotla, Samba, Kathua, Guler, Nurpur, and Jaswan, all in the hills close to the plains. About half a dozen chiefs were subverted in this process, and the most powerful hill principalities of Kangra and Jammu lost some of their territory. The Muslim territories annexed by Ranjit Singh included Khushab, Kachh, Sahiwal, Kusk, Attock, Makhad, Jhang, Tulamba, and Kot Nau. A few Baloch and Sial chiefs were subverted and the rulers of Bahawalpur, Multan and Kabul lost some of their territories. Thus before the conquest of Multan, the lower hills and the upper and middle portions of all the five *doabs* fell under the effective control of Ranjit Singh.

In order to comprehend adequately the political process during this phase of Ranjit Singh's career, it is useful to make a distinction between administrative and political control. Ranjit Singh asserted his suzerainty over many a chief between 1809 and 1818 before his territory was taken over. The only difference between Fateh Singh Ahluwalia and Jodh Singh Ramgarhia or Sahib Singh Bhangi or Buddh Singh Faizullapuria or Kahn Singh

Nakkai or Jiwan Singh of Rawalpindi, was that his territory was left under his own administration whereas the territories of the others were eventually taken over. Similarly, the Rajput chiefs of Nurpur and Jaswan had ruled in subordination to Ranjit Singh for a number of years before their principalities were annexed. The Baloch chiefs of Khushab and Sahiwal too had ruled as vassals before the annexation of their territories.

For retaining the administration of his territories in his own hands the subordinate chief had to fulfil certain obligations. He had to pay regular tribute to the Maharaja. He had to serve the Maharaja with contingents at his own expense. Succession to the position of a subordinate chief was recognized by the Maharaja on payment of *nazrāna* by the successor. Disapproval implied the removal of a potential successor. The subordinate chief had no right to have political relations with a sovereign or subordinate power. A default on the part of a subordinate chief on any of these accounts could result in punishment in the form of a fine, enhancement of the *nazrāna*, confiscation of a part, or outright annexation of his territory.

The chiefs were obliged to take their subordination seriously. Delay in the payment of tribute invited a General of the Maharaja with forces adequate to deal with a chief. Raja Sansar Chand of Kangra, Raja Jit Singh of Jammu, and several other chiefs were found serving with their contingents in one campaign or another. When after the Kashmir campaign they returned to their territories without the permission of the Maharaja, they were fined. The Raja of Chamba was fined for entertaining Shah Shuja against the wishes of the Maharaja. The hill chiefs were not the only subordinate chiefs to serve the Maharaja. Fateh Singh Ahluwalia, Jodh Singh Ramgarhia, Jiwan Singh of Rawalpindi, Buddh Singh Faizullapuria and Kahn Singh Nakkai fought in the campaigns of the Maharaja with their own contingents at their own expense. The Muslim chiefs were no exception to this either.

Ranjit Singh was able to establish his political control over a large number of chiefs far beyond the area under his administrative control. The chiefs of Kulu, Chamba, Rajauri, and Punchh, among many others in the hills, were paying tribute to him and serving him with their contingents. This outer ring of vassal territories in the north virtually left only Kashmir out. However, even the Afghan governor of Kashmir was asked to pay tribute. The Nawabs of Mankera, Multan, and Bahawalpur were paying *nazrāna* to the Maharaja, extending his political influence far beyond the limits of his actual dominions. The case of Bahawalpur, like that of Bilaspur, was rather interesting. The Nawab was paying tribute to the Maharaja for his territories on the west of the Sutlej. The case of Multan was perhaps the most important. Its Nawab owed formal allegiance to the kings of Kabul at the beginning of the nineteenth century. Ranjit Singh invaded his territory even before the Treaty of Amritsar to extort *nazrāna.* He became more assertive and insistent after the Treaty. Before long the Nawab of Multan was obliged to shift his formal allegiance from Kabul to Lahore. He accepted to pay a fixed annual tribute to the Maharaja. The conquest of Multan was, therefore, a case of annexation of the territories of a subordinate.

Both for establishing his control over vassals and for new conquests Ranjit Singh made increasingly effective use of his new infantry and new artillery. Mian Ghausa, Misar Diwan Chand, Mazhar Ali, Sultan Mahmud, Ilahi Bakhsh, Shaikh Basawan, Dhaunkal Singh, and Mihan Singh figure prominently in the pages of Sohan Lal during this phase, and he does not fail to make specific mention of battalions and *topkhānas* dispatched for the reduction of forts or the collection of *nazrāna.* The forts of Sardar Buddh Singh Faizullapuria in Jalandhar and Patti, for instance, were reduced with the help of the *topkhāna* and infantry battalions. Sohan Lal's reference to the little known fort of Muhiyuddinpur near Qasur, and the time of its reduction and demolition, is very significant in this context. Ranjit Singh had thought of capturing this fort from Sardar Gurbakhsh Singh during his expedition to Ferozepur before the Treaty of Amritsar, but held back in face of the massive and high walls of the fort. At the death of Sardar Gurbakhsh Singh within three years of the Treaty, the Maharaja asked his son Duna Singh to hand over all his forts to the functionaries of Lahore. On his refusal, the Maharaja sent the *topkhāna,* and Duna Singh surrendered after the first bombardment. Infantry battalions and artillery were used to collect revenues from Nakka, to collect *nazrāna* from Fateh Khan of Sahiwal and the hill chiefs, and to defeat the forces of Wazir Fateh Khan in an open battle near Attock. Jamadar Mihan Singh was specially honoured for his part in this battle. It was due largely to the effective use of infantry and artillery that the distant vassal chiefs and the Nawab of Multan felt obliged to make more or less regular payment of the annual tribute, and of arrears from former years. It may indeed be suggested that the expansion of Ranjit Singh's infantry and artillery in the third decade was due to its known effect during the decade after the Treaty of Amritsar, and the successful campaigns of Multan, Kashmir, and Peshawar.

Another important aspect of Ranjit Singh's policy during this phase was the effective use he made of diplomacy. There are frequent references in the *Umdat ut-Tawārīkh* to exchange of emissaries (*vakīls*) between the Maharaja and the British, the rulers of Kabul, the Nawabs of Mankera, Multan, and Bahawalpur, and the chiefs of Haidarabad, Khairpur and Shikarpur, besides the Sikh chiefs of the Sutlej-Jamuna Divide and the vassal chiefs in the hills. Partly through this exchange, Ranjit Singh could form an independent assessment of the political situation from time to time, which enabled him to isolate the immediate object of his aggression. He appears to have been fully aware of the loosening control of the kings of Kabul over their governors and vassals, the conflicting interests of the rival claimants to the throne of Kabul, and the factional interests of Afghan *sardārs* based partly on clan considerations. He gave political asylum to Shah Zaman in Rawalpindi which was then held by Sardar Jiwan Singh Thehpuria as a vassal, assigned Bhera to the Shah later for subsistence besides a daily allowance of fifty rupees from the treasury of the *kārdār* of Pind Dadan Khan, and eventually lodged him and his family in the *havelī* of Dila Ram in Lahore.

Shah Shuja, who was more active and more promising from the viewpoint of the Maharaja, was shown greater consideration and given more importance. It was suggested to Shah Shuja that Multan could be conquered for him. This was a diplomatic gesture in self-interest. Tulamba was actually taken over from the Nawab of Multan and given to Shah Shuja for subsistence. Later on, when Shah Shuja decided to go to Kashmir, the Maharaja induced him to leave his family in Lahore. The Generals sent to Kashmir, in support of Wazir Fateh Khan against the Afghan governor of Kashmir who was supporting Shah Shuja, were instructed to get hold of the person of Shah Shuja at all costs. The Afghan governor of Attock was induced to hand over the fort against the interest and wishes of Wazir Fateh Khan. It was held by force, and the Wazir was told every time that if Multan was first conquered for Ranjit Singh, Attock could be returned to him. Apparently for the help given to Shah Shuja in a crisis, the *koh-i nūr* diamond was taken from him. The Afghans were losing ground not only on the field of battle but also in the field of diplomacy.

In his conflict with the Afghans during this phase Ranjit Singh knew that the sympathies of the British were with him rather than with the rulers of Kabul. But he was careful enough to cultivate the British diplomats and administrators concerned with the affairs of the Punjab. His invitation to Ochterlony for the wedding of Prince Kharak Singh, and then to Lahore, had a diplomatic dimension. Nevertheless, Ranjit Singh was not prepared to accept any help from the British in his conflict with the Afghans. According to Sohan Lal, Metcalfe offered the assistance of British battalions to Maharaja Ranjit Singh when Wazir Fateh Khan was threatening Attock. This offer was gracefully declined. The Maharaja was jealous of his sovereignty and the integrity of his dominions.

The political idiom of the times is rather interesting. No pretext was needed for the assertion of suzerainty over others because every one subscribed to the legitimacy of conquest by those who could conquer and rule. In the very first year after the Treaty of Amritsar, Ranjit Singh entered into a formal understanding with the Gurkhas that all the territories on the west of the river Sutlej belonged to him. But these territories were not in his actual possession. Soon afterwards he declared that all the hill chiefs were subject to his control. At the beginning of the phase, Raja Sansar Chand was treated as a sovereign ruler; before the end of the phase, he too was reduced to the status of a vassal. In the case of Bhimbar and Rajauri, during Wazir Fateh Khan's expedition to Kashmir in which he was supported by the troops of Lahore, Ranjit Singh did not object to the Wazir's statement that Bhimbar and Rajauri were dependencies of Kashmir. Afterwards, however, Ranjit Singh did not hesitate to bring them under his influence, and Sultan Khan of Bhimbar did not hesitate to submit that he would perform all his duties of *mālguzārī*, *zamīndārī*, and *ra'iyat-shu-'ārī* in accordance with the wishes of Ranjit Singh.

For annexing the territories of those who fell within the orbit of the political control of the Maharaja not only a pretext but also a justification was sought. Sardar Nidhan Singh Kanhiya, for instance, was removed on the plea of the negligence of administration due to drunkenness. Sardar Kahn Singh Nakkai's territories were given to Prince Kharak Singh on a request from him in the absence of the Sardar on a compaign to Multan. When his Diwan made a representation to the Maharaja, he was told that it was a matter which could be settled by the Prince and the Sardar because of their close relationship. The territory was taken over by Prince Kharak Singh, but when he decided to leave nothing in *jāgīr* to Sardar Kahn Singh he was rebuked and the fort and villages of Bharwal were given to Sardar Kahn Singh. Even in his case, however, Sohan Lal implies that he was removed because of mismanagement and his inability to deal with refractory *zamīndārs*. The moral principle is enunciated most clearly in the case of Fateh Khan of Sahiwal. He was asked to pay enhanced *nazrāna* and he started collecting additional revenues from the cultivators. The Maharaja announced that by shifting the burden to the subject people Ahmad Khan had lost the right to rule: the first principle of rulership was the protection and welfare of the subjects. All the 250 villages and ten strong forts of the Baloch chief were taken over by the Maharaja.

After the annexation of a territory, Ranjit Singh would appoint a trusted and experienced functionary to settle revenue affairs besides the general administration of the territory. Such a settlement was generally based on all the available records and information provided by its former administrators. The ousted chief was generally given a portion of his territory in *jāgīr* for subsistence. If he offered to serve the Maharaja as a *jāgīrdār*, larger territory was given to him. At the same time, *jāgīrs* were given to others, either to placate local interests or to create vested interests in the conquered territory. In the case of Gujrat the duty of settling the territory and its administration was entrusted to Faqir Azizuddin. His position is referred to as the *sūbadārī* of Gujrat. There is an indication here that the primary divisions of the dominions of Ranjit Singh were treated as provinces irrespective of their size. The most important functionary in the revenue administration was the *kārdār* who held a small territory under his charge, generally referred to as *pargana* or *ta'alluqa*. However, the term *ta'alluqa* was also used more literally for an area held by a minor chief. In the case of Jalandhar, Faqir Nuruddin succeeded in raising revenues from one to about three lakhs of rupees. But this was not because he enhanced the rate of assessment, or changed the methods of collection, but simply because he collected the revenue in kind and stored it well to sell when the prices were higher. Ranjit Singh appreciated the Faqir very much.

Ranjit Singh used to appoint *faujdārs* and *thānadārs* in his dominions to maintain peace and order, to support the officials in the collection of revenues, and to join a commander appointed to lead a campaign in that direction. However, one of the important duties of the *thānadār* appointed to a town or a city was to protect the inhabitants of the place against the troopers. On one occasion, when Ranjit Singh returned to Lahore at midnight, he ordered the *thānadārs* not to allow any trooper to enter the city. Even their officers had to spend the night outside the city wall. When the siege of the fort of Jalandhar was in progress while the city had fallen, Ranjit Singh appointed a *thānadār* for the city to ensure that no person in the city was molested or oppressed by the troopers, and that no trooper actually entered the city. Sohan Lal's use of the term *thānadār* for some of the vassal chiefs is justified only by the duties assigned to them at a particular time. At one place he refers to Sardar Buddh Singh Faizullapuria as the *thānadār* of Jalandhar, though we know for certain that he was a chief subordinate to the Maharaja. Similarly, Sardar Jiwan Singh Thehpuria, the chief of Rawalpindi, is mentioned at one place as the *thānadār* of Rawalpindi. We know from the pages of the *Umdat ut-Tawārīkh* itself that he was the successor of Milkha Singh who had adopted Rawalpindi as his headquarters as a chief of the first generation. In the second decade of the nineteenth century, Jiwan Singh was subordinate to Ranjit Singh. We find him serving with his contingents in Kashmir in the joint expedition with Wazir Fateh Khan. In fact, he died fighting in Kashmir. His sons were allowed to succeed to the 'old territory' on the condition of maintaining three hundred horsemen though they were eventually dislodged and Rawalpindi was annexed.

Sohan Lal refers to the replacement of one '*adālatī* by another, indicating that Ranjit Singh had started appointing special magistrates for the administration of justice, perhaps even before the Treaty of Amritsar. There are references in the *Umdat ut-Tawārīkh* to *zamīndārs*, *jāgīrdārs*, *ijāradārs*, and *dharmarth* grantees. Sohan Lal's use of the term *zamīndār* may appear to be ambiguous. Yet, quite significantly, he uses this term for vassal chiefs as well as intermediaries and owners of land.

We get a fair idea of the important persons in the dominions of Ranjit Singh during this phase: Diwan Bhawani Das, Faqir Azizuddin, Hukma Singh Chimni, Atar Singh Dhari, Fateh Singh Ahluwalia, Prince Kharak Singh, Sardar Desa Singh Majithia, Diwan Mohkam Chand, Sardar Dal Singh, Diwan Hukam Singh, Karm Singh Chahal, Misar Raja Ram, Dhanna Singh Malwai, Hafiz Ruhulla, Nihal Singh Atari, Hari Singh Nalwa, Akali Phula Singh, Ram Singh Balli, Khushal Singh, Diwan Devi Das, Lala Bhawani Das, Munshi Karam Chand, Ramanand Sarraf, Sardar Jiwan Singh, Mit Singh Padhania, Faqir Nuruddin, Bhayya Ram Singh, Diwan Ganga Ram, Jodh Singh Ramgarhia, Fateh Singh Chhachhi, Qutbuddin of Qasur, Sardar Hukam Singh Atari, Gurmukh Singh, Sardha Singh, Diwan Singh Doabia, Garbha Singh, Atar Singh Faizullapuria, Sarbuland Khan Waraich, Sham Singh, Daya Singh, Hira Singh, Sada Singh, Ram Dayal, Moti Ram, Diwan Chand, Mian Ghausa, Mazhar Ali, Sultan Mahmud, Mihar Singh, Illahi Bakhsh, Faqir Imamuddin, for instance. They all served the Maharaja directly in a civil or military capacity. Many of them became better known in the third and the fourth decades. The Faqir brothers, Diwan Bhawani Das, Khushal Singh, Sardar Dal Singh, Sardar Desa Singh Majithia, Diwan Mohkam Chand, Misar Diwan Chand and Fateh Singh Ahluwalia figure more prominently than the others in the pages of the *Umdat ut-Tawārīkh*. The broad composition of the ruling class can be seen as being formed during this phase. It is quite obvious that this class did not consist of Sikhs alone. Furthermore, the members of the ruling class exercised precisely that much power and authority as was entrusted to them by Ranjit Singh.

Evidently, Ranjit Singh was his own master in all political and diplomatic matters. There was no theoretical or practical constraint on him as a ruler. The courtiers were consulted on the clear understanding on both sides that their advice might not be accepted. All functionaries of the state exercised power and authority delegated to them by the ruler of the state. The 'Sarkār Khālsā' was no less and no more than the state of Singh Sāhib Ranjit Singh. Local and limited autonomies were allowed within a monarchical framework.

NOTES

1. Khushwant Singh, *A History of the Sikhs*, New Delhi: Oxford University Press, vol. I, p. 204.
2. Surinder Singh, *Sikh Coinage: Symbol of Sikh Sovereignty*, New Delhi: Manohar, 2004.
3. B.N. Goswamy and J.S. Grewal (eds.), *The Mughal and Sikh Rulers and the Vaishnavas of Pindori*, Simla: Indian Institute of Advanced Study, 1969, pp. 220, 224, 248, 252, 256.
4. Sohan Lal Suri, *Umdat ul-Tawārīkh*, tr. V.S. Suri, Amritsar: Guru Nanak Dev University, Dafter II, pp. 62-74.

23

From Ruler to Vassal: Fateh Singh Ahluwalia

The major historians of Ranjit Singh dwell on many facts having a bearing on the relationship between Ranjit Singh and Fateh Singh, the second successor of Jassa Singh Ahluwalia. These include the exchange of turbans and a treaty of friendship in 1802; the Treaty of Lahore signed jointly by Ranjit Singh and Fateh Singh with the English on 1 January 1806; the Treaty of Amritsar signed by only Ranjit Singh with the English in 1809; joint military campaigns of Ranjit Singh and Fateh Singh; participation of Fateh Singh in campaigns organized by Ranjit Singh; territory given to Fateh Singh by Ranjit Singh; territories taken over by Ranjit Singh; association of Fateh Singh with the administration of territories belonging to the kingdom of Lahore; Fateh Singh's flight across the Sutlej; and the treatment Ranjit Singh gave to Fateh Singh's son and successor.[1]

However, all these facts are not given by each and every historian, and each fact is not given equal importance by them all. None of them looks upon these facts in the context of suzerain-vassal relationship, but some do reveal an awareness that the relationship between Ranjit Singh and Fateh Singh changed with the passage of time. N.K. Sinha comments on Fateh Singh becoming a dependent ally after having been an equal; he also refers to his position of 'subordinate chief' without any 'formal acknowledgement'.[2] Bikrama Jit Hasrat states at one place that Ranjit Singh started treating Fateh Singh as a 'mere vassal'.[3]

The most comprehensive context for the relationship of Maharaja Ranjit Singh and Fateh Singh Ahluwalia is provided by

Indu Banga in her study of the agrarian system of the Sikhs.[4] She underlines the fact that much before Ranjit Singh and Fateh Singh became rulers, the Sikh chiefs were familiar with the political organization in which the suzerain exercised political control over the vassal without taking over the administration of his territory. Ranjit Singh subverted many hill principalities, but a large number were allowed to exist as vassals. The system was not confined to the hills but also reached the plains. It did not remain confined to non-Sikh (whether Hindu or Muslim) rulers but embraced the Sikh rulers as well.

Fateh Singh Ahluwalia is placed by Indu Banga in this comprehensive context. In 1802, he was a sovereign ruler and therefore, an equal of Ranjit Singh in political status. In 1806, however, Fateh Singh accepted the territory of Jagraon from Ranjit Singh and paid *nazrāna* like many of the chiefs of the Sutlej-Jamuna Divide. Henceforth we find Fateh Singh complying with the orders of the Maharaja, providing him contingents, and accepting *jāgīrs* from him. When his son, Nihal Singh, succeeded to the *gaddī*, he paid over 4 lakhs of rupees as *nazrāna* to Maharaja Ranjit Singh. Indeed, there is plenty of evidence in support of the conditions of vassalage enumerated by Indu Banga. The vassal paid tribute and supplied contingents and hostages to the suzerain, and the latter exercised control over the vassal in his relations with other powers and also over succession. Furthermore, he could assign revenues from the vassal territory to his own officials.

If we turn to the official chronicler of Ranjit Singh's reign, Sohan Lal Suri, we find him referring to the exchange of turbans between Fateh Singh Ahluwalia and Ranjit Singh in 1802 at Fatehabad as leading to a treaty between two equals. At this time they agreed formally to observe three conditions: each other's enemies and friends were to be regarded as enemies and friends by both; each was to assist the other with his army at his own expense; and, jointly conquered territories were to be shared, Fateh Singh getting a 'suitable *jāgīr* from every *ta'alluqa*'.[5] The anachronistic use of *jāgīr* in the last phrase should not mislead us to consider Fateh Singh in any way subordinate to Ranjit Singh. In 1802, Fateh Singh willingly entered into a treaty with Ranjit

Singh on a footing of equality, without in any way compromising his sovereign status.

By 1819, however, according to Sohan Lal, we find Sardar Fateh Singh Ahluwalia posted with his troops at Amritsar, and receiving an order from Maharaja Ranjit Singh to join Diwan Ram Dayal on a campaign.[6] In 1823, like Sardar Desa Singh and Mian Dhian Singh, he was asked to supply labour at his own expense for the wall of the city of Amritsar.[7] In 1828 Sardar Fateh Singh Ahluwalia was asked to present himself to the Maharaja, together with his son Nihal Singh, for service.[8] It is in this larger context that Sohan Lal Suri places the flight of Fateh Singh Ahluwalia across the Sutlej in 1826. When Fateh Singh fell a prey to delusions and went to Jagraon across the Sutlej, Sardar Buddh Singh and Khalifa Nuruddin were appointed to take over the administration of his territories.[9] Ranjit Singh conferred *rājgī* on Mian Dhian Singh, and appointed him and Prince Nau Nihal Singh to escort Fateh Singh to Amritsar. Fateh Singh was persuaded to return. He met the Maharaja at Amritsar in the garden of Sardar Jawala Singh Padhania on the 27th of Baisakh in 1827, handed over his sword and, with tears in his eyes, submitted that he had been misled by others to cross the river Sutlej, but was firm in his loyalty to the Maharaja.[10] His territories were restored to him on the condition that he paid 5,25,000 rupees to the Maharaja as *nazr.*[11]

Henceforth, Sardar Fateh Singh Ahluwalia was assigned many duties by the Maharaja which he performed with diligence, and complied with all kind of orders.[12] When he died in 1836, the Maharaja thought of getting 10 lakhs of rupees from his eldest son Nihal Singh as *wajah-i dastār* for recognizing his succession,[13] but he was actually asked to pay 5 lakhs as *nazrāna.*[14] Henceforth, he was treated as a vassal. Jāgīrs were assigned from his territory to officials serving Ranjit Singh.[15] He was himself posted at different places to maintain law and order.[16] He was ordered to give *jāgīrs* to his brother,[17] and was sent on a campaign to Peshawar.[18]

If from the official chronicler of Ranjit Singh we turn to the official chronicler of Fateh Singh Ahluwalia, we find first of all that they agree in their accounts of the treaty of 1802. Ram Sukh

Rao, as it may be expected, does not use the word *jāgīr* while referring to Fateh Singh's share in conquered territories. He uses the word '*ahdnāma* for the treaty and states that it was meant to be observed in perpetuity. Before long, however, according to Ram Sukh Rao, Ranjit Singh started deviating from the terms of this treaty: the officials appointed by Fateh Singh were encouraged to shift their allegiance to Ranjit Singh; defaulters from Kapurthala were given protection and some of Fateh Singh's possessions were taken over by Ranjit Singh's men. Jāgīrs from Ahluwalia territories were given to Ranjit Singh's officials and, on their death or removal, the territories were retained by the Lahore Darbar; the attitude of the Maharaja and his courtiers towards Fateh Singh underwent a radical change[19] and he was no longer treated as an equal, or as a sovereign ruler.

According to Ram Sukh Rao, Fateh Singh was misled by his own agents in Lahore to believe that Ranjit Singh meant to deprive him of all his territories and to ill-treat him. When some troops from Lahore were dispatched towards the Doaba, Fateh Singh decided to cross the Sutlej. According to his own instructions, his *thānadārs* did not offer any resistance to Sardar Buddh Singh Sandhanwala when he took over the Ahluwalia treasury and territories.[20] In 1827, Fateh Singh agreed, to send his representative, Saudagar Mal,[21] to the Maharaja. He was advised, however, to meet the Maharaja personally.[22] The Maharaja on his part gave assurances to Sher Ali as an agent of Fateh Singh that he would observe the old practices.[23] Eventually, the Maharaja had an '*ahdnāma dharm kā* prepared, impressed with the saffron mark of his palm and bearing his personal seal.[24] Kanwar Nau Nihal Singh, Raja Dhian Singh, Sardar Desa Singh, Shiv Dayal, who used to keep the Maharaja's seal, Jawahar Singh and the Sodhis of Anandpur – Uttam Singh, Ran Singh and Ranjit Singh – were sent to escort Fateh Singh to Amritsar. When Fateh Singh met the Maharaja at Amritsar, the old style of *tajīm* (*ta'zīm*) and *tawājiā* (*tawāzu*) was maintained.[25] In other words, Fateh Singh acknowledged his subordination to the Maharaja and the Maharaja was gracious towards him. Ram Sukh Rao is clearer even than Sohan Lal Suri on the point that the sovereign status of Fateh Singh had been undermined long before his flight across the river Sutlej, and Fateh Singh was reconciled to this.

Fortunately, the '*ahdnāma dharm kā*, which Maharaja Ranjit Singh had sent to Fateh Singh in 1827, can be seen in the Public Library at Patiala. This document bears the seal of Ranjit Singh with the usual phrase 'Akal Sahai'. It bears also the palm impression of Ranjit Singh, indicating the solemnity of its contents and the esteem in which the addressee was supposed to be held by him. The term used for the document in the text is *dharmpatrā*, and Ranjit Singh binds himself to his promise with an oath on the Harmandir Sahib, Guru Har Rai, Guru Granth Sahib and Jwala Ji. It was issued on the 5th of Baisakh in Sammat 1884 (AD 1827) from Ram Bagh in Amritsar.

According to this document, Fateh Singh Ahluwalia had, through his intermediaries, expressed the desire to present himself before Maharaja Ranjit Singh. In response, the latter sent Sodhis Uttam Singh, Ran Singh, and Jit Singh of Anandpur, Prince Nau Nihal Singh and Raja Dhian Singh to escort Fateh Singh and his family to Amritsar, with the solemn promise that his honour, life, property, and status would remain safe on the condition of loyalty, submission, and service. It is explicitly stated in the text that Fateh Singh Ahluwalia would do nothing without Ranjit Singh's approval. In other words, Fateh Singh Ahluwalia was clearly told to regard Ranjit Singh as his overlord, or suzerain. This position had been accepted in practice by Fateh Singh even before his flight across the Sutlej. When he recrossed the river Sutlej to meet Ranjit Singh at Amritsar, he had finally and deliberately passed from any pretence to sovereignty into the subordination of a vassal. The issue was settled once and for all for him and his successors. In the Treaty of Lahore, signed by Ranjit Singh and Fateh Singh with the British, Fateh Singh was 'Raja'. But in the *dharmpatrā* of 1827 he is referred to as 'Sardar'.[26]

NOTES

1. G.L. Chopra, *The Panjab as a Sovereign State*, Hoshiarpur: Vishveshvaranand Vedic Research Institute, 1960 (2nd edn.). N.K. Sinha, *Ranjit Singh*, Calcutta: 1980. Khushwant Singh, *A History of the Sikhs*, Princeton: Princeton University Press, 1963. Bikrama Jit Hasrat, *Life and Times of Ranjit Singh*, Hoshiarpur: V.V. Research Institute Book Agency, 1977.
2. N.K. Sinha, *Ranjit Singh*, pp. 17, 23.

3. Bikram Jit Hasrat, *Life and Times of Ranjit Singh*, pp. 336-7.
4. Indu Banga, *Agrarian System of the Sikhs: Late Eighteenth and Early Nineteenth Century*, New Delhi: Manohar, 1978, pp. 39-62.
5. Sohan Lal Suri, *Umdat ul-Tawārīkh*, Lahore: New Imperial Press, 1888-89, Daftar II, pp. 50-1.
6. Ibid., p. 269.
7. Ibid., p. 306.
8. Ibid., p. 362.
9. Ibid., pp. 329, 331-40.
10. Ibid., p. 343.
11. Ibid., p. 354.
12. We find Fateh Singh in Darband, and subsequently presenting himself to Ranjit Singh to report on the campaign. Ibid., pp. 272, 275, 283. He rendered services to the Maharaja against Sada Kaur: ibid., II, p. 292; he agreed to send his son Nihal Singh to the Maharaja at Amritsar: ibid., II, pp. 330, 352; Fateh Singh's *havelī* and garden were used by Ranjit Singh to entertain state guests: ibid., pp. 337-8; he was posted at Amritsar and participated in a campaign in the Peshawar region: ibid., pp. 373, 407.
13. Ibid., Dafter III, Part III, p. 342.
14. Ibid., pp. 343, 345-6.
15. Ibid., p. 347.
16. Ibid., Daftar III, Part IV, p. 396.
17. Ibid., pp. 420, 421, 423, 424, 431.
18. Ibid., p. 447.
19. Ram Sukh Rao, *Jassa Singh Binod*, M/772, Punjab State Archives, Patiala, ff. 89 a-b.
20. Ibid., ff. 323 b-326a.
21. Ibid., f. 333 b.
22. Ibid., f. 335a.
23. Ibid., f. 337 b.
24. Ibid., ff. 337 b, 338 a.
25. Ibid., ff. 339-40 a.
26. For a photographic copy and transcription of the *dharampatrā*, see J.S. Grewal, *From Guru Nanak to* Maharaja *Ranjit Singh*, Amritsar: Guru Nanak Dev University, 1982 (2nd edn.), pp. 166-7.

24

Creation of New Rajas: Jamwals

About a dozen documents of the Chattar Singh Collection in the Punjab State Archives at Patiala relate to the kingdom of Lahore under Ranjit Singh and his successors. One of these contains a long list of the civil and military functionaries of the state of Lahore in 1833 when Hira Singh was formally given the title of *farzand-i khās.* Another document issued four days later contains the details of Hira Singh's *jāgīrs.* Another document refers to the *jāgīrs* of Gulab Singh, Dhian Singh, and Suchet Singh. In 1837, Hira Singh was made the Raja of Jasrota and Basohli, and he was given a seat in the Darbar as well as the insignia of the fly-whisk (*chaurī*). Yet another document relates to the confirmation of Dhian Singh as the *wazīr* under Kharak Singh, with the titles of Mukhtār-i Kul and Nā'ib al-Saltnat. As directed in another document, all petitions to the Maharaja were to be submitted through the *wazīr.* All these documents have a bearing on the structure of power in the kingdom of Lahore.

We propose to give English translations of three documents in the 'Chattar Singh Collection' because of their obvious relevance for the polity of Ranjit Singh. The first of these is a copy of the royal order of 1820 by which a large *jāgīr* was conferred on Mian Kishora Singh and his three sons on some general and specific conditions. Much more significant are the other two documents. One of these is a copy of the royal order of 1822, by which Gulab Singh, Dhian Singh, and Suchet Singh, the sons of Mian Kishora Singh, are created Rajas on certain conditions. The third document is a copy of the royal order by which Dhian Singh was made Rājā-i Rājgān in 1827.

These three documents are so clear in their import and significance that only a few comments are needed for further elucidation. The first mentions the areas which were to form the *jāgīr* of Mian Kishora Singh and his sons: the Chakla of Jammu, Bhoti, Bandraltha, Chenini and Kishtwar. The postscript to this document suggests that some of these areas were yet to be occupied by the newly created *jāgīrdārs.* They were to maintain 400 horsemen to be placed at the disposal of Ranjit Singh at all time. They were to present horses, falcons, slave girls and saffron annually to Ranjit Singh. They were to protect the caravan route to Kashmir and to extirpate Mian Dido. Some of the minor chiefs in the area covered by the *jāgīr* were to be made subordinate to the grantees. On the other hand, two fortresses in these hilly areas were to serve as garrisons for the troops of the government of Lahore. The formality with which this grant is conferred upon the grantees and accepted by them is worth underlining; the methodical detail of its provisions suggests that it was a well calculated measure of Ranjit Singh.

The second document is equally formal and more important from our present viewpoint. The Jamwal brothers accept the conferment of *rāj-tilak* on clearly prescribed conditions. They take the oath to remain faithful to the suzerain, to serve him with their contingents, to regard their position as entirely dependent upon the suzerain, to accept the duties assigned even under some other Raja or Sardar, and to serve in distant campaigns. The suzerain takes the further precaution of keeping Dhian Singh's family as virtual hostages in Lahore. It is worth noting that *rājgī* appears to be conferred upon the three brothers jointly. We are not sure if this was the actual position. If so, the document is extremely valuable in so far as it refutes the generally held notion that at first Gulab Singh alone was created *raja.* But even in the body of this document, and in the seal impressios it bears, Gulab Singh alone is called 'Raja'; Dhian Singh and Suchet Singh are called 'Miān'.

Titles and territories, incentives to faithful service and cooperation, earned for Dhian Singh the further distinction of becoming Rājā-i Rājgān under his suzerain. This would make Dhian Singh in fact the premier vassal of Ranjit Singh. By 1827, thus, Ranjit Singh succeeded in creating not only new vassals but also a hierarchy of vassals.

The historians of Ranjit Singh refer to him as 'Maharaja', the supply of contingents by the vassal chiefs, or to the conferment of *rājgī* by him, but such references are rather casual. This aspect of Ranjit Singh's polity has not received serious attention. His concept of suzerainty, with all its practical implications, must be seen not merely as an expression of his imperial pretensions but also as the acceptance of an old institution. In establishing his suzerainty over a considerable number of vassals he was adopting the position of the Mughal emperors before him. Some of the old chiefs were wiped out, but many more were retained as vassals. The position of the Jamwal brothers was a little peculiar. They belonged to an ancient royal family but, at the same time, were not the direct heirs to the *gaddī* of Jammu. They were aware of the strength of the tradition and as the new chiefs of Jammu were anxious to get the formal declaration from Jit Singh, the successor of Ranjit Dev in Jammu, that he had renounced all claims and rights to the territory of Jammu and its dependencies in favour of the new vassals of Ranjit Singh.

Whatever the category of a vassal, his acceptance of the suzerainty of Ranjit Singh meant that he was not free to pursue an independent policy in relation to other states without the approval of the suzerain. Though a very large measure of autonomy was given to the vassal in the internal administration of his territory, the suzerain in theory possessed the right of intervention. Even when *rājgī* was granted in perpetuity, a new succession was to be formally ratified by the suzerain. The vassal supplied token tribute and contingents to the suzerain. On the whole, Ranjit Singh's position as a suzerain was very close to that of the Mughal emperors.

DOCUMENT 1

We, Mian Kishora Singh, Mian Gulab Singh, Mian Dhian Singh and Mian Suchet Singh, the devoted slaves of the bountiful Sarkār, do solemnly declare that:

At this auspicious time the *ta'alluqa* of the Chakla of Jammu with the exception of the country in the south of Kashmir, (along with) Patti-Bhoti, Bandraltha, Chenini, and Kishtwar has been conferred upon us by way of *jāgīr* by the Source of Honours as a royal favour to exalt (His Majesty's) humble slaves, on the condition that we maintain in readiness for service four hundred well-equipped and valiant horsemen at all times in strict accordance with His Majesty's wishes and in accordance with the following detail:

(a) The *jāgīrdārs* of the Chakla of Jammu: 100 horsemen
(b) Others, on behalf of the aforementioned *jāgīrdārs* of the Chakla of Jammu: 300 horsemen
(c) The Prince of the Lofty Fortune: 200 horsemen
(d) Those of His Majesty's choice: 100 horsemen

(We) the devoted servants, who are exceedingly grateful and wholly satisfied, accept most willingly the *jāgīr* which has been bestowed upon us and undertake to maintain the above mentioned 400 horsemen always in readiness for the service of the exalted Sarkar and in accordance with His Majesty's orders. (This force) in prompt readiness is at the disposal of His Majesty's orders according to the regulations governing the powerful armies of the honourable *sardārs*, like the *ujjal-dīdār, nirmal buddh, muqarrab-i bārgāh* Jamadar Khushal Singh Ji, Sardar Jawala Singh Jio and Sham Singh Atariwala. We shall always remain intent upon service in accordance with the descriptive rolls of the Exalted Daftar. We shall not in the least neglect (our duties) in wishing well (of the Sarkār), in fidelity, sacrifice, devotion and servitude. In all humility, we shall deem it our good fortune to obey the commands of the Noble Sarkār. We undertake to protect the road to Kashmir which is used by the caravans of the *pashmīnah* traders and others, and also by travellers and wayfarers. If, in spite of these precautions, any one suffers a loss it will be our responsibility to compensate. We shall either capture the contumacious Dido to be brought to (His Majesty) or to kill him or force him to cross the river Sutlej.[1]

(Furthermore) we shall continue to present year after year to His Majesty seven *bāzes* and five *chitrahs* and other articles and horses of good quality (as detailed below):

(a) Bāz: 7 *dastah*
(b) Chitrah: 25 *dastah*
(c) Mian Gulab Singh: 2 (*dastah baz*)
(d) Bandraltha: 1 (*dastah baz*)
(e) Dayal Chand: 1 (*dastah baz*)[2]
(f) Bhoti: 1 (*dastah baz*)
(g) Kishtwar: 2 (*dastah baz*)
(h) Jāgīrdārs of the Chakla of Jammu : 5 (*dastah baz*)
(i) Mian Gulab Singh: a caparisoned horse with golden saddle on the day of the Dusehra, besides the horse of Mian Dhian Singh
(j) Saffron from Kishtwar: pucca maund
(k) Beautiful and accomplished slave girls
(l) In the fortresses of Sumergarh[3] and Kotli[4] to be the *thānas* of the Sarkār

Inscribed on the 15th of Maghar, Sammat 1877.

(Postscipt) On account of this, these few words have been written and handed over by way of acceptance (*qabūlīat*)[5] so that they serve as a *sanad* in the future. Whenever there is any increase in territory through the grace of Satguru Ji, it will be reported to His Majesty.

Inscribed on the 5th of Poh, Sammat 1877.

DOCUMENT 2

We, Raja Gulab Singh, Mian Dhian Singh and Mian Suchet Singh, all the three Jamwal brothers, who are the slaves of the Noble Sarkar, do hereby declare that:

His Majesty had, through the grace of Sri Wāhegurū Jī and out of his generosity and kind munificence, raised these persons of no consequence to a position of honour and nearness (to the Court) by granting to these humble slaves the country of Jammu and other territories on the condition of maintaining (a number of) horsemen. And now His Majesty, adding to his gracious favours of the past and out of his excessive kindness, has bestowed the *rāj-tilak* of the country of Jammu upon these slaves and exalted them to a position of pre-eminence. After expressing our deep gratitude for this great favour we hereby submit our agreement on solemn oaths and in accordance with the conditions fixed (for the purpose) as detailed below:[6]

1. We take oath on Sri Satguru Ji, Sri Maharaj, Sri Devi Ji, and Sri Ram Ji that we shall serve the Noble Sarkar, generation after generation, with submission, obedience, fidelity, sincerity, devotion and selflessness, wishing well of the Sarkār and dedicating ourselves wholly to the service of His Majesty. We shall never turn or deviate from the conditions of this agreement.
2. We shall always keep in readiness well-equipped and valiant horsemen, maintained in strict accordance with His Majesty's wishes in connection with the grant of *rāj* of the countries of Jammu, Kishtwar, Bandraltha and others, to serve His Majesty in all circumstances and wherever His Majesty may command.
3. We shall regard our life, property and territory as due to the Noble Sarkar and we shall never be oblivious of the great favours of His Majesty.
4. The family and the retainers of Mian Dhian Singh, along with his son Hira Singh, shall reside permanently in the capital of Lahore.
5. If and when His Majesty commands these slaves to honour any of the Rajas or any Hindu or Muslim Sardar by working in subordinate association with him, we shall deem it our good fortune to obey the orders of His Majesty and we shall strive to the utmost to perform our duties in accordance with His Majesty's commands.
6. Called upon to perform service in Kashmir[7] or in any other near or distant country according to the orders of His Majesty, we shall zealously render service wherever it is required and we shall always strive in every way to meet the wishes of His Majesty without the slightest hesitation, thereby justifying the favours received from him.
7. Of our own accord we have submitted to His Majesty this written agreement on the solemn oaths recalled above and bearing the saffron marks of our palms, to serve as a *sanad*, generation after generation.

Inscribed on the 3rd of the auspicious Hāṛ, Sammat 1879, at Akhnur[8] on Friday at midday.

(Seals – with *sahī* on margins)
May Sri Ram Ji be the Protector: Mian Dhian Singh
Raja Gulab Singh
Mian Suchet Singh
(Seal)
May God be the Protector: Ranjit Singh
(in the margin)
Has been examined: *sahī*

DOCUMENT 3

At this auspicious time, through the grace of Sri Akal Purkh Ji, His Bountiful Majesty has in kindness and appreciation (of merit) conferred the favour of the title of Rājā-i Rājgān Rājā-i Kalān Bahādur[9] upon the *ujjal-dīdār, nirmal buddh, muqarrab-i khās al-khās*, Rājā-i Rājgān Rājā Dhian Singh Bahādur Jamwal, in recognition of his commendable services and selfless exertions. Along with the favour of this auspicious and august title, the chieftaincy (*rāj-o riyāsat*) of the country of Bhimbar and Chhibal is granted in perpetuity to the aforementioned *muqarrab-i khās al-khās* by the Magnanimous Sarkār. As the recipient of these favours through the grace of Sri Satguru Ji let him ever remain intent upon serving with devotion and fidelity, rendering all appropriate service with promptitude and wishing well of His Exalted Majesty. The *sanad* of the grant of *rāj* and the title is being bestowed (upon him).

Inscribed on the 7th of the auspicious Hāṛ, Sammat 1884, at Ram Bagh.[10]

NOTES

1. Mian Dido belonged to a branch of the ruling family of Jammu. The local tradition presents him as a brave and fearless fighter and an irrconcilable opponent of Ranjit Singh's sway in the hills. The present document substantiates the local tradition insofar as Ranjit Singh is obliged to take special notice of Mian Dido's activities; they must have created a serious problem for Ranjit Singh. For more detail, K.M.

Pannikar, *Gulab Singh,* London: 1930, p. 27; J. Hutchison, and J. Ph. Vogel, *History of the Punjab Hill States,* Lahore: 1933, vol. II, pp. 549-50; Narsingh Das Nargis, *Gulab Singh,* Jammu: 1961, pp. 88-112.

2. Dayal Chand was the Raja of Chenini. In spite of his assistance to Gulab Singh during the attack on Kishtwar, his territory was later partitioned by Jamwal brothers and only a fourth was left to him. Hutchison and Vogel, *History of the Punjab Hill States,* vol. II, p. 583.
3. Sumergarh could be the fort of Samarth in the territory of Bhadu to the east of Jammu. For some detail, Narsingh Das Nargis, *Gulab Singh,* pp. 135, 147; K.M. Pannikar *Gulab Singh,* p. 37.
4. The fort of Kotli was strategically situated on the road to Kashmir. It was a possession of Raja Sultan Khan of Bhimbar who had spiritedly resisted Ranjit Singh's armies during the first invasion of Kashmir. Hutchison and Vogel, *History of the Hill States,* vol. II, pp. 727-8. Chattar Singh Collection, Punjab State Archives, Patiala, Documents M/529 and M/532.
5. Formal 'acceptance' (*qabūlīat*) is suggestive of a certain degree of formality involved in the agreement. Probably such acceptance was taken before the grant was made. For instance the *sanad* of acceptance of the *gaddīs* of Jammu and Bandraltha by Gulab Singh and Suchet Singh respectively was inscribed on the 3rd and the ceremony of *rāj-tilak* took place on the 4th of Hāṛ, Sammat 1879. K.M. Pannikar, *Gulab Singh,* pp. 32-4.
6. The use of the term *dafa'āt-i muqarrarah* clearly implies that these provisions were generally included in the documents drawn up for a formal acceptance of vassalage.
7. Kashmir had been conquered in 1819, and Ranjit Singh had yet to consolidate the conquered territory. He could call upon the Jamwal Rajas, therefore, to serve in Kashmir if necessary.
8. The choice of Akhnur may not be incidental. Gulab Singh had strong support in that area, and probably Jit Singh, the direct descendant of Ranjit Dev, was still present in Jammu.
9. The full title granted to Dhian Singh, as given here is *rājā-i rājgān, rājā-i kalān.* He was frequently referred to only by one or the other part of this title. Cf. G.L. Chopra *The Panjab as a Sovereign State,* Hoshiarpur: Vishveshvaranand Vedic Research Institute, 1960, (2nd edn.), 96n.
10. The date given here would show that the title was formally given to Raja Dhian Singh not before he was sent to bring back Fateh Singh Ahluwalia but after he had brought him from the other side of the Sutlej in 1827.

25

The Sikh State

Generally the Sikh state is equated with the state created by Ranjit Singh in the early decades of the nineteenth century. We must, however, take into account at least two other historical situations: the decade after Guru Gobind Singh's death in 1708, when a sovereign state under the leadership of Banda Bahadur was established (or claimed to have been established), and the late eighteenth century, when a large number of Sikh leaders re-established Sikh rule in the former Mughal province of Lahore and the Sutlej-Jamuna Divide.

It is relevant first of all to note that contemporary writers, both Sikh and non-Sikh, underscore the political aspect of Guru Gobind Singh's life. Muhammad Qasim, for example, refers to his magnificence in terms of his material and martial resources: 'he was not behind the nobles of 5,000 (*zāt*) or even rulers of principalities in anything concerned with greatness of splendour or accumulation of resources'.[1] Ratan Singh Bhangu projects the idea that Guru Gobind Singh's purpose in instituting the Khalsa was to make them the rulers of the land.

Significantly, Sikh rule was established by the Khalsa within two years of Guru Gobind Singh's death. A report from Bahadur Shah's court refers to their battle with the *faujdār* of Sirhind on 24 May 1710, after which the 'Sikhs of the Khalsa' established their control and government from the river Sutlej upto Karnal. A Jatt named Baz Singh from the *pargana* of Patti Haibatpur in the province of Lahore assumed the *sūbadārī* of Sirhind and appointed officers over the *parganas*.[2] Banda Bahadur established himself in the fort of Mukhlispur (renamed Lohgarh) near Sadhaura.[3]

As a Persian proverb has it, coins are struck in the name of those who strike the sword with effect. A Persian writer refers to a coin struck by the Khalsa, which carried the implication that the Khalsa claimed to have established a sovereign state. These coins have been discovered and examined. They refer to the second and the third year of Sikh rule, carrying the implication that the first coin was struck presumably after the conquest of Sirhind in 1710. The Persian inscription on the coin refers to the 'sword of Nanak' as the bestower of power. Guru Nanak is thus believed to be the source of all power. The victory of Gobind, the king of kings, is a mark of the grace of the True Master. No earthly superior or source of authority is acknowledged. The coin clearly symbolizes the declaration of sovereign rule. Reference to the Khalsa on the reverse indicates that the political success of the Khalsa was seen as the victory of Guru Gobind Singh.[4] The inscription on the seal of 1710 also refers to Guru Nanak as the bestower of power.

The idea that the Khalsa were meant to rule is attributed to Guru Gobind Singh. It finds expression in the *Gursobhā* in 1711. In a manuscript of 1718-19, the phrase *rāj karegā khālsā* is used.[5] It became a part of the Sikh anthem recited after the formal Sikh prayer (*ardās*). For half a century after Banda's execution in 1716, the Khalsa waged a relentless struggle for freedom. Confident of their success against Ahmad Shah Abdali, they struck a coin at Lahore in 1765. It bore the inscription that had been used on the seal in the time of Banda Bahadur. Another coin was struck at Amritsar in 1775, bearing the legend that had been used in the third year of Sikh rule in the time of Banda Bahadur. This coin refers to 'the eternal throne' (*takht akāl bakht*).[6] Both legends remained in use throughout the late eighteenth century when a number of mints were established at places other than Lahore and Amritsar.

Sikh coins were meant to replace the coinage made current by Ahmad Shah Abdali to symbolize the establishment of his rule in the former Mughal territories. The Ahmad Shahi coin had become current in the former Mughal provinces of Kabul, Kashmir, Lahore, and Multan, and the Sarkar of Sirhind. Deriving his authority from God, Ahmad Shah Abdali was laying claim to sovereignty.

It is asserted sometimes that the Sikh coins embody the concept of collective sovereignty of the Khalsa Panth.[7] The doctrines of Guru Panth and Guru Granth, the *gurmatās* (resolutions of the Guru) adopted at the Akal Takht in Ramdaspur (Amritsar), and the collective action of the Sikh army (*dal khālsā*) on the basis of *gurmatās* can be seen as reinforcing the idea of collective sovereignty. It has been pointed out, however, that these doctrines and institutions, like the institutions of *rākhī* and *misl*, were effectively operative during the period of struggle for the acquisition of power and not for the exercise of power. There was an essential difference between the phase of struggle for territorial occupation and the phase of actual rule after territorial occupation. It has been aptly stated that 'the derivation of sovereignty from the Gurus and God enabled each individual to assert his independence of any temporal lord.' For all practical purposes, 'the individual chief became a sovereign ruler not in spite of the coin but because of it'.[8]

The orders issued by the Sikh rulers in the late eighteenth century clarify the issue. We may take the example of Jai Singh Kanhiya who was an eminent Sikh ruler of this period. The inscription on his seal carries the name Jai Singh without any title. The only other words on the seal are *akāl sahāi* (may God protect, or under God's protection). God alone is the protector of Jai Singh who is wielding power in his own name. His rule is referred to as the 'rule of Khālsā Jio'.[9] His rule is also referred to as 'the exalted government' (*sarkār-i mu'allā*).[10] He is posthumously referred to as 'Singh Sāhib, the late Sardar Jai Singh'.[11] Among the Sikh rulers of the late eighteenth century, dynastic succession was the rule that enabled even a widow to wield power on behalf of her deceased husband. Sons succeeded to the founding fathers as a matter of routine.

The orders we have referred to relate to *dharmarth* grants. It is evident that every Sikh ruler could alienate revenue from land in favour of religious institutions and personages without any reference to others. The ruler confirmed old grants and gave fresh grants in accordance with his own inclinations and interests. Revenue from land was alienated also in favour of those who served the Sikh ruler. There is hardly any doubt that he appointed his own *diwāns*, *kārdārs* and *qānūngos* from the very beginning of territorial occupation. The Sikh rulers used their discretion in giving subsistence or *in'ām jāgīrs* as well. That the Sikh ruler of the late eighteenth century was independent in his political relations with others is evident from the suzerain-vassal relationship. There are numerous examples of Sikh rulers collecting tribute from non-Sikh chiefs of the hills and the plains. Among them were founders of states such as Charhat Singh Sukarchakia, Hari Singh Bhangi, Jassa Singh Ramgarhia, Jai Singh Kanhiya, and Gujjar Singh. Thus, the suzerain-vassal relationship remained an essential feature of polity in the Punjab during the late eighteenth century. We can see that every Sikh ruler was autonomous in his political relations with others as much as in his internal administration.[12]

The most that can be said about the Sikh rulers of the late eighteenth century is that they professed to rule on behalf of the Khalsa or as Khalsa. They paid homage to the Gurus not only on their coins but also through the construction of Gurdwaras at places associated with the Gurus. They assigned revenue-free lands to Granthīs, Rāgīs, Rabābīs and Ardāsiās as well as to Gurdwaras. There was hardly a Sikh ruler who did not send regular or occasional offerings for the Harmandir at Ramdaspur (Amritsar) which became a common concern of the Sikh rulers and the foremost place of pilgrimage for Sikhs in general.

The Sikh rulers gave revenue-free lands to the descendants of the Gurus, notably the descendants of Guru Nanak who were known as Bedis, and the descendants of Guru Ram Das who were known as Sodhis. Next to them were the Udasis who claimed to be closely associated with Guru Nanak through his elder son, Sri Chand (whom they regarded as the head of their orders). However, grants were not confined to Sikh, or professedly Sikh, institutions and individuals. Shaiva, Vaishnava, and Shakta temples and their custodians were patronized as well as learned Brahmans and priests. Similarly, *shaikhs* and *saiyids*, *dargāhs* and *masjids* continued to hold old grants and received some fresh ones. It is difficult to quantify the grants given by the late eighteenth-century Sikh rulers to various categories of grantees. The general impression we get is that Sikh institutions and individuals received the largest share of fresh grants, while the largest number of grants to be confirmed were obviously those of Muslim individuals and institutions.[13]

Presumably, the Sikh rulers had begun to associate Hindus and Muslims with the administration of their territories. The *diwāns* employed by Charhat Singh Sukarchakia, Gujjar Singh Bhangi, and Milkha Singh of Rawalpindi, for example, were non-Singhs, Khatris like Shiv Dayal, Gullu Mal, and Sulakhan Mal. There were *qāzīs* in Wazirabad, Gujrat, Gujjranwala and Batala. Qazi Abdul Rahman was holding a service *jāgīr* in Ram Nagar in the late eighteenth century. Ismatullah was the *qānūngo* of Gujrat under Gujjar Singh. Khudadad Khan was given a few villages in *jāgīr* by Mahan Singh for maintaining 20 horsemen for service, and Mian Khan received a *jāgīr* worth 15,000 rupees a year from Sada Kaur. Muslim and Hindu *chaudharīs* and *muqaddams* remained associated with the collection of revenues under the Sikh rulers.[14] These known examples make it clear that Hindu and Muslim individuals performed various services for the Sikh rulers of the late eighteenth century and were, like the Sikh functionaries, paid by the state. They performed military as well as civil services.

Turning to the Sutlej-Jamuna Divide we find that there were two categories of Sikh rulers: those who originally belonged to the province of Lahore and those who belonged to the province of Delhi. The rulers of Patiala, Nabha, Jind, Kaithal, and Faridkot belonged to the latter category. It is interesting to find that the last two are not associated with any *misl* in regional historiography. The founders of Patiala, Nabha, and Jind are said to have formed the Phulkian *misl.* We know, however, that each one of them started his career as a *zamīndār* of the Mughal empire and made use of its framework to rise into power. When Ahmad Shah Abdali was ascendant in the 1760s, Ala Singh, the founder of Patiala, accepted the title of Raja from him and paid tribute to him. He acknowledged the suzerainty of Ahmad Shah Abdali by striking a coin also in his name. His successor, Amar Singh, received the title of Rājā-i Rājgān from Ahmad Shah Abdali to distinguish him from the other Rajas of the Divide who had accepted Afghan suzerainty. The Ahmad Shahi coin remained current in the territories of Jind as well as Patiala. Only the rulers of Nabha struck a coin with the inscription used on the coin of Lahore in 1765. Thus, whereas the founders of Patiala and Jind accepted the status of vassals, the founder of Nabha claimed a sovereign status, though his father too had started his career as a *zamīndār* under the Mughals.[15]

There was no important differences in the government and administration of Nabha and the government and administration of Patiala and Jind. Political power was vested in an individual who used the services of other individuals at subordinate levels. There was no need to make any change in the administrative framework. Hindu and Muslim individuals were associated with government and administration from the very beginning. On the whole, thus, there was no appreciable difference in the government and administration of the Sikh rulers of the late eighteenth century on the two sides of the river Sutlej.

Ranjit Singh was born in 1780. His father Mahan Singh was a Sikh ruler of the second generation. When Mahan Singh died in 1791, Ranjit Singh was recognized as his successor as a matter of course. In the face of Afghan aggression, Ranjit Singh occupied Lahore in 1799, ousting three Sikh rulers. The event was important in his political career, but it was not the beginning of his rule. Making use of matrimonial and political alliances he started subjugating Sikh, Hindu, and Muslim chiefs on both sides of the Sutlej. In 1809, the Governor-General of the East India Company obliged him to confine his activities to the right side of the Sutlej but recognized him as the sole Sikh sovereign on his side of the river. Within ten years then, Ranjit Singh unified the Punjab under his rule and extended his territories towards Multan, Kashmir, and Peshawar at the cost of the Afghans. Eventually, his state became larger than all the Sikh territories of the late eighteenth century put together. The extent of his dominions, which also meant much larger resources in men and revenues, and more complex politics and administration, distinguished him from his Sikh predecessors. The difference was so large that it could easily be seen as a difference of kind. In the popular idiom, Ranjit Singh the *misldār* became Ranjit Singh the Maharaja.

However, Ranjit Singh continued to strike the coins struck at Lahore in 1765 and at Amritsar in 1775. No coin was ever issued in his name. On one exceptional coin he is shown sitting reverentially before Guru Nanak, reinforcing the idea that he claimed to derive his authority from Guru Nanak. In fact the coins came to be called 'Nanak Shahi'. These coins were minted in Multan, Kashmir, and Peshawar, as well as Lahore and Amritsar. The inscription on the seal of Ranjit Singh is the simple 'Akāl Sahāi Ranjit Singh'. He is referred to as 'Singh Sāhib' or 'Khālsā Jio'. However, he is also referred to as *sarkār-i 'ālī* and *huzūr-i anwar.* His order is referred is as *parwāna-i wālā.* Such phrases are used in the orders of the princes as well, which bear the seal impression of 'Akāl Sahāi Kharak Singh' or 'Akāl Sahāi Tara Singh'. 'Akāl Sahāi' is used on the seals of some Sikh functionaries of the state, like Mangal Singh and Dasaundha Singh. It is interesting to note that Diwan Moti Ram uses 'Dayā Karo Bhavānii' and Misar Ram Dayal uses 'Bhavānī Sahāi' on their seals.[16] In a medal instituted by Ranjit Singh in the 1830s he is called 'Maharaja Ranjit Singh'.[17] But even in his orders of 1834 he is still referred to as 'Khālsā Jī'.[18] There is no doubt that Ranjit Singh used personal discretion in the exercise of power, but, contrary to the general impression, he never assumed the title of Maharaja formally. His position in this respect was close to that of his predecessors.

Ranjit Singh subverted a large number of principalities but allowed a considerable number of them to exist in subordination to him. Most of them were in the hills. He created new rajas as well. The Jamwal brothers – Gulab Singh, Dhian Singh, and Suchet Singh – were given the *rāj* of Jammu and its neighbouring principalities. In 1827, Raja Dhian Singh was given the title of *Rājā-i Rājgān, Rājā-i Kalān Bahādur,* with the *rāj* of Bhimbar and Chhibal. His son, Hira Singh, was given the title of *rājā* in 1837, with the territories of Jasrota and Basohli. All the vassal chiefs enjoyed a large measure of autonomy in the administration of their territories. Significantly, many of the Sikh and Muslim rulers too became tributary to Ranjit Singh before their territories were taken over. The only Sikh ruler to survive as a vassal chief was Fateh Singh Ahluwalia of Kapurthala.

The vassal chiefs formed an important section of the ruling class. Some of them were among the foremost *jāgīrdārs* of Ranjit Singh, with a large share in the revenues of the state and a considerable role in its administration. Among the *jāgīrdārs* of Ranjit Singh were also some of the former Sikh and non-Sikh rulers, and their *jāgīrdārs*. However, a larger number were picked up all afresh on the basis of merit and loyalty. They were drawn from different ethnic and religious groups and from different parts of the state. The choice was not confined to the Punjab. Apart from well-known European officers like Allard, Avitabile, Court, and Ventura, there were Diwan Bhawani Das, Diwan Ganga Ram, Diwan Dina Nath, Diwan Ajudhya Prashad, Jamadar Khushal Singh and his nephew Tej Singh who did not belong to the Punjab. The foremost *jāgīrdārs* were ranked as sardārs, *sardārān-i nāmdār*, and *sardārān-i kalān*. Their *jāgīrs* ranged from 25,000 to 800,000 rupees a year.[19]

The composite character of the ruling class is well reflected in the orders of Ranjit Singh addressed to General Tej Singh in 1834. To figure in these orders are the Europeans like Allard, Avitabile, Court and Ventura; the Rajas and their kinsmen, like Rājā-i Kalān Dhian Singh, his son Raja Hira Singh, Raja Gulab Singh and his son Mian Labh Singh, Raja Suchet Singh, Raja Jodhbir Singh, Mian Naudh Chand, and Wazir Kesari Singh; Prince Kharak Singh and his son Prince Naunihal Singh, and Prince Sher Singh; Diwans Bhawani Das, Kirpa Ram, Prabh Dayal and Devi Sahai; Misars Beli Ram, Jassa Mal, and Mul Raj; General Sultan Mahmud Khan and Colonels Mahtab Singh, Amir Singh Mann, Mehnga Singh Kakar, Mihan Singh, Gulab Singh Pahuwindia, Mian Illahi Bakhsh, Shaikh Illahi Bakhsh and Imam Shah; the Saiyids Faqir Nuruddin Ansari, Faqir Azizudin Ansari, Faqir Imamuddin Ansari, Faqir Tajuddin Ansari, and Fakir Shah Din Ansari; Bhais Ram Singh and Gobind Ram; Sardars Mangal Singh Ramgarhia, Kahn Singh Nakkai, the Sandhanwalias Atar Singh and Lehna Singh, the Majithais Gujjar Singh and Hem Singh, the Attariwalas Jai Singh and Chatar Singh, the Manns Kahn Singh, Fateh Singh and Sham Singh, the Rangar Nanglias Arjan Singh and Wazir Singh, Sardars Hari Singh Nalwa, Hukma Singh Chimni, Jawala Singh Padhania, Ishar Singh Sandhu, Gurmukh Singh Lamma, Chatar Singh Kalianwala, Ratan Singh Garhjakhia, Diwan Sawan Mal, and Raja Fazl Dad. Several countries and regions are represented here, and many castes and communities. Amidst all these, the Sikhs appear to be preponderant, and among them the Jatts. But they were not predominant.[20]

A similar pattern appears to emerge when we turn to the grantees. The most conspicuous among them were the Sodhi collaterals of Guru Gobind Singh. Important among them were Bhai Wasti Ram and his sons Bhai Ram Singh and Gobind Ram, and Sodhi Sadhu Singh of Kartarpur. The Bedis were not far behind the Sodhis. The most prominent among them were Bedi Sahib Singh of Una and his son Bikram Singh. The *granthīs, rāgīs, rabābīs, ardāsiās* and the *mutasaddīs* of Harmandir Sahib (the Golden Temple) enjoyed grants all over the Punjab. The small establishments around the Harmandir Sahib and shrines of local importance received numerous grants. The Udasis, like the Akalis and the Nihangs, were also the beneficiaries of state patronage. Extensive grants were received by Nirmala *sādhs.* The *dharmarth* lands of the Udasis were scattered over all the *doābs.* Then there were Purohits and Brahmans, Shaiva and Vaishnava establishments, the Jwalamukhi Temple, and many other Devidwaras and Thakurdwaras. The descendants of Shaikh Farid received fresh grants and the number of Muslim grantees in Kashmir ran into thousands. The most notable among them were the shrines of Hazratbal, Shah Hamdan and Muhammad Shah Naqshbandi. All the old grants of the *saiyids,* the ulama, the *qāzīs* and *faqīrs* were confirmed by Ranjit Singh in the trans-Indus territories. The Gardezi *saiyids* of Multan retained much of their wealth and influence. Quantitatively, the revenue-free grants enjoyed by non-Sikh institutions and individuals were almost as important as the grants received by Sikh individuals and institutions. If we keep in view the fact that Sodhis and Bedis held a large proportion of their lands as *jāgīrdārs,* the purely *dharmarth* grants of the Sikhs could be less important than those of the non-Sikhs. Qualitatively, Ranjit Singh made no difference between one community and another so far as state patronage was concerned.[21]

A tangible continuity with Mughal times is evident in the administrative arrangements made by Ranjit Singh and his Sikh predecessors. The village remained the smallest unit of administration in the late eighteenth century and *pargana* the basic unit. Since the territory under every Sikh ruler was rather small, the *pargana* served as the primary unit, with the exception of Multan in the 1770s when it was treated as a province. When Ranjit Singh conquered the former Mughal province of Lahore, for which the term Punjab was used, he did not treat it as a single unit. However, he did combine a number of *parganas* into primary units which, though small, could be viewed as the counterpart of the Mughal provinces. The provinces of Multan and Kashmir were larger than the other 'provincial' units. With the *nāzim* at the provincial level, the *kārdār* at the *pargana* level, supported by *chaudharīs* and *qānūngos*, and the *muqaddam* and the *patwārī* at the village level assimilated the administration of Ranjit Singh largely to that of the Mughals. The methods of assessment, *batāī*, *kankūt*, and *mushakhkhasah*, remained the same, though the rates of assessment were somewhat different. Before the end of Ranjit Singh's reign, the practice of *ijāra* was introduced on a considerable scale. In the administration of justice, the *qāzī's* court continued to function at places. Ranjit Singh appointed new '*adālātis* as well as *qāzīs* to cater to the needs of justice. We have already noticed that suzerain-vassal polity, the *jāgīrdāri* system, and the system of state patronage through grants of revenue or revenue-free lands were strengthened by Ranjit Singh.[22]

One area in which Ranjit Singh was radically different from his Sikh and Mughal predecessors was that of the army. Despite his personal liking for the cavalry, he strengthened the artillery and even more so the infantry. Furthermore, Ranjit Singh 'modernized' his army with the help of Indian officers first and then with the help of European officers, notably the French. Anticipating aggression eventually from the British, he strengthened the army much beyond the ordinary defensive needs of the state and also beyond the revenue resources of the state. Consequently, the Sikh state got more militarized in character now.

Furthermore, Ranjit Singh ensured the numerical dominance of the Khalsa in the army as the defenders of the sovereignty of the state. When his successors felt constrained to compromise on the issue of sovereignty, the army assumed an anti-British role. The Anglo-Sikh wars were fought by the army of Lahore not so much on behalf of the rulers as on behalf of the people. The Singhs and non-Sikhs fought gallantly even in the second war. Significantly, the poet who wrote movingly on the fall of the state created by Ranjit Singh was a Punjabi Muslim, Shah Muhammad, who identified himself with the Khalsa, referring to the war as a conflict between the Punjab and the foreigners.[23]

In retrospect we can see that the Khalsa claimed to have established sovereign rule under the leadership of Banda Bahadur who exercised power on their behalf in the name of the Gurus. Sovereign status for the Khalsa was claimed in the late eighteenth century as well, deriving authority from the Gurus and God. However, power was clearly exercised by individuals as representatives of the Khalsa under God's protection. In the Sutlej-Jamuna Divide, several states were established by the former *zamīndārs* of the Mughal empire, making use of its administrative framework. Most of them accepted the suzerainty of Ahmad Shah Abdali, as they had accepted the Mughal authority earlier. However, the government and administration of the Sikh rulers on both sides of the river Sutlej were very much similar.

Ranjit Singh created a large state, but he never adopted the title of Maharaja formally. He continued to strike coins already current, acknowledging the derivation of authority from Guru Nanak, which carried the implication of sovereignty for his state. The simple epithet of '*Khālsājī*' continued to be used for him nearly till the end of his reign. But all this does not mean that he did not exercise power with the restraint only of his conscience. This was exactly the position of his late eighteenth-century Sikh predecessors. The monarchical pattern was not introduced but reinforced by Ranjit Singh. His government and administration was much more complex, just as his state was far larger than that of any of his Sikh predecesssors, or the contemporary Sikh rulers. The ruling class in his reign was composite, and state patronage was extended to all categories of his subjects irrespective of their religious affiliation. There was no discrimination in principle, but Sikhs were represented in a larger proportion in the civil administration and the army than men of the other religious communities. The identification of a larger number of people of the region with the state, irrespective their religious creed and social background, was a measure of what is now regarded as its secular character.

NOTES

1. In the Sutlej-Jamuna Divide, territories along the hills were occupied by the Sikh leaders of the province of Lahore, but the southern portions were occupied by the Sikh *zamīndārs* of the province of Delhi. Indu Banga, *Agrarian System of the Sikhs: Late Eighteenth and Early Nineteenth Century*, New Delhi: Manohar, 1978, p. 21.
2. J.S. Grewal and Irfan Habib (eds.), *Sikh History from Persian Sources*, Tulika/Indian History Congress, 2001, p. 117.
3. Ibid., p. 122.
4. Surinder Singh, *Sikh Coinage: Symbol of Sikh Sovereignty*, New Delhi: Manohar, 2004, pp. 27-47.
5. Karamjit Malhotra has argued that this *Nasīhatnāma* could very well have been composed in the lifetime of Guru Gobind Singh between 1699 and 1708: 'The Earliest Manual on the Sikh Way of Life', in *Five Centuries of Sikh Tradition: Ideology, Society, Politics and Culture*, eds. Reeta Grewal and Sheena Pall, New Delhi: Manohar, 2005, pp. 55-82.
6. Surinder Singh, *Sikh Coinage*, pp. 61-72.
7. Ibid., pp. 158-98. The author does not take into account all the relevant information available on this theme, and oversimplifies the situation.
8. Indu Banga, *Agrarian System of the Sikhs*, p. 36.
9. B.N. Goswamy and J.S. Grewal (eds.), *The Mughal and Sikh Rulers and the Vaishnavas of Pindori: A Historical Interpretation of 52 Persian Documents*, Simla: Indian Institute of Advanced Study, 1969, pp. 219-21.
10. Ibid., pp. 231-3.
11. Ibid., pp. 267-9.
12. Veena Sachdeva, *Polity and Economy of the Punjab During the Late Eighteenth Century*, New Delhi: Manohar, 1993, Appendix, pp. 163, 167, 168, 169, 170, 171, 172, 173, 178, 191.
13. Banga, *Agrarian System of the Sikhs*, pp. 148-67.
14. Veena Sachdeva, *Polity and Economy of the Punjab*, pp. 71, 72, 73, 74.
15. Though not concerned with this aspect, Griffin provides enough information on the founders of Nabha, Jind, and Patiala to underline their initial position as *zamīndārs* of the Mughal empire: *The Rajas of the Punjab*, Patiala: Punjab Languages Department, 1970 (rpt.).
16. Goswamy and Grewal, *The Mughal and Sikh Rulers and the Vaishnavas of Pindori*, pp. 271-343.
17. B.N. Goswamy, *Piety and Splendour: Sikh Heritage in Art*, New Delhi: National Museum, 2000, p. 187.

18. J.S. Grewal and Indu Banga (eds.), *Civil and Military Affairs of Maharaja Ranjit Singh* (*A Study of 450 Orders in Persian*), Amritsar: Guru Nanak Dev University, 1987, documents 175, 241.
19. Banga, *Agrarian System of the Sikhs*, pp. 118-47.
20. All these names figure in Grewal and Banga, *Civil and Military Affairs of Maharaja Ranjit Singh.*
21. Scattered all over the orders in Grewal and Banga, *Civil and Military Affairs of Maharaja Ranjit Singh.*
22. Banga, *Agrarian System of the Sikhs*, pp. 63-117.
23. Shah Muhammad in his *Jangnāma* refers to the first Anglo-Sikh war as one between Hind and the Punjab, and he refers to the English as the third party (*tīsrī zāt*).

Part 4

SIKH SOCIAL ORDER

26

The Doctrines of Guru Panth and Guru Granth

Religious doctrines and institutions often serve as a source of unity and cohesion among the members of a community. The idea and institution of Guruship played a crucial role in the history of the Sikhs from the very beginning. The Sikh Panth entered a new phase of its history when Guru Gobind Singh decided not to appoint any individual as his successor. The end of personal Guruship, however, did not mean the end of Guruship itself. The doctrines of Guru Panth and Guru Granth became popular in the eighteenth century to take the place of the personal Guru. Both doctrines were intimately linked with the past and the future.

The equation of God with the Guru, the indispensability of the Guru for liberation, and identification of the Guru with the Word (*shabad*) are emphasized in the *bāṇī* of Guru Nanak. In his compositions we come upon expressions like 'He who is the infinite supreme God is the Guru whom Nanak has met', or 'Serve Hari the Guru, the Lake (of immortality), so that you obtain honour in His court'. Indeed, 'Guru is God, ineffable, unsearchable. He who follows the Guru comprehends the nature of the universe'. The Guru is compared to the ladder, the dinghy, and the raft 'by means of which one reaches God'. When the True Guru is merciful, 'faith is perfected', 'there is no fear of death', 'there is eternal peace', 'the nine treasures are obtained', and 'one blends in union with the True One'. Without the Guru, on the other hand, 'there can be no *bhakti*, no love'; there can be no access to the company of the *sants*'; 'one blindly engages in futile endeavour'; 'without the Guru there is darkness'. Finally, 'the Word is the Guru', and it is through the Word 'that I dwell on Him and so through the Guru the fire of *haumai* is extinguished'.[1] It must be added that Guru Nanak refers to himself as the minstrel (*dhādī*) who utters the speech (*bāṇī*) of God.[2] Guru Nanak's own compositions are thus an extension of the Word.

In the compositions of the successors of Guru Nanak the identification of God with the Guru is kept up. Guru Arjan, for instance, says at one place, 'the True Guru is Niranjan (God)'. So does Guru Gobind Singh: 'Know that the eternal and incarnate one is my Guru'.[3] However, there is a greater emphasis on identification of the Guru with Guru Nanak who is regarded as the originator of Guruship with a divine sanction behind his mission. 'They need no other instruction', says Guru Angad, 'whom Guru Nanak has given understanding through his guidance and who, through (God's) adoration, are blended with the Truth'.[4] 'The Guru has the key of the lock', says Guru Angad, 'the heart is the store-room, the body is its roof, Nanak; without the Guru the doors of the heart cannot be opened, since nobody else has the key'. Guru Amar Das says: 'There can be no deliverance without the true Guru'.[5] In the new context the Guru refers equally well to God and Guru Nanak, and his successors. In a composition of Guru Ram Das, 'the Guru is God and God is the Guru – there is 'no difference between them'.[6]

The *bāṇī* of Guru Nanak as the utterance inspired by God was the Word, the Guru. In a verse of Guru Amar Das there is the explicit statement, 'O Sikhs of the Guru, know that the true Guru's hymn is most true; the Creator Himself has caused him to utter it'.[7] Guru Ram Das equates *bāṇī* with the Guru and the Guru with *bāṇī*. Guru Arjan says that 'God gave Baba Nanak the Word as inexhaustible wealth, to use and spend'. Not only the *bāṇī* of Guru Nanak but also of his successors represents the Shabad Guru.

The idea of the unity of Guruship was a corollary of the installation of a successor by Guru Nanak during his lifetime. The decisions taken by the successor were as legitimate as the decisions of Guru Nanak. Therefore the person designated by the first successor was as true a successor of Guru Nanak. So were all the succeeding Gurus, till we come to Guru Gobind Singh. This idea is expressed by Guru Gobind Singh himself. 'Though not fools, the *sādhs* surely discerned Guru Nanak in Angad and Angad in Amar Das; Amar Das in turn came to be called Ram Das'.[8]

The metaphor of light for the unity of Guruship was effectively used by the Bhatts whose compositions have been included in the *Ādi Granth.* Balwand and Satta emphasize the unity: 'You are Nanak, you are Lehna and you are Guru Amar as perceived (by the wise); it is the same light and the same manner, the king has only changed his outward form'. The Guru is also referred to as the true Guru (*satgurū*). Divine sanction behind his mission is indicated by referring to him as an *avtār* and a prophet. The Guru is called the true king (*sachchā pātshāh*) who bears a heavy burden of responsibility.[9]

Most of these ideas are reflected in the *Vārs* of Bhai Gurdas. The true Guru is the true king, the king of both the worlds. Guru and God are the same: regard the Guru as God. The indispensability of the Guru and the unity of guruship are also emphasized. Without the Guru it is all darkness; without the true Guru there is no understanding; only the true Guru eradicates the disease of *haumai*; the entire world sinks without (the help of) the Guru. Lehna received Guruship from Nanak and passed it on to Amar Das. Guru Nanak, in Bhai Gurdas's metaphor, made the water run upstream by installing a disciple as the Guru. A Sikh became the Guru and the Guru became a Sikh. The equation of God with the Guru was extended to the equation of the Guru with the Sikh congregation: 'the true Guru pervades the *sādh-sangat*'. 'In the *sādh-sangat* is the Realm of Truth wherein resides the true Guru, the Formless One.' Bhai Gurdas identifies the *shabad* of the Guru with the Guru himself. And finally, the Guru is a true king of the realm of the spirit, guiding people in a new faith that was distinct from both Indic and Islamic dispensations, and was meant to transcend them all.[10]

The idea of the unity of Guruship makes the office impersonal, more important than the person. The fact that Guru Angad was a Sikh of Guru Nanak before he was designated as the Guru made every Sikh a potential Guru, and suggested an equation between the Guru and the Sikh. Bhai Gurdas's idea that the Guru was present in the *sangat* gave a peculiar sanctity to the collective body of the Sikhs. From 'the Guru is in the sangat' to 'sangat is the Guru' was a logical step. From the very beginning the Guru was equated with the Word and the Word came to be equated with the *bāṇī* of Guru Nanak and his successors. Guru Arjan compiled the Granth which, even in the presence of the Guru, was highly venerated because of the equation of the *bāṇī* with the Guru. The ground was thus prepared for the impersonal doctrines of Guru Panth and Guru Granth without impairing the idea of the unity of personal Guruship.

According to Sainapat, only a day before his death Guru Gobind Singh told his followers that the Khalsa represented his own form (*rūp*), and that henceforth he would dwell in the Khalsa. They were to seek inspiration in the *bāṇī* as the eternal Guru.[11] Writing in 1769, Kesar Singh Chhibber emphasizes the importance of both the doctrines of Guru Panth and Guru Granth.[12]

Of the two doctrines, that of Guru Panth was uncompromisingly egalitarian. All members of the Panth were equal in all respects. In the eighteenth century, this equality was interpreted chiefly in political terms. Every member of the Panth was duty bound to bear arms and he had the right to fight, and to conquer. He had also the right to participate in the deliberations of the Sarbat Khalsa.

The belief that the Guru was present among the Khalsa facilitated the institution of Gurmatā which played a vital role in their political struggle. The word *matā* in Punjabi means a decision agreed upon by common consent. Gurmatā was a resolution adopted by the Khalsa in the belief that the Guru was present among them. It was morally binding on all the participants and all the individual members who were informed about it. The most important Gurmatās were passed at Amritsar. They related to measures of defence and offence against the opponents. The Dal Khalsa came into action when the leaders of the Khalsa voluntarily pooled their resources under the command of a single leader. It was largely through the institution of Gurmatā that the followers of Guru Gobind Singh maintained their strength and integrity and triumphed over Ahmad Shah Abdali.

However, the scope of the Gurmatā was not extended to cover

the government and administration of the territories occupied by the leaders of the Khalsa. From the very beginning, the individual Sikh ruler was autonomous in the internal administration of his principality. The principle of hereditary succession was adopted by all the Sikh rulers. There was no room for exercising the right to counsel or to fight and conquer.

The role of the doctrine of Guru Panth was thus curtailed with the establishment of Sikh rule. No egalitarian institutions were evolved. Even the supposed equality between the Sikh rulers did not result in institutionalization of any kind. The Akalis had a limited role to play for some time as the representatives of the Khalsa Panth. But they possessed no institutionalized authority. A Sikh ruler could easily claim to rule on behalf of the Sikhs without a formal constitution. The doctrine of Guru Panth was never discarded in theory but it was not operative in the Sikh social order after the establishment of Sikh rule.

While the doctrine of Guru Panth was virtually relegated to the background, the doctrine of Guru Granth retained its importance. This doctrine could enable the Sikhs to preserve partial equality among themselves: they were all equal in the presence of the Guru Granth, and the established usages of religious congregation were observed by the pauper and the prince alike. Unlike the doctrine of Guru Panth, the doctrine of Guru Granth did not necessarily have radical implications for politics or for the social order in general. The concentration of political power in the hands of one person, who shared it at will with others at subordinate levels and who could in theory make arbitrary use of that power, did not find any opposition in the doctrine of Guru Granth. If the doctrine of Guru Panth enabled the Khalsa to mould their collective destiny, the doctrine of Guru Granth enabled the individual Sikh chief to rule with a clear conscience.

The end of Sikh rule prepared the ground for the revival of the idea of Guru Panth. Some of the protagonists of the Singh Sabha Movement tried to popularize the idea that the Sikh Panth was the inheritor of the early Sikh tradition, including its ideals and institutions. The aspiration and demand to manage the affairs of the Golden Temple and other historic Gurdwaras were rooted in the idea that the representatives of the Sikh Panth alone had the authority and the right to manage their religious institutions. The

Akali movement and its culmination in the Sikh Gurdwaras Act of 1925 which vested the control and management of historic Gurdwaras in the Shiromani Gurdwara Prabandhak Committee bears witness to the importance of the doctrine of Guru Panth in the twentieth century.

NOTES

1. For all these quotations from the *Ādi Granth*, W.H. McLeod, *Gurū Nānak and the Sikh Religion*, Oxford: Clarendon Press: 1968.
2. J.S. Grewal, *Guru Nanak in History*, Chandigarh: Panjab University, 1969, pp. 282-5.
3. McLeod, *Gurū Nānak and the Sikh Religion*, p. 198.
4. Grewal, *Guru Nanak in History*, p. 287.
5. Indubhusan Banerjee, *Evolution of the Khalsa*, Calcutta: A Mukherjee & Co., 1963, vol. I, p. 231.
6. Ibid., p. 239.
7. Ibid., p. 238.
8. Grewal, *Guru Nanak in History*, p. 290-1 and n 17; Banerjee, *Evolution of the Khalsa*, pp. 235-6.
9. Grewal, *Guru Nanak in History*, pp. 294-5.
10. Ibid., pp. 297-304.
11. Sainapat, *Shri Gurū Sobhā*, ed., Shamsher Singh Ashok, Amritsar: Shiromani Gurdwara Prabandhak Committee, 1967, p. 132.
12. Kesar Singh Chhibber, *Bansāvalīnāma Dasān Pātshāhiān kā*, ed., Ratan Singh Jaggi, Chandigarh: Panjab University, 1972 (*Parkh*, vol. II), pp. 163-4.

27

City of Sikh Pilgrimage

If centres of pilgrimage provide a certain degree of cohesion to religious communities, perhaps no city has been so important to any people as Amritsar to the Sikhs. The very name was derived from a vital institution established in the early history of Ramdaspur where the tank surrounding the Harmandir was known as *amritsar* (pool of nectar). Within half a century of its history, Ramdaspur saw the foundation of another important institution, the Akal Takht, which complemented the Harmandir. The twin institution of Harmandir-Akal Takht bestowed upon the town a unique importance in the eyes of the Sikhs. The role which this institution has played in the history of the Sikhs makes it far more important than any other centre of Sikh pilgrimage. To go into the history of this Sikh city *par excellence* is to delve into the social psychology of the Sikhs.[1]

We may start with the circumstances in which the town of Ramdaspur was founded in the sixteenth century. Guru Nanak had founded Kartarpur on the right bank of the river Ravi in the second quarter of the century. His successor, Guru Angad, had to leave the place because Kartarpur could be, and was, claimed by his sons. Guru Angad established his centre at Khadur in the present district of Amritsar. Similarly, when the sons of Guru Angad inherited the establishment at Khadur, his successor established his headquarters at Goindval on the right bank of the river Beas. On the main route from Lahore to Delhi, Goindval soon developed into a township. With this background, it is understandable why Guru Amar Das thought of establishing a new nucleus for his son-in-law and successor, Guru Ram Das. It was meant to be a religious centre, and the income which was bound to come from the traders and craftsmen who settled in the new township could ensure the financial independence of the Guru.

In retrospect, it is easy to see that the place where Ramdaspur was founded had certain advantages. Its short distance from Lahore at that time was an advantage. The easy availability of water was another asset. There is a strong Sikh tradition that a piece of land was purchased by Guru Amar Das and there is an equally strong tradition that revenue-free land was given to him by Akbar. There is no incompatibility between these two traditions. There was a time when it was believed that proprietary rights did not exist in India during the medieval period, but that view now stands modified. We have enough evidence to show that proprietary rights, particularly in towns, did exist. [2] There is nothing improbable about the purchase of land. Similarly, there is a great possibility that Akbar remitted the revenue due to the state. A Jogi called Udant Nath was given two hundred *bighas* of land by Akbar in 1571.[3] The Sikh tradition refers precisely to this time for Akbar's grant to Guru Amar Das. It is likely, indeed, that the revenue on the piece of land purchased by the Guru was remitted by the Emperor.

Four points in particular may be made about the early history of Ramdaspur without following any chronological order. First of all we may consider the institution of *amritsar* which was to give its name to the city two hundred years later. Guru Amar Das had entrusted the task of excavating a tank to Ram Das, his son-in-law and successor. The task was completed by Ram Das as the fourth Guru. His son and successor, Guru Arjan, enlarged the tank and built in its midst a place of worship called the House of God (Harmandir) which made the tank all the more holy and sacred. Then a third element was added. The Granth compiled by Guru Arjan in 1604 was placed in the Harmandir. These three elements in combination constituted the institution of *amritsar*, literally 'the pool of the nectar of immortality'. The institution of *amritsar* has survived to the present day as the Golden Temple, and its original name has been given to the city as a whole.[4]

There is evidence that Guru Ram Das and Guru Arjan

encouraged craftsmen and traders to reside in this place. Regular pilgrims used to come at the time of the Baisakhi and Diwali; some of them decided to settle down here. The *pargana* towns of Patti and Kalanaur find specific mention as places from where some families came to reside permanently in Ramdaspur. These were the families of traders and craftsmen. Thus it may be safely suggested that a market developed in Ramdaspur almost at the same time as the institution of *amritsar*.[5]

The institution of Akal Takht developed in Ramdaspur in the time of Guru Hargobind, the son and successor of Guru Arjan, in the early seventeenth century. The significance of this institution for Sikh history has been casually noted by some historians, but its relevance for the transformation of Ramdaspur into Amritsar has not been realized at all. After the martyrdom of Guru Arjan in 1606, Guru Hargobind decided to adopt martial measures for self-defence. Symbolically, he girded two swords, one of spiritual leadership (*pīrī*) and the other of temporal leadership (*mīrī*). To conduct the temporal affairs of the community of his followers, Guru Hargobind constructed a platform called the Akal Takht or Immortal Throne, close to the Harmandir. Whereas the Harmandir was meant for the worship of God, the Akal Takht was meant for all temporal affairs.

Consider also the administration of Ramdaspur. There is no evidence that an official of the Mughal government had anything to do with it. The administration of the town was in the hands of the Guru himself. In a sense, this new township was an autonomous pocket: the government of the day had virtually nothing to do with it. It is evident that there was scope for individual and collective initiative within the complex of the Mughal empire, as probably within the complex of all medieval states. Only on this assumption can we appreciate the founding of several towns by the Sikh Gurus, besides Ramdaspur: Tarn Taran in the Bari Doab, Kartarpur in the Jalandhar Doab, Kiratpur and Makhowal-Anandpur in the territories of the vassal chiefs of the Mughals. In the compositions of Guru Arjan, the administration of Ramdaspur and its unique position are described by the phrases '*rām rāj*' with the implication that there was no coercion or financial burden imposed upon its residents.[6]

All these features of Ramdaspur enable us to understand the subsequent history of the town and its eventual transformation into a city. Early in the reign of Shah Jahan, Guru Hargobind came into armed conflict with the Mughal administrators of the province of Lahore, and decided not only to leave Ramdaspur but also to move out of the province to settle down at Kiratpur, in a vassal principality in the Shivaliks across the river Sutlej. His successors too continued to live there. But the town of Ramdaspur survived as a centre of pilgrimage, a market, and an autonomous township, albeit under the control of the dissident Minas.

In the lifetime of Guru Arjan, his elder brother, Prithi Chand, had claimed a share in Ramdaspur. In due course he had come to claim the Guruship also for himself, a claim which could not be made good in the presence of Guru Hargobind. There were some Sikhs, however, who were not enthusiastic about Guru Hargobind's anti-government stance. After his departure from the Bari Doab in the 1630s, Prithi Chand's son and successor, Manohar Das Miharban, found it much easier to claim Ramdaspur as his religious centre. It was in his interest to maintain it as a focus of pilgrimage and trade, making his own arrangements for its administration.

A further change in the history of Ramdaspur came as a corollary of change in the affairs of the Sikh Panth. In 1699, Guru Gobind Singh instituted the Khalsa to solve the problems of internal disunity and external threat. He declared that all Sikhs were his Khalsa: they should be directly connected with him. An important implication of this declaration was the removal of the *masands* as intermediaries and the rejection of rival claimants as Gurus. The followers of Prithi Chand, among others, were thus thrown out of the pale of the Khalsa Panth. It is not unlikely that some of the Sikhs of Ramdaspur too became the Khalsa of Guru Gobind Singh before his death in 1708.

In any case, personal Guruship ended with the death of Guru Gobind Singh and the entire Khalsa Panth was believed to have become his successor. By this token Ramdaspur now belonged to the Khalsa. When Banda Bahadur rose against the Mughal government with the support of the Khalsa and established Sikh rule over a large part of the Punjab, the town of Ramdaspur was taken over by the Khalsa.[7] In the late 1720s, more than a score of *chaudharīs* and *panchas* were assisting the representatives of Mata Sahib Devi in administering the town.[8] A new phase in the history of Ramdaspur had begun.

In the struggle for survival after the execution of Banda Bahadur in 1716, Ramdaspur had become the rallying point of the politically active Khalsa. The religious sanctity of the *amritsar* and the temporal role of the Akal Takht were revived. The Khalsa started visiting Ramdaspur, particularly at the time of Baisakhi and the Diwali, as in former days. But now they were faced with the common problem of survival, and they could think of deliberating on issues of common interest. Since they believed the Guru to be present in the Panth, the collective decisions taken at the Akal Takht, called *gurmatās*, became morally binding on all. The efficacy of the institution of *gurmatā* made for its popularity, and Ramdaspur became the nerve centre of Sikh political activity in the early eighteenth century.

As in the time of Guru Hargobind so did now Ramdaspur become the target of attack by the Mughal administrators, but there was a difference. Zakariya Khan, the Mughal governor of Lahore, not only decided to execute Bhai Mani Singh, the leader of the Sikhs in Ramdaspur, but also to occupy the town. In the late 1730s and the early 1740s, Ramdaspur became a prized possession of the Mughal Governor of Lahore as well as the Khalsa. The sacrifices made by the latter for its recovery made it all the more symbolic of independence. For nearly two decades, then, all the major political decisions of the Khalsa were taken at the Akal Takht and executed by their collective forces, the Dal Khalsa. Under these circumstances there was little chance that Ramdaspur would decline as a town, though Ahmad Shah Abdali destroyed even the Harmandir once or twice.[9]

The political success of the Khalsa against Ahmad Shah Abdali ensured the prosperity of Ramdaspur. Several of the *sardārs* among the Khalsa decided to establish their own quarters close to the nucleus provided by Ramdaspur. Some of these quarters, called *kaṭras*, covered a large area, each with a market of its own besides residential buildings, administered by the *sardār* or his nominee. Some of the *sardārs* built fortresses as well, like Jassa Singh Ahluwalia, Jassa Singh Ramgarhia, Mahan Singh Sukarchakia and, above all, Hari Singh Bhangi who made his new quarters the capital of his territory. By 1800, there were nearly a dozen townships around Ramdaspur, each with its own autonomous administration.

In the early nineteenth century Ranjit Singh imposed unity upon this conglomeration of townships in the process of unifying the Punjab under his rule. The fort of the Bhangis and their quarters were taken over in 1804. The Ramgarhias lost their possessions in the city about a decade later. In 1826, the Maharaja took over all the territories of Fateh Singh Ahluwalia; these territories were restored to him but not his possessions in Amritsar. Other autonomous quarters had already been taken over. The unification of townships into a city was complete by now, and it was re-inforced by the construction of a double wall around the city with twelve gates connecting it with the hinterland and the outside world. The administration of the city was entrusted to government officials. The fort of Gobindgarh and the Ram Bagh palace outside the city wall further emphasized the character of the city as the second capital of Maharaja Ranjit Singh.[10]

What happened to the twin institution of Harmandir and Akal Takht in this process? In theory, the entire Khalsa inherited this institution. The affairs of the Harmandir were looked after by Jassa Singh Ahluwalia on behalf of the Khalsa Panth during the late eighteenth century. His successors continued to perform this role till the city was taken over by Ranjit Singh. Thereafter the management of the Harmandir became his responsibility. The Akal Takht was claimed by the leaders of the Akalis or Nihangs as the representatives of the Khalsa. Gradually however, they lost their influence primarily because the Akal Takht had little role to play in the affairs of the Sikhs during the time of Ranjit Singh and his successors. The Harmandir now was the place where the prince and the pauper could sit as equals before the Guru Granth. It symbolized the unity of the Sikh Panth.

NOTES

1. J.S. Grewal, *The City of the Golden Temple*, Amritsar: Guru Nanak Dev University, n.d., p.19. 'Ramdaspur to Amritsar: From a Town to a

City', in *Studies in Urban History*, eds. J.S. Grewal and Indu Banga, Amritsar: Guru Nanak Dev University, n.d., pp. 114-22.

2. J.S. Grewal, *In the By-Lanes of History*, Simla: Indian Institute of Advanced Study, 1975.
3. B.N. Goswamy and J.S. Grewal (eds. and trs.), *The Mughals and the Jogis of Jakhbar*, Shimla: Indian Institute of Advanced Study, 1967.
4. References to the tank, the Harmandir, and the town of Ramdaspur are to be found in the compositions of Guru Ram Das and Guru Arjan (*Ādi Sri Gurū Granth Sāhib*, pp. 430, 623-5, 781, 783-4, 1362, 1396), and in the *Vārs* of Bhai Gurdas.
5. References to Ramdaspur during the seventeenth century and the early decades of the eighteenth occur in Kavi Darshan's *Vār Amritsar Kī*, ed., Ganda Singh, Amritsar: Sikh History Society, 1957; Kesar Singh Chhibber, *Bansāvalīnāma Dasān Pātshāhiān Kā*, ed. Ratan Singh Jaggi, Chandigarh: Panjab University, 1972 (vol II of *Parkh*, ed. S.S. Kohli).
6. *Shabdārth Sri Gurū Granth Sāhib Jī*, Amritsar: Shiromani Gurdwara Prabandhak Committee, 1999, vol. III, p. 817. The statement is explicitly made that God has created *rām-rāj* in Ramdaspur. The editor points out in note 7 that in *Srirag* (M 5, 74), Guru Arjan refers to *halemī-rāj*. As translated by Teja Singh and Ganda Singh, 'Now the order of the Merciful has gone forth that no one shall molest another'—*A Short History of the Sikhs*, Patiala: Punjabi University, 1989 (rpt.), p. 36.
7. J.S. Grewal and Irfan Habib (eds.), *Sikh History from Persian Sources*, New Delhi: Tulika/Indian History Congress, pp. 107-8.
8. Kesar Singh Chhibber, *Bansāvalīnāma Dasān Pātshāhiān Kā*, pp. 182-3.
9. The centrality of Ramdaspur, the Akal Takht, and the Harmandir during the struggle of the Khalsa for political power is underscored by Ratan Singh Bhangu in his Gurū *Panth Prakāsh*.
10. Useful for the late eighteenth and the early nineteenth century are the works of Ram Sukh Rao and Ganesh Das and Sohan Lal Suri's *Umdat ut-Tawārīkh* (Lahore: 1885-86), Daftars II & III. Contemporary observations by European visitors such as Baron Charles Hugel's *Travels in Kashmir and the Punjab*, Patiala: Punjab Languages Department, 1970 (rpt.). Useful among the secondary works are Anand Gauba, *Amritsar. A Study of Urban History (1849-1947)*, Jalandhar: Cosmic Printers, 1988 and V.N. Datta, *Amritsar. Past and Present*, Amritsar: The Municipal Committee, 1967.

28

Social Order in *Bansāvalīnāma* and *Gurū Panth Prakāsh*

The doctrines of Guru Panth and Guru Granth figure in the Sikh literature of the eighteenth and early nineteenth centuries. However, the scope of this literature is wider than these doctrines. It contains ideas which have a bearing on social differentiation as well as equality. We propose to analyse the work of two writers who responded in different ways to the establishment of Sikh rule and its implications for the Sikh social order.

One of these writers was Kesar Singh, a Chhibber Brahman, who did not participate in the Sikh struggle for political power but whose ancestors had been associated with the Gurus. Looking for patronage from the Sikh rulers in his old age he assumed the role of a mentor, trying to suggest how they should exercise power. The second writer was Ratan Singh, a Bhangu Jatt, who was born after the establishment of Sikh rule but whose ancestors had participated in the Sikh struggle for power. Concerned about the threat to Sikh rule in the Punjab from the British, particularly after the death of Ranjit Singh, he tried to demonstrate how sovereign rule of the Khalsa Panth was established and what the Khalsa Panth stood for.

Born around 1700, Kesar Singh was taken to Delhi by his father Gurbakhsh Singh after the evacuation of Anandpur by Guru Gobind Singh in 1704. In Delhi, the father and the son were associated with the establishments of Mata Sundari and Mata Sahib Devi, the widows of Guru Gobind Singh. Kesar Singh accompanied his father to Ramdaspur (Amritsar) in the second decade of the eighteenth century. He stayed there to see the beginning of a long political struggle of the Khalsa of Guru Gobind Singh against the Mughal administrators of the province of Lahore. However, he does not appear to have stayed long in Ramdaspur. Probably in the 1730s, he left for his home in Jammu and wrote his *Bansāvalīnāma* in 1769.

The full title of Kesar Singh's work is *Bansāvalīnāma Dasān Pātshāhiān Kā*. It is not confined, however, to the ten Gurus. There are four chapters on the eighteenth century. The alternative title *Kursīnāma* underlines Kesar Singh's interest in genealogies, but the scope of his work is larger in terms of content. His work combines the features of Janamsākhī, Gurbilās and Rahitnāma literature in Gurmukhi. The bulk of his text is in *dohras* and *chaupaīs*, but there are also several quotations from the *Ādi Granth* and compositions attributed to the Tenth Master. There are occasional quotations from the *Vārs* of Bhai Gurdas and the work of a 'court poet' of Guru Gobind Singh. There are references also to Tulsidas's *Ramāyana*, the *Bhagvat Gītā*, *Yog Vashishtha* and the *Bhogal Purāna*.

Kesar Singh was impelled to write his *Bansāvalīnāma* by the political change which brought the Singhs of Guru Gobind Singh to the top. He writes on the assumption that Sikh rule had come to stay. Though a rule mainly of Jatts, it is legitimate: Guru Gobind Singh himself had decided to confer rulership on the Shudras. However, Kesar Singh is not exactly jubilant about this development. Perhaps the clue lies in his personal predicament. He expresses regret that he knows no ruler and has received nothing for his subsistence. He is contemptuous of those writers who take their compositions to the rulers and pander to them for patronage. He does not mind the patronage given to the descendants of the Sikh Gurus, but they were not the only grantees under Sikh rule. Kesar Singh believed that the Brahman Sikhs were entitled to receive state charity and, therefore, he feels unhappy about the situation in which their claims were being neglected. His own claim to patronage, he felt, was stronger than those of others because of the great services rendered to the Gurus by his illustrious ancestors.

Kesar Singh was unhappy also about the acquisition of power for its own sake. For one thing, power and piety did not go together.

He was afraid that the Singhs would become more and more engrossed in earthly pursuits and forget their faith (*sikhkhī*). He gives the impression at places that the doom of *sikhkhī* was imminent. On the whole, however, the situation was not yet beyond redemption. The foremost duty of a ruler was to be just, and the Sikh rulers could work for justice and avoid oppression. Their power could be sanctified by charity (*punn dān*). Kesar Singh advised them not only to devote their time to the worship of God but also to disburse the revenues of their territories generously by way of *dharmarth*.

Kesar Singh sets himself up as a mentor of the Sikh rulers, telling them whom to associate and whom not to associate with their government. Since the Sikh rulers had associated non-Sikhs with their administration from the very beginning, Kesar Singh does not miss the opportunity to question the association of Khatris and Muslims with Sikh administration. They are presented as the enemies of Guru Arjan, Guru Hargobind, and Guru Gobind Singh. In fact, nothing good had come from them to the Gurus and their followers, according to Kesar Singh, Khatris are occasionally equated with the Hindus in general, but Kesar Singh's consistent and vehement animosity is directed towards the Muslims in general. Indeed, according to him, the sins of an individual become associated with the class or community to which he belonged. Thus the acts of the Mughal rulers and their administrators are ascribed to Muslims in general. Since the use of Persian in administration enabled the Muslims as well as the Khatris to continue serving the new state at various levels, Kesar Singh does not approve of it. It is interesting to find Kesar Singh making use of Guru Nanak's denunciation of the Khatris of his day for taking to Persian, the language of the *mlechha*. He appears to react to the liberal policies of the Sikh rulers more as a Brahman than as a Sikh.

Kesar Singh's presentation of *sikhkhī* too is Brahmanized. Members from amongst the erstwhile Brahmans, Khatris, Vaishyas, and Shudras were a part of the Sikh Panth; they all shared a common faith, bound together by the ties of *sikhkhī*. This did not mean, however, that all other ties were snapped. Kesar Singh narrates the incident of a Mazhabi Sikh who pretended to be a Sandhu Jatt, ate with Jatt Sikhs, and on that account was punished by Kahn Singh Trehan, a descendant of Guru Angad. In the past, the Singhs who had given their lives in the cause of the Panth did not have to bother about the distinctions of caste for matrimonial alliance. All that was insisted upon was that a Sikh should marry a Sikh. Similarly, they could put aside the sacred thread and *dhotī* and disregard notions of ritual purity in eating. Among the contemporary Sikhs, however, a Brahman should marry a Brahman and a Khatri should marry a Khatri. No one should be forced either to wear or to remove the sacred thread, and a Brahman Sikh need not put it aside. In support of the ties of caste, Kesar Singh invokes the authority of the *Ādi Granth* as well as the *Gītā.* For him, each *varna* has its own peculiar *dharma* which is not affected by the common bond of the Sikh faith. Caste distinctions can, and should, be upheld because there is no contradiction between the equality of faith and the inequality of social position in the Sikh Panth.

Kesar Singh divides the Sikhs into four categories, two belonging to the past and two to the present. In the past, there were Sikhs who had lived a life of piety in the presence of the Gurus; they were *dīdārī* Sikhs. Their legacy was preserved by the *murīd* Sikhs, who were living a life of piety and detachment in the present. These two categories of Sikhs were not necessarily Singhs. Among the Singhs too, there were two categories: the *muktā* and the *māikī.* The former were always ready to lay down their lives in the cause of the Sikh faith; they belonged to the past. The latter were the contemporary Singhs who were involved in *māyā* or earthly pursuits. For Kesar Singh, the distinction between the *māikī* Singhs and the *murīd* Sikhs is rather basic. As he puts it, *sikhkhī* was instituted by Guru Nanak on the bank of the river Ravi and *singhī* was instituted by Guru Gobind Singh in the shade of the Shivaliks. Whereas the *māikī* Sikhs are accountable to Dharamraj for what they do, the *murīd* Sikhs enjoy immunity from any such accountability. Kesar Singh's own preference is for the latter.

Kesar Singh's concern for *sikhkhī* is no proof of his good understanding of Sikhism. He appears to hold on to Brahmanical beliefs and attitudes with remarkable tenacity. Besides one God, he believes in gods and goddesses of the Hindu pantheon. In a longish episode, the Mother Goddess is invoked by Guru Gobind

Singh, with the help of a Brahman from the south, to avenge the martyrdom of his father by creating the Khalsa. The blue dress of the Khalsa was the dress of the Goddess. Kesar Singh subscribes to the idea of incarnation. Guru Gobind Singh is presented at one place as the *avtār* of Vishnu. Taking the doctrine of transmigration rather literally, Kesar Singh explains the enmity between Prithi Chand and Guru Arjan, between Ram Rai and Guru Har Krishan, and between Aurangzeb and Guru Tegh Bahadur in terms of the law of *karma*. In combination with his belief in transmigration, this law explains much of the relationship between Guru Nanak and his successors. To Kesar Singh, the Vedas and the Puranas are nearly as important as the Sikh scripture. He can bracket the *Ādi Granth* and the *Gītā* as equally authoritative texts.

On the whole, Kesar Singh Chhibber appears to propose an alliance between Sikh rule and a Brahmanized Sikhism, in which there is no contradiction between religious equality and social differentiation. Instead of enlarging the scope of equality, he is keen to curtail it.[1]

For Ratan Singh Bhangu, Guru Gobind Singh became one with his disciples when he asked 'the cherished five' to baptize him through the rite of *khande-pahul*. He became at once the disciple-and-the-Guru (*āpe gur chelā*). The individual Singh was all important in the eyes of Guru Gobind Singh, but any five Singhs collectively were much more important. Like 'the cherished five', they could initiate others into the Khalsa fold. The prayers of 'the five' were regarded as efficacious because of the presence of the Guru among them. Indeed all the power that is in *gurbāṇī* is present also in 'the five'. That was why Kapur Singh accepted the robe of honour after it had been placed at the feet of the five Singhs. The 'five' were not more important than a whole congregation (*sangat*), they only represented the congregation. 'The Guru and the Sangat are one; there is no difference between them.' The congregation in turn is representative of the entire Khalsa. That is the sense in which the Guru is the Khalsa and the Khalsa are the Guru. In other words, the five represent the Guru Panth in certain situations just as a whole congregation represents the entire Panth in some others. It is extremely significant to note that Ratan Singh Bhangu compares the vesting of Guruship in the Panth by Guru Gobind Singh with the vesting of Guruship in Angad by Guru Nanak. Personal Guruship ends with Guru Gobind Singh but the institution and the doctrine of the unity of Guruship remain intact.

There are frequent references to general meetings (*dīwāns*) held by the Khalsa and the resolutions (*gurmatās*) passed by them. Such resolutions were passed in a variety of situations on specific issues of immediate concern. They were binding on everyone present and also on those who were informed about them, precisely because the Guru was believed to be present in the Khalsa. The term *gurmatā* itself is suggestive of special significance attached to these resolutions. They were often passed in the presence of the Guru Granth but this was not the only or primary reason why they were called 'the resolutions of the Guru'. Ratan Singh uses the term *mata* in its ordinary connotation of decision or intention. The term *gurmatā* is reserved for the occasions when a large number of the Khalsa deliberated on a certain issue. The times of Baisakhi and Diwali at Amritsar provided the occasion for many a *gurmatā*.

Though the *gurmatās* related generally to specific and immediate issues, their implications were not necessarily of short duration. The resolution to attack Zain Khan, the Afghan governor of Sirhind, for instance, did not merely mean his elimination; it also involved the occupation of his territories on a lasting basis. In this connection, Bhangu's reference to another resolution passed by the Khalsa at the Akal Takht carries even greater significance. According to this *gurmatā*, the Singh who occupied a certain territory first had the right to retain and adminster it. No one, however powerful, was supposed to oust him from that position. That was why there was a tendency among the important leaders to occupy cities and towns or large chunks of territory, while the smaller leaders and even individual Singhs occupied villages or small pockets of territory. This was made possible by the sanctity attached to the doctrine of Guru Panth. By contrast, actions taken by a *misl*, an association based on kinship, personal, or local ties, did not have the sanctity which the *gurmatā*-based action possessed.

Ratan Singh Bhangu's aim was to demonstrate how subjects

became kings: how the Sikhs became sovereign. This development is traced to the mission of Guru Nanak who made it possible for 'sparrows to kill hawks', and for 'lambs to kill lions'. Guru Nanak was the only saviour of the Kaliyuga, his position being comparable to that of Rama in the Tretayuga and of Krishna in the Dwaparyuga. He was the saviour of both Hindus and Muslims. His message was in fact meant for the entire world. The faith he promulgated was worth fighting for. That was how the struggle of the Khalsa became a war in the cause of faith. Ratan Singh Bhangu makes it clear that the Singhs who were fighting against their contemporary rulers belonged to the Panth of Guru Nanak. This indeed is built into the very little of his work, *Gurū Panth Prakāsh.*

This did not mean, however, that the Khalsa of Guru Gobind Singh had no special role to play. According to Ratan Singh Bhangu, the Khalsa was instituted by Guru Gobind Singh to raise the Sikh and to destroy the un-Sikh. The latter included the Mughal rulers and their supporters. It was necessary to prepare the Sikhs to take up arms against their rulers. That was why *charanpahul* was replaced by *khande kī pahul.* The Khalsa was made manifest to fight and to rule. This idea was embodied in the very form of greeting, *Gur-fateh* (victory for the Guru). The Khalsa were convinced that collectively they were invincible and they were destined to establish sovereign rule.

This conviction was based, among other things, on a decision attributed to Guru Nanak. When Babur approached him for blessings, the throne of 'Hind' was bestowed upon him on the condition that he would not oppress the followers of Guru Nanak. This compact ended when Jahangir had Guru Arjan executed through his subordinates. The fall of the Mughal empire after the seventh emperor was believed to be imminent. A prophecy attributed to Guru Gobind Singh specifically made every Khalsa horseman a potential ruler. One of the charges against Banda Bahadur is precisely that he wanted to confine rulership to himself. Ratan Singh Bhangu refers to situations in which the Khalsa refuse to accept a subordinate position whatever its importance in terms of political power and economic advantage. From the very beginning the Khalsa was meant to be sovereign.

This conviction was supported by incessant action. Armed

struggle was raised to a principle: 'fight' (*dangā*) was the 'surname' (*got*) and 'caste' (*jāt*) of the Singhs. Armed action against the rulers of the day and their supporters was an assertion of sovereignty. In this context the decision of a single Singh to levy an anna from every cart and a paisa from every donkey on the highway to Lahore was meant to be a challenge to the supremacy of the Mughal Governor of Lahore. The Singh who did this was also inviting martyrdom. Sovereignty thus demanded its price. The example of Guru Gobind Singh, who sacrificed all his four sons, served as a source of inspiration. At any rate the Khalsa were prepared to make sacrifices and to undergo suffering in the cause of sovereign rule. Ratan Singh Bhangu makes the explicit statement that Khatris, Jatts, Tarkhans, and Kalals attained to rulership because they did not abandon the goal of sovereign rule in the face of unbearable suffering.

Ratan Singh Bhangu evolves a metaphysics of martyrdom. He has great appreciation for Tara Singh who defied the Mughal authorities and died fighting. But his admiration for Bhai Mani Singh and Bhai Taru Singh is much greater; though, passive their martyrdom was almost deliberate, like that of Guru Tegh Bahadur. They both became *deoṛīdārs* of the sons of Guru Gobind Singh in heaven. The roots of the Mughal empire withered after Guru Tegh Bahadur's martyrdom. The Pīrs and Paigambhars of the Turks were removed from Sachkhand to a backyard, and they were no longer able to intercede. The mundane events become a reflection of decisions taken in Sachkhand. The idea of sovereignty was closely linked with the metaphysics of martyrdom. Those who die in the cause of the Panth go to paradise, or they are reborn to become rulers. Ratan Singh Bhangu attaches great significance to the martyrdom of Gurbakhsh Singh Nihang who had died fighting the Afghans to protect the Harmandir; he was reborn as Ranjit Singh.

Notwithstanding the metaphysics of martyrdom, the political struggle of the Khalsa is waged on firm ground. Ratan Singh Bhangu attaches crucial importance to the guerilla tactics of the Khalsa. To offer a running fight, or to attack and retreat, is an essential feature of their tactics. Out of the two-and-a-half points of battle, Ratan Singh gives one point each to attack and retreat, but only half a point to 'fight-unto-death'. He invokes the authority and example of Guru Gobind Singh for this. The Khalsa increases in numerical strength due to the oppression of the peasantry by the Mughal administrators. Many a destitute individual joins the fold of the Khalsa. Many others join them in the hope of plunder. After the initial success of the leaders of the Singhs, soldiers and servants are employed by them for the occupation of territories. The Khalsa get support from the non-Singhs just as Mughal administrators get support from the non-Sikhs. Ratan Singh Bhangu clearly states that the Mughal governors of Lahore did not get any support from Delhi. They were weakened by the invasions of Nadir Shah and Ahmad Shah Abdali, while the governors of the latter were weakened by the invasion of the Punjab by the Marathas. Ratan Singh Bhangu does not ignore the adverse effect of the heat of the sun on the Afghans of Ahmad Shah Abdali, or that of fasting during the month of Ramzan; nor does he ignore the stimulating effect of *bhang* and opium on the Singhs when they fight their battles.

The Khalsa Panth, according to Ratan Singh Bhangu, was meant to be egalitarian. Guru Gobind Singh deliberately turned to the lower castes because he was convinced that Rajputs would not be willing to carry out his mission. More than a score of social groups are mentioned in this connection: Brahmans, Bhatts, Khatris, Aroras, Banias, Bakals, Karars, Suds, Jatts, Gujjars, Kambohs, Sainis, Lohars, Tarkhans, Kumars, Sunars, Jhiwars, Nais, Chhimbas, Kalals, Behrupiyas, Churhas and Chamars. They obviously include not merely the low caste but also the outcaste, those marginalised by the prevalent social order. Among the 'cherished five', Ratan Singh mentions a Khatri, a Jatt, a Chhimba, a Nai, and a Jhiwar to underline that persons from all the *varnas* were included in the Khalsa Panth. He states explicitly that all distinctions were abolished when the Singhs drank from one vessel; the notion of *varna* and *ashrama* was discarded when the sacred thread and the sacred mark were put aside. When the fortress of Ram Rauni was constructed at Ramdaspur, all the Singhs contributed their labour irrespective of their importance in the Panth. The rationale given for egalitarianism is significant: the difference of caste and the notion of ritual purity did not suit the conditions of war, defence, hardship, and hunger.

Among those who died fighting by the side of Tara Singh, there were Brahmans, Nais, and Tarkhans as well as Jatts; there were also Multani and Peshawari Singhs who were presumably Khatris or Aroras. The leaders of the five *jathās* constituted by 'Nawab' Kapur Singh in the 1730s consisted of two Jatts, two Khatris, and one Ranghreta. Bir Singh Ranghreta is mentioned elsewhere also as the leader of 1,300 horsemen always fighting in the van. Throughout the period of political struggle, we find incidental references to Khatris, Jatts, Tarkhans, Lohars, Ranghretas and Mazhabis as active members of the Khalsa Panth. The preponderance of Singhs from the countryside is implied in the tendency among the leaders of the Khalsa to first occupy their own villages and the surrounding territory. The preponderance of Jatts among the Singhs is evident from a casual remark of Jassa Singh Ramgarhia that the number of Jatts in the Khalsa Panth was a hundred times more than that of the Tarkhans. Jatt preponderance is assumed in fact by Rattan Singh Bhangu when he says that the provinces wrested from the Mughals by Ahmad Shah Abdali were in turn wrested from him by the Jatts.

Nevertheless, differences of caste was discounted by the Jatts themselves. Sukha Singh, a Tarkhan, was 'brought up' by Shiam Singh, a Sandhu Jatt. Jassa Singh Ahluwalia, a Kalal, was similarly 'brought up' by Kapur Singh, a Virk Jatt. Just as the service of the Panth led Charhat Singh Sukarchakia to the pinnacle of eminence among the Khalsa, so did the service of the Panth make Jassa Singh Kalal the Patshah of the Panth. However, differences of caste were not completely abolished, particularly the stigma of the 'outcaste' groups. Ratan Singh Bhangu admires Sardar Shiam Singh for giving *pahul* to everyone who came to him for this purpose. Also, he ate with them all. Though he patronized and protected the *nīch*, he did not eat with them.

In the work of Ratan Singh Bhangu, the egalitarianism of the Khalsa Panth is matched by his insistence on the Singh identity, implying his reluctance to admit ideological differentiation within the Sikh Panth. The Khalsa, the Panth, and the Singh stand equated. From the very beginning Guru Gobind Singh had excommunicated the Minas, the Masands, the Ram Raiyas, and those who smoked or killed their infant daughters. The Khalsa were instructed not to have any connection with them. The Khalsa were not to wear the sacred thread or the *dhotī*. They were to worship Akal Purkh alone, not ghouls and ghosts, Gugga or Sakhi Sarwar; they were not to visit graves or cremation grounds. There are several other items of the Khalsa code of conduct that are mentioned by Ratan Singh Bhangu. In a reference to preparation for the ceremony of marriage there is an indication that the services of Brahmans were not required, and the *Guru Granth Sahib* occupied the central place in the ceremony.

The bonds of faith were more important than ties of caste or class for the Singhs. Ratan Singh Bhangu refers to the traditional animosity between the Jatts and the Rajputs, but the Rajputs in question are outside the Panth. The Singhs who are praised as good Singhs attend to worship regularly, render personal service to others, and remain ready to fight. Distinguished further are the Nihangs, dressed in blue, who remained celibate and did not acknowledge anyone as their master. Praised also are those who took the initiative in constructing Gurdwaras at places associated with the Sikh Gurus, particularly Guru Gobind Singh and his family.

Ratan Singh Bhangu refers to the tradition of awarding punishment (*tankhā*) to those of the Khalsa who deviate from the code in any way. It is interesting to note in this connection that Sukha Singh was excommunicated by the Khalsa at one time on the suspicion that his wife had killed her infant daughter. It is even more interesting to note that Diwan Kaura Mal used to pay five rupees a day as a fine (*tankhā*) for smoking the *hukkā*. This was a special concession. The non-Singhs were regarded as members of the Khalsa Panth only if they did not infringe certain basic norms. It is obvious that the *sahajdhārī* Sikhs, as much as the *keshdhārī* Singhs, were regarded as members of the Sikh Panth. In contrast to Kesar Singh Chhibber, then, Ratan Singh Bhangu shows a clear preference for the Singhs. His identification with them is almost complete, but his freedom from prejudice against any category of Singhs or Sikhs is equally remarkable.[2]

The increase in the number of Singhs was regretfully noted by Kesar Singh Chhibber; their preponderance is taken for granted by Ratan Singh Bhangu. Sikhkhī was subsumed by '*singhī*'. Guru Nanak was the source ultimately of both. Political activity, government, administration, and fighting on behalf of the state were some of the important concerns of the Singhs. They subscribed to the doctrine of Guru Panth, but the days of the *gurmatā* were over. However, the importance of 'the five' was still there in various situations. The most important legacy of the idea of sovereignty was not only the establishment of a large number of Sikh principalities in the late eighteenth century but also the establishment of a large Sikh state in the early nineteenth. The prophecy of Guru Gobind Singh justified the rulership of a single Singh.

By the mid-nineteenth century the Sikh social order was marked by social and ideological differentiation. While there was no 'caste system' among the sikhs, all considerations of caste were not set aside, especially for matrimony. The Sikhs of caste background did not eat with the former 'untouchables'. However, social stratification among the Sikhs was largely due to differences in the economic means of the individuals and groups and classes which constituted the Sikh social order. Much more egalitarian than what Kesar Singh Chhibber had liked it to be, the Sikh social order was less egalitarian in practice than the ideal social order of Ratan Singh Bhangu.

NOTES

1. Kesar Singh Chhibber, *Bansāvalīnāma Dasān Pātshāhiān kā*, ed. Ratan Singh Jaggi, Chandigarh: Panjab University, 1972 (*Parkh*, vol. II, ed. S.S. Kohli). For a brief analysis of Chhibber's treatment of the Khalsa, J.S. Grewal, 'Brahmanizing the Tradition: Chhibber's Bansāvalīnāma', *The Khalsa: Sikh and Non-Sikh Perspectives*, ed. J.S. Grewal, New Delhi: Manohar, 2004, pp. 59-87.
2. Ratan Singh Bhangu, *Prachīn Panth Prakāsh*, ed. Bhai Vir Singh, New Delhi: Bhai Vir Singh Sahit Sadan, 1993 (rpt.). For a brief analysis of Ratan Singh Bhangu's treatment of the Khalsa, J.S. Grewal, 'Valorizing the Tradition: Bhangu's Panth Prakash', *The Khalsa: Sikh and Non-Sikh Perspectives*, pp. 103-22.

29

A Theory of the Sikh Social Order

In the late nineteenth century, the Namdhari Baba Ram Singh recommended the *Prem Sumārg* to his followers as a religious text.[1] Bhai Kahn Singh of Nabha published extracts from his manuscript copy of the *Prem Sumārg* in an anthology of Sikh codes of conduct.[2] In the present century, Mohan Singh was flushed with his rediscovery of this interesting piece of Punjabi prose; he underlined its importance by characterizing the period between the death of Guru Gobind Singh and the birth of Ranjit Singh as the age of *Prem Sumārg*.[3] The text of the *Prem Sumārg* has been published with an elaborate introduction by Bhai Randhir Singh. He argues that this work was composed in the early decades of the eighteenth century.[4] Recently, however, it was argued that this work is a modern forgery, because many of the ideas expressed in it could not have become current before the establishment of colonial rule in the Punjab.[5] Yet there is credible evidence about the existence of a copy of this work at least in 1815.[6]

Bhai Randhir Singh equates the *Prem Sumārg* with the Khalsa way of life and sees its relevance for Sikh political aspirations in the present.[7] Mohan Singh appreciated its great impact in the past, looking at the early nineteenth century Sikh history largely as a historical corollary of the author's vision of the future.[8] Assuming the work to be a direct statement of historical facts, Teja Singh has approached it as an 'authority' on contemporary Sikh community.[9]

According to Mohan Singh, the author of the *Prem Sumārg* had foreseen a time when a better, nobler, purer class (*khālsā*) would come to power and rule for 'the good of all'. He presented a vision of the ideal Sikh state, to be actualized in the early nineteenth century. 'We have to note', says Mohan Singh, 'that long before a Punjabi King rose in the person of Maharaja Ranjit Singh, this artist of vision had imaginatively conceived of a state, which would simultaneously take up and solve the linguistic, ethical, cultural, political, military, and financial problems of the people'.[10] This view of the *Prem Sumārg* does not find support from empirical evidence on the early nineteenth century.

Teja Singh invokes the evidence of the *Prem Sumārg* in support of the view that Guru Gobind Singh vested Guruship in the Khalsa. 'If anybody wishes to see me', says Guru Gobind Singh (in the *Prem Sumārg* as quoted by Teja Singh), 'let him go to an assembly of Sikhs, and approach them with faith and reverence; he will surely see me amongst them'.[11] This statement cannot be attributed to Guru Gobind Singh because the *Prem Sumārg* is an apocryphal work attributed to Guru Gobind Singh. In fact the anonymous author presents the whole work as the address of the Immortal Being to Guru Gobind Singh before the Khalsa was created. With his standpoint in the past, the author professedly projects his vision into the future.

The *Prem Sumārg* may be regarded as a 'theory' of Sikh social order. The author expresses his views on the purpose and goal of this social order and presents the ideal norm to which the private and public life of the members of the society should conform. He talks of the ideal Sikh state. His work thus envisions a Sikh society under Sikh rule.

For a general analysis, the *Prem Sumārg* may be conveniently divided into three unequal parts. The opening four or five pages serve as a sort of prologue to the main work which sets out in detail what is expected of each member of the Sikh community in the religious, social, and political spheres. The last chapter of six pages may be regarded as an epilogue.

From a purely literary point of view, the prologue is an artistic device to underline the importance of the main work. The comprehensive code of conduct becomes obligatory because of the nature and purpose of the Panth presented in the prologue. With a direct divine sanction behind it, the Khalsa was created to dispel all evil and ignorance and to spread the right religion among the whole world. The end, however, was not near at hand: the people in the Kaliyuga were still to suffer oppression leading to complete moral anarchy. Only those who would follow the code of the Khalsa would survive into the Satyuga, to be brought to earth by divine intervention in human affairs. All this is foretold by God.

The artistic device was made possible by the experience of the Sikh community. Before the Khalsa was instituted, Guru Gobind Singh's mission was proclaimed through the *Bachittar Nātak*, a work which was certainly known to the author of the *Prem Sumārg*. The Immortal Being had told Guru Gobind Singh: 'I have cherished you as My son to propagate the *panth*, to extend true religion, and to restrain people from senseless acts'.[12] The opening paragraph of the *Prem Sumārg* is a paraphrase of this claim to divine authority for the mission of Guru Gobind Singh. An important purpose of his mission was to put an end to oppression: 'I have come into the world for the sake of true religion, to spread *dharm* and to extirpate the wicked and the oppressor'.[13] A period of persecution is forecast and the triumph of the Khalsa is postponed to a not very distant future.

The prologue could give reassurance to the Khalsa in their faith to suffer for the sake of true religion, hoping for better days to come. Whoever follows the code instituted by Guru Gobind Singh will not only save himself but also become the agent of liberation for his associates in this world, and abide eternally in the Sachkhand in association with the Sant Khalsa in the life hereafter. In following the way of life presented in this book, the Khalsa would be obeying simply the will of God. The prologue provides the author with a standpoint from which he can invoke the authority of Guru Gobind Singh. For the readers of the *Bachittar Nātak* there was nothing extraordinary in God addressing Guru Gobind Singh before his birth.

In the epilogue, the individual is asked to be pleased with whatever happens to him. The root of all suffering is egocentricism; the remedy lies in the realization of God's omnipotence and submission to His will. Therefore, complete submission to the will of God and indifference to both pain and pleasure formed the essence of the 'the way of love'. However, this way of *sahaj-jog* could be followed only by the few. The Khalsa are included in the elect, if not equated with them.

The bulk of the work covers the religious, social, and political aspects of the ideal Sikh community. In this part of the book, the author outlines the religious beliefs and practices to be followed by the Khalsa. He explains in some detail how *pahul* should be administered to initiate a person into the Order of the Khalsa. The ceremonies to be performed at the birth of a child in a Sikh family, at the marriage of a person, and at a person's death are detailed. The author deals with the occupations to be pursued by the Khalsa, and what they should do with their property. He gives an exposition of the ideal Sikh government and administration. The scope of discussion in these chapters is often wider than what is suggested by their headings. In the formal treatment of these themes there is a good deal of repetition and some minor contradictions.

The author of the *Prem Sumārg* was not writing a formal treatise on Sikh social order. Nevertheless, his conception of an ideal Sikh society can emerge from answers provided by the work to some relevant questions. What are the personal religious beliefs of the members of an ideal Sikh community? What are their moral duties as individual persons? What are their obligations towards the other members of the community? What is their attitude towards women? and towards caste? What is their attitude towards the members of communities different from their own? What is an ideal Sikh state? What kind of social structure emerges from the author's conception of an ideal Sikh society?

The author inculcates belief in the Immortal Being as the only omnipotent and omnipresent God. A member of the Order of the Khalsa should devote his body, mind, and wealth to the Immortal Being, always remembering Him and accepting His will. He should attribute his good deeds to God's grace and not to himself. He should have no faith in gods and goddesses or in the worship associated with them in temples or homes. He should not care for fasting, pilgrimages, thaumaturgy, necromancy, or astrology. He should believe in no *pīr* or guru other than the ten Sikh Gurus who embodied one and the same light of Truth inspired by God. Devotion to the Gurus was little short of submission to God's will. The Khalsa should love the Word (Gurbāṇī). The recitation of select portions of the *Granth Sāhib* and the writings of Guru Gobind Singh, four or five times a day, accompanied by personal prayers, was obligatory for the Khalsa. They should take *pahul*, bear arms, keep the *kesh* unshorn, and wear *kaṛā* and *kachhā*.

The spirit of the Sikh *rahit* was as important as the form. The essence of the Sikh way of life could not be reduced merely to formal observances. A Sikh should be immune to sensual temptation and indulgence. He should always speak the truth (except when it was likely to cause harm to somebody). The watchwords of a Sikh should be truth, continence, contentment, duty, mercy, humility, and service. He should never live on charity: he must earn his own living through honest means.

A Sikh should associate himself with the Sant Khalsa and serve them as he would serve his Guru. Sikhs should love one another and work in harmony. They should all come to the aid of a person who is in danger. For a Sikh, the communal brotherhood was more important than ties of kinship. A Sikh should always be ready to share his food, clothes, and other belongings with the needy; if he is in a position to be of any service to others, he should jump at the opportunity, regarding it as a sign of God's grace. Indeed, the best way to please the Guru was to serve his Sikhs.

A Sikh woman was to share with men their religious beliefs and practices, and all formal observances. She was to take *pahul* to be initiated into the Order of the Khalsa, whether unmarried, married, or widowed. She must marry. Not all widows were debarred from remarriage. Certain restrictions were placed on the woman in the social sphere. A life of domesticity was her chief concern and in public she was to move around preferably veiled. The author gives expression to the common prejudice that the woman is inferior to man because of her weak intellect and her helplessness against sexual urges. However, he uses her weakness as an argument in support of remarriage of widows.

The author believes that all men and women were equal in the eyes of their Creator. All mankind is the progeny of the Immortal Being.[14] There was to be no distinction between the high and the low among the Khalsa and there was to be only one caste, that of the Sodhi Khatri, the caste of Guru Gobind Singh, to which one came to belong immediately on one's initiation into the Order of the Khalsa. This however was the ultimate objective and in the interim some concessions could be made to prejudice in favour of caste and subcaste. Marriage was as permissible within the same caste and subcaste as among castes. Again, there were some Sikhs from whom the Khalsa should not eat, like the Chūhṛās, Chamārs, and Sansīs. But this exception was made only because of the nature of their occupations; otherwise there was nothing bad about their caste as such. The ideal of the Khalsa was: *ek panth, ek parsād.*[15]

The Khalsa Panth was not only a distinct but also a unique community in so far as it was in the sole possession of undiluted religious truth. All other religions, though ordained by God for the salvation of mankind, had deviated from their true purpose and were doomed to disappear sooner or later. It was not for the Khalsa, however, to become active agents of their destruction. It was open to the adherents of other religions to join the Panth to save themselves. They could co-exist with the Sikhs in amity. A Sikh was never expected to eat alone; if he did so, then he must keep a meal for the first visitor, whether a Khalsa, a Hindu, or a Muslim. If *jhatkā* meat were not available, a Sikh could eat *halāl.* With a few minor and specific exceptions, all food as a rule was pure for the Khalsa, whether it came from a Hindu or a Muslim. Sikh women must be married into Sikh families but Sikh men could be married to non-Sikhs, Hindu or Muslim. In all cases, however, brides were to be 'purified' by initiation into the Order of the Khalsa. The Khalsa was expected to avoid armed conflict, but if there was no chance of escape, 'he should not lose a moment and should not show his back'.[16] The author visualized armed fight only with Muslims and vaguely hoped for the political success of the Sikhs in the future.

In the ideal Sikh state, political power was to remain in the hands of the Sikhs. However, it was to be vested not in the Panth but in a single ruler: the Maharaja or the Pādshāh assisted by a sagacious *wazīr* who could be trusted with delegated authority. Several pious and learned councillors were to remind the ruler constantly of his duties to his subjects, there being no checks on his power except that of his conscience. In fact the foremost duty of the ruler was to safeguard his own authority and to punish the slightest disregard of his commands (even by the closest of his relatives or the highest of his officials, including the *wazīr*) with certain death. Royal commands were to be received by the officials with a ceremonial deference. No official was to be allowed to overstep the bounds of his position.

The kingdom was to be divided into provinces, each consisting of twenty-one *parganas.* Provincial administration was to be run with the help of a *faujdār-i 'umdah,* a governor, *a diwān,* an officer of justice, a newsletter-writer, and an audit officer. This provincial administration was almost a replica of the central government. The ruler must establish an elaborate system of *mansabdārī* in the army. The payment of revenue was to be in kind, but all assessments were to be carefully made in terms of cash even for the tracts of land granted in *jāgīr.* A *kotwāl* was to be appointed in every important town and city. Much in the author's description of the administrative set-up reminds us of the Mughal government more than the government of Ranjit Singh.

An important aspect of the government of the Sikh state was the administration of justice. The department of justice was personally supervised by the Maharaja. An official guilty of denial of justice to any one was to be removed from service. The Maharaja was to be accessible to all his subjects and in judicial decisions no favour or partiality was to be shown to anyone. The chief officer of justice was in a sense placed above the Maharaja himself. This officer was given a seal of office on his appointment, with the inscription, 'seal of justice, through the command of the Immortal Being'. And even the Maharaja (or his son, grandson, or his highest official) was obliged to appear before the court of justice on receiving sealed summons.

Indeed, the *raison d'être* of the Sikh state was justice. The ruler should remember that power was granted to him for the administration of justice. In life hereafter in the court of the True King he would not be questioned about his devotion to God, but be asked how many under his rule had received comfort and how many had suffered misery. He would be held responsible for nothing but justice in a very comprehensive sense. 'What is justice? It is this: that the ruler should not appropriate to himself what is not his by right, and he should not permit others to do so either. As far as it may lie in his power, he should not tolerate anyone's suffering: this is called justice'.[17] Religious devotion was less important than justice. Power without justice was hell.

In a limited sense, the ideal Sikh state was to be a welfare state. In accordance with the understanding of justice in this text, the ruler should institute a department of charities with its offices in all cities, towns, and even villages. He should take care that none in his kingdom was without food, dress or occupation. He should help all indigent parents to enable them to give their daughters in marriage. In fact he should fulfil every kind of want, particularly that of a householder. The ruler as a guardian of his subjects should constantly look after their welfare. The underlying principle of revenue assessment should be the lightest of burdens on the cultivator. The state taxes should be few and light. The ruler should always pray to God to grant him the capacity of discharging the duty of protecting and comforting his subjects.

Although the ruler was to work without discrimination on the basis of religion in most of his public activities and patronage, he was to give special attention to the Khalsa Panth. Gurmukhi (Punjabi) was to be the official language of the state. All Sikh children were to be given instruction in the code of the Khalsa. This religious education was the ruler's personal responsibility, for he would have to account for the good and bad deeds of his subjects. The ruler should not permit any other worship, presumably among the Khalsa, than that of the Immortal Being.

The Khalsa Panth though casteless had a social stratification of its own which was based on differences in economic advantages. The ruler and his kinsmen were at the top of the social pyramid. The civil officials and *mansabdārs,* with their large *jāgīrs,* formed the social elite: they were to be instructed and enabled to live in a good style. The best of all occupations was trade, as distinct from petty shop-keeping which was not permitted to the Khalsa. That the traders were expected to be prosperous is evident from the recommended plan of their houses in cities and their way of life. Next to trade was agriculture. But the condition of the peasant was probably not expected to be better than that of the artisan. There are indications that the artisans were numerous. They were not to be addressed by their occupational name; the deriders of their occupations were to be severely dealt with. However, they were required to stick to their family occupation; no new openings were allowed to them. No service was allowed to the Sikhs, except in the army. But mention is made also of Sikh domestic servants. The keeping of slaves, both male and female, was permissible.

From the foregoing analysis of the *Prem Sumārg* it is clear that its hypothetical nature is explicable in terms of the author's personal situation and his anxiety to influence the members of his community. The author accepted and perpetuated the idea that the mission of the Sikh Gurus was divinely inspired and that personal Guruship had come to end with the death of Guru Gobind Singh. There is a suggestion that Gurbani (including the writings of Guru Gobind Singh) was to be the solace and guide (almost the Guru) of the Sikhs. Interpreting the mission of the Sikh Gurus to their followers, the author works out the social and political implications of Sikh religious ideals. There is a persistent attempt at mutual conciliation between the ideal and the actual. Thinking primarily in religious terms, the author insists on equality within the Khalsa. This ideal could lead perhaps to social mobility. But the author does not visualize an egalitarian society. In fact, social stratification based on differences in wealth is built into his presentation of the Sikh social order. As in the social, so in the political sphere, the author does not see any relevance of the idea of equality for Sikh institutions. The ideal Sikh state is not democratic or republican in character: it is a benevolent but authoritarian monarchy in which there is no institutional check on the power of the ruler and the use of his power. On the whole, the Sikh social order visualized by the author is not exactly egalitarian but is more egalitarian than the Sikh social order of the early nineteenth century.

NOTES

1. Baba Ram Singh's letter of 1877 to his followers, quoted by Randhir Singh (ed.), *Prem Sumārg*, Amritsar: Sikh History Society, 1953, pp. 77-8.
2. Bhai Kahn Singh, *Gurmat Sudhākar*, Amritsar: 1922 (3rd edn.), pp. 445-63.
3. Mohan Singh, *An Introduction to Punjabi Literature*, Amritsar: 1951, pp. 111-42.
4. Only a few complete copies of the *Prem Sumārg* are known to be in existence and they are not very old (*Panjābī Hath-Likhtān dī Suchī*, vol.

I, pp. 334-5; vol. II, p. 299). However, S.S. Kohli states that a manuscript of AD 1718 is in existence: *Panjābī Sāhit dā Ithās,* Ludhiana: Lahore Book Shop, 1955, p. 216. Mohan Singh too places the work among the early eighteenth-century writings in Punjabi: An *Introduction to Punjabi Literature,* pp. 111-42. Though based mainly on internal evidence, Bhai Randhir Singh has given an elaborate argument in support of his view that the *Prem Sumārg* was written shortly after Banda's execution in AD 1716, probably by a younger contemporary of Guru Gobind Singh and a learned associate of Bhai Mani Singh: *Prem Sumārg,* pp. 71-99.

5. Surjit Hans, 'Prem Sumārg: A Modern Forgery', *Punjab History Conference Proceedings,* Patiala: Punjabi University, 1982, pp. 180-8.
6. W.H. McLeod, *Prem Sumārg: The Testimony of a Sanatan Singh,* New Delhi: Oxford University Press, 2006, p.6.
7. Randhir Singh, *Prem Sumārg,* pp. 99-101.
8. Mohan Singh, *An Introduction to Punjabi Literature,* pp. 111, 121-3.
9. Teja Singh, *Sikhism: Its Ideals and Institutions,* Delhi: Orient Longman, 1951, p. 26.
10. Mohan Singh, *An Introduction to Punjabi Literature,* pp. 121-3.
11. Teja Singh, *Sikhism: Its Ideals and Institutions,* p. 26.
12. *Sri Dasam Granth Sāhib Jī,* ed., Ratan Singh Jaggi and Gursharan Kaur Jaggi, New Delhi: Gobind Sadan (Mehrauli), vol. 1, pp. 57, 148. Cf. M.A. Macauliffe, *The Sikh Religion,* Delhi: Low Price Publications, 1995 (rpt.), vol. V, p. 299.
13. *Sri Dasam Granth Sāhib Jī,* p. 152. Cf. M.A. Macauliffe, *The Sikh Religion,* vol. V, p. 301.
14. Randhir Singh *Prem Sumārg,* pp. 3, 4, 6-23, 18-19, 24, 42, 43, 44-5, 48-52, 61, 66-7, 84-96, 98-103, 111, 127-8, 131-3, 137.
15. Ibid., pp. 44, 45, 46.
16. Ibid., p. 12.
17. Ibid., p. 96.

30

Sikh Raj and the Sikh Social Order

A comprehensive hypothesis on Sikhism in the period of Sikh rule has been constructed by Harjot Oberoi. The late eighteenth century, according to him, was marked by an 'extraordinary fusion of Khalsa and non-Khalsa identities'. Both the Khalsa and the Sahajdhārīs (non-Khalsa) controlled Sikh shrines, and articulated theology and mythology in a religious framework of their own. Sikh thinking and religious practices were transformed into what Oberoi calls 'Sanatan Sikhism'. Primarily a 'priestly' religion, Sanatan Sikhism made a critical distinction between religious intermediaries and the lay people. All Sikhs required formal initiation through either *khande kī pahul* or *charnamrit.* Guruship was vested in Gurbāṇī (the holy word of the Sikh Gurus), but the religious specialists were regarded as *gurus* or religious guides. Their religious establishments helped ordinary Sikhs to seek worldly fortune, overcome sorrow, and receive moral and religious instruction. The Sanatan tradition was primarily the religious universe of the Sikh élite, a sort of 'official religion' closely aligned to the Sikh kingdom of Lahore and its elite. It was rooted in large urban centres like Amritsar and in small towns like Anandpur. An extensive peasant and artisan class, living mostly in villages, practised 'popular religion' with its own ritual intermediaries. The Sanatan and popular forms of religious expression appeared to have worked out 'a comfortable relationship' that was marked by 'a reciprocal influence between the cultures of the powerful and subordinate'. Sanatan Sikhism thus embraced all kinds of religious beliefs and practices among the Sikhs, and spread an umbrella over religious diversity.[1]

The Sikh writers of the period were not necessarily linked with the state. They wrote for the people. The Gurbilās literature of the period, written in praise of the Gurus, insists on the end of personal Guruship after Guru Gobind Singh and the vesting of Guruship in the Khalsa and the *Granth*. 'You can see me in the Khalsa', says Guru Gobind Singh in Koer Singh's *Gurbilās Pātshāhī 10*. 'Regard the Khalsa as the Guru'. 'Serve the Khalsa who is your father, mother, and Guru rolled into one'. 'The Panth is equal to the Guru'. At the same time, the true Sikh regards the *Granth* as the Guru, has faith in *Granth* as the Guru.[2] Kesar Singh Chhibber states that Guru Gobind Singh gave Guruship to *Granth Sahib*. Therefore, 'the *Granth Sahib* is our Guru now'. At the same time, 'the Guru is Khalsa, and the Khalsa is Guru'.[3] According to Sarup Das Bhalla, 'Guru Granth' takes the place of 'Sri Gurū Jī Sāhib' after the ten Gurus.[4] According to Sukha Singh, the Guru and the Sangat are one; the Guru is in the Sangat.[5] Ratan Singh Bhangu talks of 'Sri Gurū Granth Sāhib' or simply 'Guru Granth'. For him, 'the Guru is Khalsa and the Khalsa is Guru; there is no difference between the Gurū and the Khālsā'. The Guru gave Guruship to the Khalsa.[6] All of these contemporary writers equate the *Granth* with the *Ādi Granth*. Kesar Singh Chhibber says that the *Dasven Pātshāh Kā Granth* was the younger brother of the *Ādi Granth*. Therefore, both could be regarded as Guru. But Chhibber also says explicitly that Guru Gobind Singh vested Guruship in the *Ādi Granth*.[7] On the whole, thus, our authors believe in ten Gurus and uphold the doctrines of Guru Granth and Guru Panth. By implication, a personal Guru is ruled out.

Our authors uphold the belief in Akal Purkh as the only God. However, they subscribe also to the view that Guru Gobind Singh invoked the Mother Goddess for instituting the Khalsa to destroy the Turks. Koer Singh invokes the goddess for aid in his undertaking as a writer, referring to her as the primal force (*ād saktī*) who made the Panth powerful. He calls her *devī*, *mātā*, *jaggmātā* and *kālkā*, and uses several other names. However, he talks of 'Ād Purkh' as the only creator of the universe, praises the Gurus and the Sangat.[8] Similarly, Kesar Singh Chhibber invokes 'Satgur Purkh' and all the deities, including 'Mātā Surastī' and 'Mātā Gaurī' for inspiration, and gives an elaborate account of how Guru Gobind Singh invoked Bhavani (also called Devi Mata Kali) for making the Panth powerful in order to destroy the wicked.[9] Sukha Singh's invocation is close to that of Koer Singh. Guru Gobind Singh worships the *devi* (called Chandi and Bhavani) to institute the Khalsa Panth and to make it victorious.[10] According to Sarup Das Bhalla, both the Turks and the Hindus were opposed to the Sikhs. The Guru did not wish to reveal his own *siddhī.* Therefore he invoked Chandi Mata to create Chhatrīs (Kshatriyas) for destroying the *mlechh.*[11] Ratan Singh Bhangu refers to 'the awakening of Chandi' who as Kali could be satisfied with 1,25,000 heads.[12] Evidently, the goddess is not the supreme deity; she is closely linked with an event and invoked for a specific purpose: to sanctity the use of arms by the Khalsa.

As we noticed earlier, the *Vār* composed by Gurdas towards the end of the eighteenth century underscores the unity of God and the unity of Guruship, equates the Sikh with the Khalsa, and celebrates the establishment of Sikh rule. The annihilation of the Turks was a prelude to an era of justice, peace, and the freedom of conscience under Sikh rule. A refrain of the *Vār* praises Guru Gobind Singh for being at once the Guru and the discipline. 'Sikh' Sangat for the author is the 'Khalsa' Sangat. Not to belong to the Khalsa Panth is to be a non-Sikh. The Sikhs believe in the unity of the ten Gurus and the Guruship of the Granth and the Panth. The religious faith and the ideology of the Khalsa is the same as that of the pre-Khalsa Panth. Both the Sikh faith and the Khalsa Panth have an identity that is different and distinct from that of Muslims and Hindus. The religious faith of the Khalsa is more important than their politics. The author prays for the boon of the Name, for association with the *sangat*, for the eradication of *haumai*, for the capacity to accept God's will (*hukam*), and for attainment of liberation. Bhagautī and Kālkā in this *Vār* clearly symbolize the power of God and do not refer to the Goddess Bhagvati or Kali.[13]

The goddess figures in the Rahitnāma of Chaupa Singh but not in the Rahitnāmas of Desa Singh and Daya Singh which were composed later. In fact a Rahitnāma compiled in this period lays down that the Khalsa should pay no heed to any god or goddess, any temple or image, any place of pilgrimage, fasting or religious vows; they should not make libation to gods, repeat the Gayatri or any other prayer; they should never wear a sacred thread or hold a *shradh*; they should have nothing to do with a Brahman; they should not seek to become well versed in Shastras. Another Rahitnāma of this period enjoins upon the Singhs to avoid *jangams* (Shaiva mendicants), *bāmīs* (tantrics), *sanyāsīs, bairāgīs, jogīs* and *udāsīs.* They should not accept as their guide a person who believed in any of the six systems of philosophy. These Rahitnāmas insist that a Singh should obliterate the authority of both Musalmans and Hindus; he should fight the Turks face to face and defeat them; he should regard the Turks as enemies and slay them; he should never bow to a Turk or serve him, trust him, or be his friend; he should have no affection for a Muslim woman. A Singh should never eat the meat of an animal slain according to the Muslim ritual. He should not associate with those who socialise with Turks.[14]

The Rahitnāmas relate primarily to the Sikh way of life and their emphasis, therefore, is on Sikh beliefs and practices. 'Accept the Khalsa as Guru, as the Guru's visible body'. This injunction appears early in the eighteenth century, and so does another: 'Every Sikh is bidden to accept the Granth as Gurū'.[15] 'The Khālsā is the Gurū', says a Rahitnāma of our period, and refers to the Guru Granth.[16] The Guru is present in both the Granth and the Panth, says another contemporary Rahitnāma; it refers to Gurū Granthjī, and looks upon the Guru's Khalsa as 'the image of Akāl'.[17] 'Regard with reverence the Granth Sāhib Jī as the Gurū', says the *Rahitnāma of Chaupa Singh.* Guru Gobind Singh had told the Sikhs that the entire body of the Sikhs (Sarbat Sangat) was his Khalsa and that 'Khalsa is the Guru'.[18] Another Rahitnāma equates *bāṇī* with the Guru, and Guru with the *bāṇī* in order to emphasize that the Khalsa should believe in nothing else but the *shabad* of the Guru; they should read the *shabad*, hear the *shabad*, and live in accordance with the *shabad.*[19] 'Shabad is the Gurū', reiterates an early nineteenth century Rahitnāma; the Khalsa should regard *shabad-bāṇī* as the Guru; they should serve the Khalsa as they serve the Guru; the Guru is in the Khalsa.[20]

Thus we find that the doctrines of Guru Granth and Guru Panth are underscored by the Rahitnāmas of the period, upholding belief in ten Gurus and rejecting a personal Guru.

The emphasis of the Rahitnāmas is on the religious life of the Khalsa: the daily discipline of meditation, recitation of Gurbāṇī, visit to the Gurdwara where *kīrtan* and *kathā* are held, and participation in congregational prayer (*ardās*). Initiation through baptism of the double-edged sword (*khande kī pahul*), adopting the epithet Singh, keeping uncut hair and flowing beard, wearing turban, bearing arms, specifically *kirpān*, keeping the comb (*kanghā*), and wearing an iron bracelet (*kaṛā*), and *kachh*, are made obligatory. Only a few Rahitnāmas mention *charan pahul*. The term Sahajdhārī is used only in the *Rahitnāma of Chaupa Singh*, which puts emphasis nonetheless on *kesh*, *kirpān*, *kachh*, *kanghā*, and *kaṛā* at different places.[21] Some of the Rahitnāmas explicitly refer to the visibly distinct identity of the Singhs. As one Rahitnāma puts it, the Khalsa with his *kesh*, turban, and flowing beard does not remain concealed in a gathering of a lakh of Hindus and Musalmans.[22] As Chaupa Singh puts it, the Khalsa Panth irritates Hindus and Musalmans like a mote in the eye.[23]

Indeed, most of the Rahitnāmas tend to equate the Sikh with the Khalsa or the Singh. Chaupa Singh brackets the Sahajdhārī with the Keshdhārī Sikh of the Guru for the daily religious discipline. He also refers to initiation through *charan pahul*. The Sahajdhārī Sikh is allowed to wear the sacred thread, and to cut his hair with a pair of scissors but not to cut his beard. A Sikh in the service of the Mughal government could infringe all norms but not the injunction regarding female infanticide, tonsure, and tobacco.[24] The Sahajdhārī Sikh of the *Rahitnāma of Chaupa Singh* is different from the Keshdhārī, but the two share a very large space in terms of doctrine and religious practice. They subscribe to the doctrines of Guru Granth and Guru Panth and look upon the Gurdwara as their sacred place. Furthermore, preference for the Keshdhārī position is made quite obvious. The Sahajdhārīs do not include the followers of Prithi Chand, Dhir Mal, Ram Rai and the Masands. They are regarded as reprobate, and the Khalsa are told not to have any kind of association with them.[25]

Though a celibate Sikh is visualized as a member of the Panth,[26] the Udasis do not seem to be included among the

Sahajdhārīs. Thus, the Sahajdhārī is not merely a non-Singh or a non-Khalsa. He shares all essential religious doctrines and practices with the Singh. The Rahitnāma of Bhai Desa Singh was meant only for the Singhs.[27] Bhai Daya Singh, who tends to equate the Sikh with the Singh, suggests sanctions (*tankhā*) for those who follow Dhir Mal or Ram Rai.[28] Thus, a line was drawn first between the Khalsa (Singhs) and the non-Khalsa (Sikhs) and then between these two and the reprobate groups even if they regarded themselves as Sikh.

The Rahitnāmas contain instructions regarding the rites of passage. Chaupa Singh assigns no role to a Brahman in connection with the ceremonies to be performed at the time of death; he recommends reading of the Granth, and performance of *kīrtan* and *ardās*. However, the ashes were to be taken to Hardwar to be immersed in the Ganges. The marriage ceremony should be performed by a Brahman (Sikh?).[29] The Rahitnāma called *Sākhī Rahīt Kī* has no role for a Brahman: 'all the *karam* and *kiryā* of my Panth have been performed by Akāl Purkh Jī', says the Guru who has forbidden (Brahmanical) *kirya* and *karam* for his Sikhs.[30] According to Bhai Daya Singh, a Sikh should make an offering of a rupee and a quarter at a birth, marriage, and death. 'When a Sikh dies put on him a new *kachh*, bathe him, and tie a turban on his head. Recite *Japuji* continuously at that time'. 'Do not celebrate a marriage without using the Anand order'. A Sikh of the Guru should not eat the food of anyone who has a marriage performed by a Brahman.[31] The ceremonies of birth, marriage, and death recommended in the *Prem Sumārg* have no role for a Brahman.

The Rahitnāmas attach great importance to the Sikh *dharmsāla* or *gurdwāra*, where the local congregations meet for worship. According to Chaupa Singh, a Sikh should go to the *dharmsāla* every day, join the sangat, and listen to *kīrtan* and *kathā*. Association with Sikhs is beneficial in several ways, quite apart from the singing or hearing of *shabads*. A Sikh should visit the *dharmsāla* on returning home from travel. Wherever there are five, seven, ten or a hundred homes of Sikhs they should build a *dharmsāla* as the Guru's place where wayfarers may get food and accommodation. A good Sikh should be appointed as a *dharmsālia* (the person in charge). Sikh women should also go to the congregation (*darbār*).[32] 'Worship only where there is *shabad* of the Guru', says a Rahitnāma attributed to Bhai Nand Lal.[33] Not to attend the *satsang* regularly was a grievous fault.[34] A Singh must have *darshan* of the *Granth Sahib* before commencing his daily work.[35]

Gurdwaras are regarded as the places of pilgrimage for the Sikhs. Chaupa Singh recommends to the Sikhs of the Guru to visit the places of the Gurus.[36] Bhai Desa Singh is more specific: Amritsar, Anandpur, Patna, and Abchalnagar (Nander) are the places *par excellence* for Sikh pilgrimage. However, a Sikh should circumambulate and make offerings at 'any place associated with a Guru – east or north or west or whatever direction'.[37] It is not without interest that Bhai Desa Singh used to stay in a *bunga* at Amritsar and he went to Patna to have *darshan* of the Harmandir Sahib where he saw Guru Gobind Singh in a dream and received instruction for writing his Rahitnāma.[38] Bhai Daya Singh is equally emphatic about places of pilgrimage. '*amritsar* is equal to countless Gangas'. 'A Sikh who has not bathed in *amritsar* is as impure as unwashed clothes'. Without visiting Anandpur and Keshgarh, 'you cannot obtain knowledge of the Sikh faith'. The heavy *tankhā* of twenty-five rupees is levied on a Singh who visits Jagannath before he proceeds to Sikh holy places like Abchalnagar.[39] A wide range of literature was produced exclusively on *amritsar* during the late eighteenth and early nineteenth centuries.[40]

The Rahitnāmas lay down norms for the Sikh social order. The doctrine of Guru Panth carries the implication of equality among the Sikhs. In the *sangat* and the *langar*, concern for equality is made explicit. Distinctions are made on the basis of piety in terms of the Khalsa or Singh norms. In matters of matrimony and commensality, however, distinctions are made on the basis of social background. Chaupa Singh recommends marriage within the Sikh order but according to *varnashrama* and *kul*. In general too, the Sikh of the Guru should conduct his affairs in accordance of the *maryāda* of *varnashrama*. He should associate with others in such a manner that he does not become polluted. All the four *varnas* are welcome to become the Sikhs of the Guru and their way of life in terms of *rahit* and *kurahit* is the same, but they should relate to one another socially according to their *varna*.[41]

A Nand Lal Rahitnāma emphasizes the importance of the fellow-Sikh (Gurbhāī): he should be regarded as equal to the Guru. To turn away from a fellow-Sikh is to turn away from the Guru. Service of a Gurbhai is the source of prosperity.[42] However, the Rahitnāma is silent about matrimony and commensality. The *rahit* of Bhai Desa Singh is meant for Singhs of all the four castes (*varna*). The category of people not to be associated with the preparation of *langar* are *nāīs* and *jhīwars*, weavers and potters, and others of low caste. But 'everyone can share food in the *langar*': Brahmans and Khatris, and all devotees.[43] Bhai Daya Singh states that any member of the four castes who takes *amrit* would attain to liberation, and so would he whose status is lowly. 'Any member of the four castes can take *amrit* initiation'. All four castes should be seated on the mat to receive *parsād*. 'To adopt the forms of caste is not to our taste'. 'When a Singh gives his daughter to anyone other than a Singh it is like giving a goat to a butcher'.[44] According to the *Prem Sumārg*, the entire Khalsa constitutes a single caste (*baran*), but if for any reason they cannot act in accordance with this principle they could stick to their own caste: Khatri, Brahman, Sud, Arora, Suniar, Bhatia, Rajput, Lohar-Tarkhan, Jatt, and others. This distinction could be observed only for matrimony, not anything else. The daughter must be married to a Khalsa in spite of the difference of caste. The son could be married to even a non-Khalsa, or anyone. Intercaste marriage was justified also because the married state was obligatory for the Khalsa boys and girls. The Khalsa was forbidden to eat food from a *chūhṛā*, a *chamār*, a *sānsī*, a *dhānak* or a *kalāl*. This exception was made on account of the nature of their occupation; otherwise there was nothing bad about them. They could serve food to the Khalsa through the Khalsa by contribution in cash or kind. All the Khalsa of Sri Akal Purkh are one in following the same path.[45]

Chaupa Singh makes several observations which have a direct bearing on gender relations. The husband is like God (*kartā*) and the wife should remain devoted to him, regarding all other men as father, brother, or son. She should not associate with another man, nor with a woman of loose character. She should not spurn the advances of her husband. A Sikh woman should observe cleanliness, especially when cooking. She should not bathe in a naked state, nor throw water towards the sun while bathing. She should learn to read *Granth Sahib* and sing Gurbāṇī; she should not sing popular songs, nor participate in the singing of immodest songs at the time of wedding. She should go to the *dharmsāla* twice a day, and make offerings in kind. She should not read *Granth Sahib* in the congregation (*darbār*) of men but she can do so in a congregation of women. She should not associate with the women of the five reprobate groups. She should recite only the Guru's word (*mantar*) and should have no faith in tombs and sepulchres. In short, the life of a Sikh woman should revolve around the Guru, the *sangat*, and the husband. Since men are prone in the Kaliyuga to listen to women, the Sikh woman should give sound instruction (*updesh*) to her husband.[46] A Sikh of the Guru should not repose trust in any woman, not even her own; he should not divulge any secret to her, regarding her untrustworthy. A Rahitnāma attributed to Bhai Nand Lal favours detachment in a life of house-holding, and recommends that a Sikh should not trust a woman with a secret. He should not eye any woman with lust.[47] This is reiterated in another Rahitnāma with reference to women who come to the *sangat*. The Sikh is also forbidden to lie with a woman other than his wife. [48] On the whole, thus, a Sikh woman's place is in the home (which is patriarchal); conjugal fidelity is mutual; religious life in general and the *dharmsāla* are accessible to her.

The chronicles of the period of Sikh rule provide information on state patronage and religious practices of the rulers. Revenue-free lands were confirmed or granted to persons and institutions of all religious systems: Sikh, Hindu, and Muslim. The largest share went to the Sikh institutions and the descendants of Guru Nanak and Guru Ram Das, that is the Bedis and the Sodhis. However, many of the Bedis and Sodhis held *jāgīrs*, with the implication that they maintained troops, generally horsemen, for the service of the state. All the important Sikh rulers 'served' the Darbar Sahib at Amritsar with revenue-free lands and other contributions from time to time.[49] Maharaja Ranjit Singh continued this policy as well as the practice of visiting the Darbar Sahib rather frequently, making offerings to the *Granth Sahib* and various other places near the Darbar Sahib. The evidence of the *Umdat ut-Tawārīkh* is enough to underline that the Maharaja and his successors showed utmost devotion to the Darbar Sahib and other sacred places in Amritsar.[50]

Ganesh Das refers to Amritsar as the foremost pilgrimage centre of the Sikhs with several sacred places: Harmandir Sahib, Dukh Bhanjani, Akal Bunga, Baba Atal, Bibeksar, Kaulsar, Ramsar, and Santokhsar. There were other places in the western Punjab associated with the Gurus and regarded as sacred: Panja Sahib near Rawalpindi, Choa Baba Nanak near Rohtas, Dharmsala of Bhai Qandhara Singh in Gujrat (associated with Guru Hargobind), Ber Baba Nanak and Baoli of Baba Nanak in Sialkot, Ghalotian near Daska (associated with Guru Har Rai), and Rori Baba Nanak near Eminabad. Ganesh Das was thoroughly familiar with the *rahit* of the Khalsa. He makes a general statement about the contemporary Sikhs. The book which contained the compositions of Guru Nanak and his successors was called *Granth Sahib* and the person who attended to it was called Bhai. To read or hear the Granth was regarded as meritorious. The place where *Granth Sahib* was installed was called *dharmsāla.* At the beginning of every lunar month, the *halwā*, called *kaṛhā parshād,* was prepared with equal quantities of *ghee,* sugar and flour and offered to *Granth Sahib.* After the prayer (*arzdāsht*), the Bhai distributed *kaṛhā parshād* among all the Sikhs present, who meditate on God in accordance with the teachings of Guru Nanak. The Sikh of Ganesh Das is the Khalsa Singh.[51]

Far more detailed information is provided by Ram Sukh Rao on the rulers of Kapurthala, the successors of Jassa Singh Ahluwalia. His own 'services' for Harmandir Sahib are highlighted, and he is said to have been responsible for the management of the Sikh sacred places in Amritsar. This position was later taken up by Maharaja Ranjit Singh. Ram Sukh Rao creates the impression that it was customary for the rulers of Kapurthala to offer revenue-free land and cash to Sikh sacred places on all important occasions such as birth, marriage, death, and coronation. Besides Harmandir Sahib and other sacred places in Amritsar, both Maharaja Ranjit Singh and Fateh Singh Ahluwalia made such offerings to Anandpur, Nander, Goindval, Sultanpur, Muktsar, Rawalsar, Paonta Sahib, Dera Baba Nanak, and Kartarpur in the Jalandhar Doab. Both rulers showed great regard for the descendants of Guru Nanak, especially the Bedis of Una, the descendants of Guru Amar Das, especially the Bhalla Bawas of Goindval, and the descendants of Guru Ram Das, especially the Sodhis of Anandpur. The Sodhis of Anandpur are referred to as '*gurūs*'. Offerings were sent to all their branches on all important occasions. Their mediation was sought by Maharaja Ranjit Singh to persuade Fateh Singh Ahluwalia to return to Kapurthala when he had sought protection with the British in 1826. However, Gulab Singh Sodhi of Kartarpur, a descendant of Dhir Mal, had to request Jassa Singh Ahluwalia to intercede with the Khalsa to treat him as one of them. Significantly, Gulab Singh is said to have joined the service (*naukarī*) of Jassa Singh Ahluwalia. The forts of Sodhi Sadhu Singh, son of Gulab Singh, were destroyed by Fateh Singh Ahluwalia for sacking some Ahluwalia possession. A few other Sodhis served Fateh Singh Ahluwalia as well as Ranjit Singh. Many of the Sodhis were actually *jāgīrdārs*, and they were treated like other *jāgīrdārs*. The attitude of Maharaja Ranjit Singh and Fateh Singh Ahluwalia towards the Bedis was no different: they were treated with respect but not when it came to mundane matters. Sahib Singh Bedi of Una held considerable territories and received *jāgīrs* from the Sikh rulers. Offerings were sent to him, and his mediation was sought in disputes. Nevertheless, Fateh Singh obliged Sahib Singh to relinquish his control over the villages that he had usurped. Fateh Singh intervened also in the disputes between the sons of Sahib Singh after his death. Ranjit Singh treated the Bedis like other Sikh *sardārs*. He did not hesitate to resume a certain territory after Sahib Singh Bedi's death. The attitude of Maharaja Ranjit Singh and Fateh Singh Ahluwalia towards the Akalis was very much similar: it was respectful but authoritative.[52]

Fateh Singh Ahluwalia's interest was not confined to the Sikh places of worship or to the Sodhis, Bedis, and the Akalis. He is stated to have visited some Sufi shrines. Along with Maharaja Ranjit Singh he visited the temple at Jawalamukhi. Fateh Singh visited the shrine of Mansa Devi near Mani Majra. When he had suffered from small pox as a prince, his father, Raja Bhag Singh, made arrangements for the worship of Sitala during his illness and also on his recovery. Brahmans were employed to conduct all rituals, and astrologers were consulted for auspicious moments. Customary charities were lavishly made. Above all, Fateh Singh is presented as a great Vaishnava; like Ram Sukh Rao, he was a devotee of Lord Krishna. Temples dedicated to him were constructed at Kapurthala and Vrindavan, with adequate support for their maintenance. Vaishnava Puranas and epics and other Vaishnava works were regularly read in Raja Fateh Singh's daily assembly.[53]

What is important to note about the religious practices of the rulers is that they ignored some of the norms of Sikhism, especially the negative ones. Their example could be followed by the members of the ruling class. But the state did not impose any restrictions on the religious beliefs and practices of the people. Their own concern for Sikh institutions never decreased. Ranjit Singh's preference for the Khalsa Singh identity is evident from his insistence that the Sikhs who joined his army be the baptized Khalsa. Even the non-Sikh functionaries of the state tended to wear turbans and keep flowing beards.

There was a certain degree of tension in the Sikh norms and the Sikh praxis. Out of this tension appear to have risen the Nirankari and the Namdhari movements before the end of Sikh rule. The protagonists of both these movements placed Guru *Granth Sahib* at the centre of religious life and they had nothing to do with Brahmans for the performance of the ceremonies of birth, marriage, and death. In this respect, they were close to the norms of the Rahitnāmas though the movements were Sahajdhārī.

In the late eighteenth century, the European observers generally talk of the Khalsa, equating the Sikh with the Singh and looking upon them as distinct from both Hindus and Muslims. One of them refers to the Sikh scripture (*Ādi Granth*) used in daily worship in which formal prayer (*ardās*) was made and sacred food was distributed. He also refers to another book (presumably the book of the Tenth Master) which was held in 'almost as much reverence' as the *Ādi Granth*.[54] The initiation ceremony was seen by all as distinguishing the Khalsa from the Hindus because it obliterated all differences of caste. It was open to all castes and even to Muslims. Only one of the European observers refers to the initiation ceremony in a manner that suggests *charan pahul*, but even he is actually talking of initiation of the Khalsa (and not of Sahajdhārīs). He also says that some Sikhs respect idols or go to the Ganges for pilgrimage but the majority revered the Gurus and went to Amritsar for pilgrimage.[55] The Khalsa never shaved their heads or beards, and wore turbans generally of blue colour. They wore drawers (*kachh*) and iron bracelet (*kaṛā*), and they carried arms. They ate all kinds of meat but never beef. They used *bhang*, opium and spirits but never tobacco.[56]

Early in the nineteenth century, John Malcolm refers to non-Khalsa Sikhs, called the *khulāsā*, who are 'non-conformist Sikhs' because they believe in the *Ādi Granth* but do not conform to the institutions of Guru Gobind Singh. The word *khulāsā* was interpreted by some as 'the purest, or the select' and by others as 'exempted from the usages imposed on the other Sikhs'. They were not devoted to arms but they were entrusted with the management of revenues and the conduct of negotiations by the Sikh Chiefs; they had all the art of the lower classes of Hindus from whom they could not be easily distinguished. 'Their character differed widely from that of the Singhs'. The Singhs whether merchants or cultivators differed little from the soldier. Initiated by five Singhs through baptism of the double-edged sword, the Singh wore blue dress and attached great sanctity to his hair. The initiation ceremony, destruction of the distinctions of caste, and pursuit of arms as a religious duty separated the Singhs from the Hindus.[57] 'Wherever the religion of Guru Gobind prevails, the institutions of Brahma must fall. The admission of proselytes, the abolition of the distinctions of caste, the eating of all kinds of flesh, except that of cows, the form of religious worship, and the general devotion of all Singhs to arms, are ordinances altogether irreconcilable with Hindu mythology, and have rendered the religion of the Sikhs as obnoxious to the Brahmans, as it is popular with the lower orders of that numerous class of mankind'.[58]

Malcolm refers to the Book of the Tenth Master at several places. The term *Ādi Granth* is used for the Granth compiled by Guru Arjan to distinguish it from the *Dasam Pādshāh kā Granth* believed to have been composed by Guru Gobind Singh. The latter was not confined to religious subjects: it contained accounts of his own battles to stir up a spirit of valour. It was 'at least as much revered, among the Sikhs, as the Adi-Granth'. It was 'considered, in every respect, as holy as the Adi Granth'. Both the Granths were placed before the principal leaders when they met for adopting *gurmatās*. The Khalsa were directed to read the *Ādi Granth* and *Dasam Pātshāh kā Granth* every morning and every evening. It is important to note that Malcolm does not mention the latter in his description of the Sikh sacred place called *dharmsāla* where the writings of Guru Nanak incorporated in the *Ādi Granth* were read or recited upon 'every solemn occasion'. The 'dying words' of Guru Gobind Singh were: 'Read the *Granth*, and attend to its tenets'. At that time, there was no *Granth* of the Tenth Master. In any case, Malcolm does not refer even to the *Ādi Granth* as the Guru. Therefore, the question of the other Granth being regarded as the Guru is not raised.[59]

Apart from the Khalsa Singhs and the *khulāsā* Sikhs, Malcolm talks of the Bedis, Nirmalas, Shahids, and Akalis. The Bedis were 'greatly revered' by the Singhs as descendants of Guru Nanak, even though they did not acknowledge the institutions of Guru Gobind Singh. Mild and inoffensive in character, they did not carry arms. If not mendicants, they were generally travelling merchants. The Shahids and Nirmalas, especially the latter, were of peaceable habits and many of them were said to be learned. Both had their Bungas at Amritsar and explained the *Ādi Granth* to the Sikhs. Any one could join their order. The Akalis held the strangers in contempt and their aggressive deportment was 'hardly tolerant to the other Sikhs'. They were desperate soldiers and fanatic priests. They had usurped the sole direction of religious affairs at Amritsar, and played an important role in the council of the Singhs held at Amritsar for adopting *gurmatās*. They wore blue chequered clothes and bracelets of steel round their wrists; they initiated converts and directed the religious ceremonies at Amritsar. They could impose fines even on chiefs. They were staunch supporters of the religion of Guru Gobind Singh. In the councils of the Singhs convened by the Akalis all ate together, including converts from Muslims and the sweeper caste.[60]

According to Malcolm, the Sikh converts continued to practise all the civil usages and customs of the castes or tribes to which they belonged if they did not infringe on the tenets of Guru Nanak or the institutions of Guru Gobind Singh. With regard to marriage, the old traditions of the castes or tribes were followed. The Hindu usage regarding commensality too was followed except at the time of *gurmatās*. The Jatt and Gujjar Sikhs could intermarry and interdine with non-Sikh Jatts and Gujjars. Malcolm cites the example of a marriage between the Sikh Jatt house of Patiala and the non-Sikh Jatt house of Bharatpur. The Brahman and Khatri Sikhs did not intermarry or interdine with Hindu Brahmans and Khatris. Similarly, the Muslim converts to Sikhism severed all connections with Muslims in general, and intermarried or interdined among themselves. The conduct of the Sikhs towards their women was not different from that of the Hindus and Muslims in any material respect. The main thrust of Malcolm's observations is that the Sikhs generally followed the old patterns of matrimony and commensality among themselves.[61]

Harjot Oberoi quotes from *A History of the Sikhs* by J.D. Cunningham as one of the most informed individuals on the Sikh faith to show that Sikhism was a living faith in the 1840s:[62]

> The Sikhs do not form a numerous sect, yet their strength is not to be estimated by tens of thousands, but by the unity and energy of religious fervour and warlike temperament. They will dare much, and they will endure much, for the mystic Khalsa or commonwealth.

Cunningham was familiar with the Granth of the Tenth Master. In his view, it was only partly composed by Guru Gobind Singh. It was treated as a scripture but Guruship was believed to have been vested only in the *Ādi Granth*. Furthermore, the Sikhs did not regard even the most revered of their holy men as Gurus because Guruship had been declared by Guru Gobind Singh 'to rest in the general body of the Khalsa'. The two Rahitnāmas known to Cunningham depicted the Sikh Panth as a distinct entity, and underlined Sikh belief in the sovereignty of the Khalsa (*rāj keregā Khālsā*) and the vesting of Guruship in the *Ādi Granth* and the Khalsa. Not only in the literature held in high esteem by the Sikhs but also on the ground, the Khalsa were visible everywhere. Cunningham had no doubt that the Sahajdhārī Sikhs, the *khulāsā* Sikhs of Malcolm, were almost unknown in his day.

They were seen in the cities of British India but 'the warlike Singhs of the tenth king' were predominant in the Punjab.[63]

Cunningham lists at least eighteen sects or denominations of the Sikhs in the 1840s. But all of these even according to him were not 'sects': neither the Bedis, Trehans, Bhallas and Sodhis, nor the Ranghretas, Ramdasis, and Mazhabis. Only some Sodhis claimed to be *gurus.* The Bhais and Gianis were simply the pious and learned Singhs. The Akalis and Nihangs were distinguished from the rest of the Khalsa by their asceticism and spirit of independence. The Nirmalas too were known for administering the baptism of the double-edged sword. A few groups had been excommunicated by Guru Gobind Singh or the Khalsa. We are left with only the Suthra Shahis and the Udasis. The latter were proud of their association with the Sikhs and held the *Adi Granth* in reverence but they were essentially a 'Hindu sect'. Cunningham is emphatic, therefore, that 'the great development of the tenets of Guru Gobind has thrown other denominations into the shade'.[64] Their enthusiasm as converts to 'a new religion' was still fresh; their faith was 'still an active and a living principle'. They continued 'to make converts'.[65]

The Singhs figure prominently among the topmost *jāgīrdārs* of the kingdom of Lahore. Of nearly two scores of Generals and Commanders in the army of Lahore before the first Anglo-Sikh war, a little more than half were Khalsa Singhs. More significantly, all the Sikhs who joined the army were Singhs. There was hardly any unit of cavalry, infantry or artillery which did not have Singh soldiers and Singh officers. Panchayats of Singhs from each batallion or company as the representative body of the Khalsa could interfere in the nomination or removal of their rulers.[66] Cunningham equated the Sikh virtually with the Singh. A careful reading of his history leaves hardly any doubt that he was actually counting the Singhs in estimating the number of Sikhs.

The contemporary evidence considered in the foregoing pages leaves little doubt about the numerical superiority of the Khalsa Singhs in the Sikh community. The doctrine of Guru Granth was the most important doctrine for them, followed by the doctrine of Guru Panth. The Granth was explicitly identified with the *Ādi Granth.* The Sodhis were sometimes referred to as *gurus,* but they had joined the Singhs and their importance was due primarily to their large *jāgīrs* and their descent from Guru Ram Das. The position of the Bedis, the descendants of Guru Nanak, was similar to that of the Sodhis. The respect and consideration shown to them by the Sikh rulers did not place them outside the authority of the state: they were at par with the other *jāgīrdārs.* The section of Singhs who laid claim to be the representatives of the Khalsa Panth were actually the Akalis, also called Nihangs.

Belief in one God was central to the Sikh faith. By far the most important institution for Sikh worship was the Gurdwara. The existence of gods and goddesses was recognized by some, and a limited role was assigned to the goddess as Chandi, Durga or Bhagauti. The Sikh rulers patronized Sikh and non-Sikh religious institutions and individuals, including Shaiva, Vaishnava and Shakta establishments, and Sufi *dargahs.* They visited Sikh and non-Sikh places of worship. The rites of birth, marriage and death were performed with the help either of the Guru Granth or of Brahmans, or both. There was no scriptural or formal approval of the visit of a Singh to the shrines of Sitala, Gugga, or Sakhi Sarvar. Matrimony within the community was preferable and there was no bar on intercaste marriage. The general pattern of matrimony, however, remained confined to the tacitly approved castes for matrimonial ties. Commensality among all the four castes was not uncommon among the Singhs. The sacred food was meant for all. Outside the sacred space, however, the Singhs with the caste background did not eat with the outcaste Singhs. However, the outcaste Singh was regarded as a part of the Sikh social order as a member of the Khalsa Panth.

The manuals on the Sikh way of life (Rahitnāmas) were meant primarily to propagate the norms of personal and social life among the Singhs. All of them underscored the importance of the essential Sikh beliefs, and religious life centred on *kīrtan* and *kathā* in the Gurdwaras and the reading of Gurbāṇī. There was no institutional authority to resolve the issues of religious belief and practice for the collectivity, but individual Singhs invoked the authority of the Gurus, including the Guru Granth, in support of the views they wished to propagate. The number of such individuals was very considerable.

The beginnings of the Nirankari and the Namdhari movements before the end of Sikh rule indicate that departure from the teachings of *Guru Granth Sahib* and the importance given to the Brahmans in Sikh social life were seriously objected to by some of the Sikhs themselves. Exclusive importance given to the *Ādi Granth* and the Sikh rites of the passage, coupled with Singh identity, would form the core of the Singh Sabha Movement a quarter of a century later.

NOTES

1. Harjot Oberoi, *The Construction of Religious Boundaries: Culture, Identity and Diversity in Sikh Tradition,* New Delhi: Oxford University Press, 1994, pp. 89-91, 137-8, 201-03.
2. Koer Singh, *Gurbilās Pātshāhī 10,* ed. Shamsher Singh Ashok, Patiala: Punjabi University, 1968, pp. 138, 139, 283, 286.
3. Kesar Singh Chhibber, *Bansāvalīnāma Dasān Pātshāhiān Kā,* ed., Ratan Singh Jaggi, Chandigarh: Panjab University (*Parkh,* vol. II), 1972, pp. 163, 164, 198, 215, 221.
4. Sarup Das Bhalla, *Mahimā Prakāsh,* eds. Gobind Singh Lamba and Khazan Singh, Patiala: Punjab Languages Department, 1970, vol. II, p. 892.
5. Sukha Singh, *Gurbilās Pātshāhī 10,* ed. Gursharan Kaur Jaggi, Patiala: Punjab Languages Department, 1989 (rpt.), p. 451.
6. Ratan Singh Bhangu, *Prachīn Panth Prakāsh,* ed. Bhai Vir Singh, Delhi: Bhai Vir Sahit Sadan, 1993 (rpt.) pp. 58, 81, 297, 298, 389, 417.
7. Kesar Singh Chhibber, *Bansāvalīnāma Dasān Pātshāhiān Kā,* pp. 136, 215.
8. Koer Singh, *Gurbilās Pātshāhī 10,* pp. 17-21, 10-26.
9. Kesar Singh Chhibber, *Bansāvalīnāma Dasān Pātshāhiān Kā,* pp. 1, 102-8, 113-16.
10. Sukha Singh, *Gurbilās Pātshāhī 10,* pp. 1-3, 126-37.
11. Sarup Das Bhalla, *Mahimā Prakāsh,* pp. 820-4.
12. Ratan Singh Bhangu, *Prachīn Panth Prakāsh,* pp. 50, 132, 151-2.
13. Bhai Gurdas, *Vārān Bhāī Gurdās,* ed., Giani Hazara Singh, Amritsar: Khalsa Samachar, 1962 (4th edn.), Vār 41. For a brief analysis of this Vār, J.S. Grewal, 'Celebrating Liberation: the Var of Gurdas', *Journal of Regional History,* Amritsar: Guru Nanak Dev University, 2002, (New Series vol. III), pp. 15-24.
14. W.H. Mcleod, *Sikhs of the Khalsa: A History of the Khalsa Rahit,* New Delhi: Oxford University Press, 2003, pp. 297, 298, 299, 300, 302, 313, 316, 317, 318, 321, 322.

15. Ibid., pp. 288, 289.
16. Ibid., pp. 297, 306.
17. Ibid., pp. 316, 317, 318.
18. Ibid., pp. 76, 98, 100.
19. Ibid., pp. 6, 18.
20. Randhir Singh (ed.), *Prem Sumārg*, Jalandhar: New Book Company, 1965, pp. 6, 18.
21. W.H. McLeod, *The Chaupa Singh Rahit-Nāma*, Dunedin: University of Otago Press, 1987, pp. 58, 68, 232.
22. Ibid., p. 134.
23. Ibid., p. 92.
24. Ibid., pp. 57, 60, 64, 67.
25. Ibid., pp. 210-11.
26. Ibid., pp. 65-66.
27. McLeod, *The Sikhs of the Khalsa*, pp. 318, 320, 321, 322.
28. Ibid., p. 319.
29. McLeod, *The Chaupa Singh Rahit-Nāma*, pp. 63, 72.
30. Ibid., pp. 135, 137.
31. McLeod, *The Sikhs of the Khalsa*, pp. 318, 320, 321, 322.
32. McLeod, *The Chaupa Singh Rahit-Nama*, pp. 57, 58, 64-5, 68-9, 70, 71, 72, 76-7, 102-113.
33. Ibid., p. 133.
34. McLeod, *The Sikhs of the Khalsa*, p. 280.
35. Ibid., p. 297.
36. McLeod, *The Chaupa Singh Rahit-Nāma*, pp. 70, 72.
37. McLeod, *The Sikhs of the Khalsa*, p. 297.
38. Ibid., pp. 308-9.
39. Ibid., pp. 317, 318, 324.
40. Swaran Singh, 'Amritsar in Medieval Ṗanjabi Literature: An Historical Analysis' (Punjabi), Ph.D. Thesis, Guru Nanak Dev University, Amritsar, 1994.
41. McLeod, *The Chaupa Singh Rahit-Nāma*, pp. 59, 60, 72, 73, 117.
42. Ibid., pp. 134, 135, 137.
43. McLeod, *The Sikhs of the Khalsa*, pp. 300, 306.
44. Ibid., pp. 311, 314, 315, 319, 321.
45. Randhir Singh (ed.), *Prem Sumārg*, Amritsar: Sikh History Society, 1953, pp. 44, 45, 46.
46. McLeod, *The Chaupa Singh Rahit-Nāma* pp. 58, 69, 113, 114, 115-16.
47. Ibid., p. 137.
48. McLeod, *The Sikhs of the Khalsa*, pp. 281, 283.
49. Indu Banga, *Agrarian System of the Sikhs*, New Delhi: Manohar, 1978, pp. 148-67.
50. Sohan Lal Suri, *Umdat ul-Tawārīkh*, translated into English by V.S. Suri and published by Guru Nanak Dev University.

51. Ganesh Das, *Chār Bāgh-i Panjāb*, ed. Kirpal Singh, Amritsar: Khalsa College, 1965, pp. 105-6; for the Khalsa *rahit*, pp. 114-16.
52. Ram Sukh Rao, *Sri Fateh Singh Pratāp Prabhākar*, ed. Joginder Kaur, Patiala: 1980, pp. 61-3.
53. Ibid., pp. 63-4.
54. Ganda Singh (ed.), *Early European Accounts of the Sikhs*, Calcutta: Indian Studies Past and Present, 1962 (rpt.), pp. 71-5.
55. Ibid., pp. 63, 64, 65.
56. Ibid., pp. 18-19, 63-5, 71-5, 79, 83, 92.
57. John Malcolm, *Sketch of the Sikhs*, London: 1811, pp. 91-92n, 125, 129-32, 133, 180, 186, 189.
58. Ibid., p. 151.
59. Ibid., p. 31 note, pp. 51-52, 120, 168, 173, 185, 196.
60. Ibid., pp. 115-23, 133-35.
61. Ibid., pp. 135-39.
62. Harjot Oberoi, *Construction of Religious Boundaries*, pp. 215-16.
63. J.D. Cunningham, *A History of the Sikhs*, Delhi: S. Chand and Company, (rpt.), 1955, pp. 81n1, 137-38, 321-47.
64. Ibid., pp. 81 n1, 347-9.
65. Ibid., pp. 11-12, 16, 75-6.
66. Ibid., pp. 245, 289, 383-90.

Glossary

'adālatī:	one who performs justice; a touring justice under Sikh rule.
Ādi Granth:	the Sikh scripture, compiled by Guru Arjan in 1604 (containing the compositions of the first five Gurus and of a number of *bhaktas, sants,* and *Sufis*) and authenticated by Guru Gobind Singh with the compositions of Guru Tegh Bahadur added. Now known as *Guru Granth Sahib*.
'Ahdnāma:	an agreement mutually agreed upon by two or more parties; a treaty between rulers.
Akal Takht:	the platform constructed by Guru Hargobind to preside over the temporal affairs of his followers. The practice was revived by the Khalsa in the early eighteenth century. A structure raised on a spot that came to be known as Akal Bunga where all important meetings of the Khalsa were held. It served as the headquarters of the Akalis till the early nineteenth century.
Akali:	a staunch follower of Guru Gobind Singh; equated with the Nihang in the early nineteenth century; in the twentieth century, initially a volunteer to take over Sikh Gurdwaras and afterwards a member of the Shiromani Akali Dal.
'āmil:	an administrator; a revenue collector; interchangeable with *kārdār* as the administrator of a *ta'alluqa* under Sikh rule.
amritsar:	literally the pool of the nectar of immortality; the term originally used for the tank constructed by Guru Ram Das; the usage was extended to the town of Ramdaspur (Amritsar) by the early nineteenth century.
anna:	a small coin, 1/16 of a rupee, and equal to 4 *paisas* or 12 *pies*.
ardās:	a formal and collective prayer of the Sikhs, noticed by the author of the *Dabistān-i Mazāhib* in the seventeenth century; probably going back to the time of Guru Nanak.
ardāsiā:	literally one who offers *ardās* (prayer); a person employed by Sikh rulers and *jāgīrdārs* for this purpose.

arzdāsht: a memorial or address from an inferior to a superior; wrongly supposed to be the original term for the Sikh prayer called *ardās*.

āshramas: any of the four stages of life according to the Shastras; hermitage, monastery, residence or institution for philanthropic purposes.

avtār: 'descent'; incarnation of a deity, usually Vishnu.

Bābarbāṇī: four compositions of Guru Nanak, assumed to have been composed in connection with the sack of Saidpur (later Eminabad) by Babur; the phrase is used in one of the compositions in the sense of 'Babur's order'.

Bakhshī or Mīr-Bakhshī: the officer in charge of the army affairs in the Mughal times; he was directly responsible to the emperor.

bairāgī: a renouncer, usually a Vaishnavite.

bāṇī: speech; the utterances of the Gurus and the *bhaktas* recorded in the *Ādi Granth*; the amplified form *gurbāṇī* or *bhagat-bāṇī* is commonly used.

batāī: division of produce between the cultivator and the state, also called *ghalla-bakhshī*.

bhāī: a brother; a Sikh formally connected with religious affairs; an epithet of respect.

bhandār: a place for the preparation and distribution of food in religious institutions; store; a storehouse.

bhog: conclusion of reading of the *Ādi Granth*, followed generally by singing of hymns and always by an *ardās*.

bigha: a measure of land generally considered equal to 20 *biswās* or 2 *kanāls*; also one half of a *ghumāon*; the actual size varied from region to region.

Buddha Dal: the old army; the term used for a combination of the early fighting units of the Khalsa when new units had been formed in the third quarter of the eighteenth century; the latter in combination were called Taruna Dal or the young army.

chahārumī zamīndār: originally a partner in conquest entitled to a fourth part of the revenue but later reduced to the status of a *jāgīrdār*.

Chamar: a leather tanner; an untouchable caste of leather tanners and workers.

charan pahul: a form of baptism in which the person to be initiated drank the water in which the toe of the *guru* has been dipped, symbolizing humility and dedication on the part of the initiate. Also called *charanamrit* or nectar of the feet.

charanamrit: wash of the *guru's* feet. Also called *charan pahul*.

Chhatrīs (Kshatriya): the warrior or ruling caste of traditional Hindu society; the Khatris in medieval Punjab derived their origins from the Kshatriya, but followed trade, shopkeeping and other professions, including administration.

chaudharī: the headman of a group of villages for collecting revenues on behalf of the government.

chobdār: a staff holder; a messenger, a gate-keeper; an authorized watchman.

dafa'āt-i muqararah: the articles agreed upon; the fixed terms and conditions.

dal khālsā: a term used during the eighteenth century for the combined forces of the Sikh leaders.

dānishmand: wise, learned; a philosopher who bases his arguments on rationality.

dargāh: the place of a *pīr* who is no longer alive ; a holy place, court.

dārogha: a superintendent or head of an organization.

darvesh: a pious Muslim, generally a Sufi; a pious person.

Dasam Granth: the term used for the compilation earlier called the Book of the Tenth King (*darven pātshāh kā granth*); its compilation is attributed to Bhai Mani Singh; the authorship of its contents (a number of independent compositions) and the date of its compilation have been the subject of debate.

deoṛīdār: gatekeeper of the residence of an exalted person, the keeper of royal residence in the time of Maharaja Ranjit Singh.

derā: camp; encampment; a unit in the army of Maharaja Ranjit Singh and his successors; the place of a religious personage.

dhādī: a ministral; important among the Sikhs as the singer of Sikh lore.

dharma: the appropriate moral and religious obligations attached to any particular section in Hindu society; duty, moral obligation; a righteous cause.

dharmsāl: the place for earning merit; Sikh sacred space or the Sikh place of worship in early Sikh history; synonymous with Gurdwara.

dhūṇī: fire kept burning; a practice of the Gorakh Nāthī *jogīs* to keep fire burning all the time.

ḍīwān: the keeper of a treasury; the head of the finance department; an honorific given to Hindu nobles by Maharaja Ranjit Singh and his successors.

dīwānī: the office of the *dīwān*, in charge of revenues and finance under a ruler or the master of an estate.

dohrā: a rhyming couplet of a certain measure, popular in Punjabi poetry.

faqīr: a pious person; a devotee of God; used generally for a Muslim mendicant.

farzand-i khās: a specially dear son; a title given to a young person by the ruler.

fatiha: the opening *sūrah* of the *Qur'ān* used at the beginning of an undertaking, and in prayer for the dead.

faujdār: one who keeps troops; a military officer under the Mughals whose duty was to maintain law and order and to assist civil authorities; the office survived into the early nineteenth century Punjab.

gaddī: a cushioned seat; a throne; the seat of the head of a religious fraternity.

giānī: one who possesses knowledge (*giān*); among the Sikhs, a person well versed in the scriptures.

gopī: the wife or daughter of a cowherd; a milkmaid; any girl of Braj in love with Krishna.

gotra: subcaste; subdivision of a caste

granthī: a professional reader of the *Granth*; the functionary in charge of a *gurdwāra*.

gurbāṇī: an utterance of the Guru.

gurbhāī: disciples of the same *gurū*, given great importance in the Sikh tradition.

Gurbilās: a poetic work written in praise of the Gurus or one of the Gurus.

gurdwāra: 'the door of the Guru'; a Sikh place of worship, generally the centre of social activity too.

gurmatā: decision of a general congregation of Sikhs, generally taken in the presence of *Guru Granth Sahib*.

Guru: an epithet used for the founder of Sikhism and each of his nine successors, and also for the *Granth Sahib* and the Panth; preceptor; religious teacher.

gurz-bardār: a mace-bearer, used generally as a special messenger of the emperor.

habshī: an Abyssinian; negro, black slave.

halāl: the traditional Muslim mode of slaughtering animals for meat; anything lawful, as opposed to *harām* (prohibited).

Harmandir: 'the temple of God'; the central Sikh shrine in Amritsar popularly called the Golden Temple.

haqq: truth; God; a right; a rightful claim.

haumai: the psyche of self-centredness, arising out of attributing to oneself what actually is due to God's will.

hukam: an order; the divine order operative in the natural and the moral world as an expression of God's omnipotence.

hukamnāma: 'a written order'; used generally for the letters of the Sikh Gurus to their followers.

ijāra: an arrangement in which a certain source of income was placed in the charge of a person on the condition of his paying a stipulated sum to the state. The person in charge was called *ijāradār*, the holder of an *ijāra*.

in'ām: literally, a reward; an assignment of revenue distinct from *jāgīr* and *dharmarth*, and implying the idea of reward.

jāgīr: an assignment of land revenue in lieu of salary for performing service for the state.

jama'dār: the leader of a band; an officer above a *havaldār* in the 'regular' army of the kingdom of Lahore.

Janamsākhī: a collection of episodes related to the life of Guru Nanak, meant primarily to project his doctrines, ethics and his spiritual status; several traditions of this genre developed in the seventeenth and eighteenth centuries.

jangam: a sect of Shaivite ascetics; a mendicant sect; a member of these sects.

janjū: the thread worn by upper-caste Hindus, regarded as a sacred symbol.

jathā: a group, a band; used particularly for the fighting unit of the Khalsa.

jhatkā: the mode of slaughtering an animal for meat with one stroke of the sword or some other instrument; the traditional non-Muslim mode of slaughtering animals in India. Unlike *halāl*, it carried no religious significance.

jogī: from yogī, or one who practices yoga; a person belonging to any of the twelve orders of the followers of Gorakh Nāth.

Kaliyuga: the fourth and last of the cosmic ages traditionally regarded as the age of degeneracy.

kalma or *kalima*: a word, discourse; the Muslim confession of faith: 'There is no god but Allah and Muhammad is His messenger'.

kanghā: the comb kept by a baptized Sikh as one of the five Ks.

kankūt: a method of assessment based on the appraisement of the standing crop.

kanpātā: 'split-ear'; a follower of Gorakh Nāth who wears rings in pierced ears as the mark of his spiritual status.

kaṛā: the iron bracelet worn by a baptized Singh as one of the five Ks.

kārdār: an official; generally used for the administrator at the *ta'alluqa* (or *pargana*) level under Sikh rule.

kaṛhā parshād: sacramental food distributed in *gurdwāras* to all present, generally cooked with equal quantities of wheat flour, sugar, and *ghee*.

karma: an act, a deed; the law of *karma*, according to which living beings take birth in different forms, the human birth being the best because it is a rare opportunity for emancipation or release from the chain of transmigration.

kathā: an exposition of the Guru's verses, generally in connection with the life of the Guru.

kaṭrā: a locality; enclosed market-cum-residential quarters, generally with a separate entrance and internal management.

keshdhārī: a baptized Singh who maintains long unshorn hair.

Khalsa: the Sikh brotherhood instituted by Guru Gobind Singh; used for an individual as well as the collective body.

khān: a title given to nobles by the rulers in medieval India.

khande kī pahul: baptism of the double-edged sword, introduced by Guru Gobind Singh for initiating all Sikhs into the Order of the Khalsa.

khānqāh: a hospice; the establishment of a Sufi Shaikh.

kharāj: the tribute paid by the vassal to the suzerain; also called *peshkash*.

Khatri: from Kshatriya; an important caste of traders in the Punjab.

khes: a kind of heavy cotton shawl or sheet, a cotton substitute for blanket.

khidmat: service.

khidmatgār: a servant; an attendant.

khil'at: a dress of honour, containing articles of costume generally numbering three to twenty-one, including even arms or horses, and bestowed by a superior on an inferior as a mark of distinction.

khulāsā: a term used for Sikhs not initiated through baptism of the double-edged sword and, consequently, they did not keep unshorn hair, and did not bear arms or the epithet 'Singh'.

kimkhāb: an embroided cloth of silk.

kīrtan: the singing of hymns from the sacred scriptures of the

Sikhs; hence *kīrtan darbār* for an elaborate performance.

kos: a measure of distance equal to 2 ¼ miles or about 3 ½ kilometres.

kotah hathiār: short weapons, for hand to hand fight.

kotwāl: the official in charge of a fort; used generally for the city official meant to keep law and order.

langar: the kitchen attached to a *gurdwāra* from which food is served to all regardless of caste or creed; a community meal; a kitchen.

lungī: a piece of cloth, tied to the waist as an article of dress and flowing down to ankles.

madad-i ma'āsh: literally aid for subsistence; most commonly used in Mughal times for land revenue alienated in favour of a religious personage or institution.

mahal: a revenue subdivision usually corresponding with a *pargana*; also applied to a source of revenue.

malāhida: plural of *mulhid*; heretics; infidels; atheists.

malik: a title of honour.

manmukh: self-oriented; one who follows his own impulses rather than the guidance of the Guru.

mansab: an office, position or rank in the Mughal administration indicating the status, obligations, and remuneration of its holder in the official hierarchy.

mansabdār: the holder of a *mansab* in the system evolved by the Mughals, called the *mansabdārī* system.

marla: a measure of land equal to 1/20th of a *kanāl* (about 425 sq. metres)

maryādā: limit, boundary; bounds (of law, usage); custom; convention; traditionally correct behaviour; generally used in connection with the Sikh code of belief and conduct.

masand: a representative appointed by the Guru to look after the affairs of a local congregation of Sikhs, or a number of such congregations.

mazār: a mausoleum; the tomb of a Sufi Shaikh regarded as a place of pilgrimage.

māyā: the material world and all that is therein, treated in the Sikh tradition as 'false' in contrast with the eternal truth of God.

mīṇā: a derogatory epithet used for Prithi Chand, the elder brother of Guru Arjan, and also for his successors and their followers.

mīrī-pīrī: leadership of both the spiritual and temporal realms associated with Guru Hargobind and his successors.

misl: a combination of fighting units under a Sikh leader in the eighteenth century for defence and occupation of territories.

mlechha: impure; a derogatory term used for an outcaste or a foreigner, both were regarded as outside the four-fold *varna* order.

muftī: an expounder of the law in Islam.

malguzārī: the payment of land revenue; the *malguzār* collected revenue from the cultivators and paid it to the state, retaining his own share.

muhalla: a distinct locality in a city or a town.

muktā: a liberated person; in Sikh history, any of the martyrs of Chamkaur or Muktsar.

muktī: release, emancipation, liberation.

mullā: a Muslim priest and teacher, generally in charge of the mosque in a village.

munāfiqa: a hypocrite, dissembler, atheist

munshī: a writer or a scribe

muqaddam: the headman of a village or a part thereof.

muqarrab: one who is admitted, allowed to approach, one near the throne, a courtier.

muqarrab-i bārgāh: one who is admitted to the presence of the ruler, allowed access to his court.

mushakhkhasah: a fixed amount, used in connection with revenue.

mutasaddī: an accountant, an official.

nadar: from the Persian *nazr*, 'sight'; grace.

nāzim: an administrator; the governor of a province.

nazr: an offering or a present; also cesses of various kinds.

nazrāna: the tribute paid by a vassal; also paid by an official on a regular basis or on special occasions.

nihang: a militant follower of Guru Gobind Singh; the Nihang Singhs regarded themselves to be the guardians of the faith; they were employed in the army of Ranjit Singh and received *jāgīrs* from the state.

Nirmala *sādhs*: the ascetics and renunciants belonging to the Nirmala order among the Sikhs.

pahul: water used for initiating a person as a Sikh (*charan pahul*) or a Singh (*khande ki pahul*).

pancha: one of five; the member of a *panchāyat*; the headman of a village or one of its subdivisions.

pandit: a learned Brahman; any Brahman.

Panth: a path, the people following a particular path; collectively the followers of the Gurus; the Sikh community.

pargana: a small unit of administration in a province under the

	Mughals; remained in use in the Punjab till the mid-nineteenth century and became synonymous with the *ta'alluqa*.
parsād:	food; sacred food.
pashmīnah:	a fine variety of wool.
pīr:	a *shaikh* or guide among the Muslim mystics who leads on the path to union with God; believed to be a bestower of blessings after his death.
pūjā:	worship, adoration of a deity, veneration; homage; idolatry.
qanūngo:	a hereditary keeper of the revenue records at the *pargana* or *ta'alluqa* level.
qāzī:	the judicial officer who administered Islamic law; the office survived into the early nineteenth century in the Punjab.
qudrat:	omnipotence; power manifested in the creation; taken also to mean 'nature'.
Qur'ān:	Islamic scripture revealed by Allah to the Prophet Muhammed.
rabābī:	one who plays on the *rabāb*, an instrument with three strings.
Rāfizī:	a sect of the Shī'as.
rāgī:	a singer, particularly of the hymns of the Sikh scriptures.
rahit:	way of life, used especially for the Sikh way of life in accordance with the philosophic and ethical principles advanced by the Gurus.
Rahitnama:	a written code; norms laid down for the Sikh way of life in accordance with the principles of Sikhism; also relate to acts infringing those principles, and therefore prohibited.
rākhī:	literally 'protection'; in the eighteenth century a Sikh leader's claim to a part of the produce from land in return for protection afforded against all other claimants.
Ramdāsiā:	the follower of Ram Das; used for a Singh whose background was that of an untouchable *chamār*.
Ranghreta:	a Singh whose background was that of an untouchable *chūhṛā*.
sādh:	a person devoted to religious pursuits; a mendicant; a recluse.
sahaj:	the state of union with God.
Sahajdhari:	a Sikh who is not baptized as a Khalsa and does not observe the Khalsa code of discipline; a non-Khalsa Sikh.
sāhibzādas:	sons of the Master, a reference of the sons of Guru Gobind Singh.

sālagrama: a small stone image or idol carried on the person or worshipped by the Vaishnavas.

sanad: royal ordinance or any deed or grant or certificate from one in authority.

sangat: assembly, religious congregation; a congregation of Sikhs; the collective body of Sikhs at one place.

sanyāsī: a renunciant, generally a Shaivite.

Sansi: a category of the outcaste.

sant: a holy man; generally a follower of the figures like Namdev, Kabir, Ravidas and Dadu; equated with Sikh in the *Guru Granth Sahib*, and now with an eminent Sikh known to be pious.

sardār: a leader; a Sikh ruler; any Khalsa Sikh.

sarkār-i ā'lā or *sarkār-i wālā*: literally His exalted Majesty; a term used for Maharaja Ranjit Singh.

sarrāf: a money-changer; a jeweller.

Satyuga: the first of the four cosmic ages, the age of truth or virtue, the golden age.

shabad: the word; a hymn; verses from the *Guru Granth Sahib.*

shahīdganj: a Gurdwara built in commemoration of a Sikh martyr or martyrs.

Shaikh: the head of a Sufi order; a respectable Muslim.

Shiqdar: a person appointed to look after the civil and military administration of a territory called *shiq* under Afghan rule and, therefore, *shiqdār.*

Shivratri: a festival in honour of Shiva and Durga.

shraddh: the rite in which the dead ancestors are fed through the mediacy of Brahmans.

siddh: a person who has attained to high spiritual state so as to command supranatural powers.

silsilah: a line, a chain, a Sūfī order.

sūba: a province or the primary division of an empire; the governor of a province was called *sūbadār*, and his office *sūbadārī.*

Sufi: a mystic of Islam subscribing to devotional theism.

sultān: the ruler, the king in the pre-Mughal times.

sunnat: the tradition of the prophet Muhammad; popularly restricted to the practice of circumcision.

ta'alluqa: synonymous with *pargana* under the Sikh rule.

tahsīl: collection, particularly of revenues from land; the revenue collector was called *tahsīldār.*

takht: a throne; one of the five important religious centres of Sikhism.

tappa: the subdivision of a *ta'alluqa* or a *pargana* containing a varying number of villages.

tat khālsā: the staunch Khalsa; used for the Khalsa of Guru Gobind Singh who opposed Banda Bahadur and his followers in the early eighteenth century, and also for the Singh reformers of the early twentieth century.

thāṇa: a place where troops are posted for maintaining peace and order, and for assistance in the collection of revenues.

thāṇadār: the commandant of a garrison or a fort.

tilak: the sacred mark on the forehead a Brahman, an upper-caste Hindu, or the member of any religious sect.

topkhāna: the artillery.

Tretayuga: the second of the four cosmic ages in which virtue began to decline.

tufang: a musket.

Udasi: a renunciant belonging to an order tracing its origin to Guru Nanak through his son Sri Chand but not through Guru Angad and his successors.

'ulama: plural of '*ālim*, a person who possesses knowledge; used generally for the learned in Islamic theology and law.

Vakil: an agent or a deputy; an envoy.

vār: a literary genre, generally used for heroic poetry; Guru Nanak used it for his religious compositions; the most famous *vārs* in Sikh literature were composed by Bhai Gurdas in the early seventeenth century, celebrating Sikh Gurus and the Sikh Panth.

varnāshrama: the fourfold division of society into *varnas* and of human life into *ashramas*.

varna: literally, colour; used for the ideal norm of the four-fold social order.

waddha ghallūghārā: the great carnage, of the Sikhs at the hands of Ahmad Shah Abdali in February 1762.

wajah-i dastār: tribute paid by a vassal on account of the recognition given to his succession by the overlord.

walī: singular of *auliyā*; used for a Sufi who has attained to the highest spiritual state of subsistence in God.

wazīr: the first or the prime minister, next in authority and importance to the king.

zamīndār: literally the holder of land; applied alike to the intermediary who collected revenue on behalf of the state and to a vassal chief and a peasant proprietor.

zāt: personal rank in the *mansabdārī* system

zikr: remembrance; reciting of God's names, the practice of Muslim mystics to remember God.

Bibliography

Ādi Sri Gurū Granth Sāhib Jī (Sri Damdami Bīṛ, various printed editions, standard pagination).

Ahmad Shah, *Tārīkh-i-Hind,* MS 1291, Khalsa College, Amritsar. The part relating to the Sikh Gurus and the history of the Sikhs has been printed as an appendix to the *Umdat ut-Tawārīkh* of Sohan Lal Suri.

Archer, J.C., *The Sikhs in Relation to Hindus, Muslims, Christians and Ahmadiyas: A Study in Comparative Religion,* Princeton: Princeton University Press, 1946.

Bajwa, Fauja Singh, *Military System of the Sikhs (1799-1849)*, Delhi: Motilal Banarsidas, 1964.

Banerjee, Indubhusan, *Evolution of the Khalsa,* 2 vols., Calcutta: A. Mukherjee & Co., 1963 (2nd edn.).

Banerjee, A.C., *Anglo-Sikh Relations,* Calcutta: 1949.

Banga, Indu, 'Ahmad Shah Abdali's Designs over the Punjab', *Proceedings of the Indian History Congress* (Patiala: Punjabi University), 1968, pp. 85-90.

——, *Agrarian System of the Sikhs: Late Eighteenth and Early Nineteenth Century,* New Delhi: Manohar, 1978.

Bhalla, Sarup Das, *Mahima Prakash,* ed. Shamsher Singh Ashok and Gobind Singh Lamba, Patiala: Punjab Languages Department, 1970.

Bhangu, Ratan Singh, *Prachīn Panth Prakāsh,* ed. Bhai Vir Singh, Amritsar: Khalsa Samachar, 1972 (rpt.).

Bhai Jodh Singh, '*Jin Prem Kiyo Tin Hī Prabh Pāyo*', *Ek Murit Anek Darshan,* ed. S.S. Amol, Jalandhar: Khalsa College, 1967.

Bhai, Kahn Singh, *Gurmat Sudhākar,* Amritsar, 1922 (3rd edn.).

Bute Shah, *Tawārīkh-i Panjāb,* MS 1128, Khalsa College, Amritsar.

Chattar Singh Collection, Punjab State Archives, Patiala.

Chhibber, Kesar Singh, *Bansāvalīnāma Dasān Pātshāhiān Kā,* ed. Ratan Singh Jaggi (*Parkh,* vol II), Chandigarh: Panjab University, 1972.

Chopra, G.L, *The Panjab as a Sovereign State,* Hoshiarpur: Vishveshvaranand Vedic Research Institute, 1960 (2nd edn.).

Cunningham, J.D., *A History of the Sikhs,* Delhi: S.Chand & Co., 1966 (rpt.).

Datta, V.N., *Amritsar: Past and Present,* Amritsar: The Municipal Committee, 1967.

Early European Accounts of the Sikhs, ed. Ganda Singh, Calcutta: Indian Studies Past and Present, 1962 (rpt.).

Farquhar, J.N., *Modern Religious Movements in India*, London: 1929.

Fauja Singh (ed.), *The City of Amritsar*, New Delhi: Oriental Publishers and Distributors, 1978.

—— (ed.), *Guru Tegh Bahadur, Martyr and Teacher*, Patiala: Punjabi University, 1978.

—— and Kirpal Singh (eds.), *Proceedings of the Panjab History Conference*, Patiala: Punjabi University, 1966.

Ganda Singh, *Banda Singh Bahadur*, Amritsar: Khalsa College, 1935.

——, *Sardar Jassa Singh Ahluwalia*, Patiala: Punjabi University, 1999.

Ganesh Das, *Chār Bāgh-i Panjāb*, ed. Kirpal Singh, Amritsar: Khalsa College, 1965.

Gauba, Anand, *Amritsar: A Study of Urban History (1849-1947)*, Jalandhar: Cosmic Printers, 1988.

Gibb, H.A.R. (tr.), *Travels in Asia and Africa*, London: 1953.

Goswamy, B.N. and J.S. Grewal, *The Mughals and the Jogis of Jakhbar: Some Madad-i-Ma'ash and Other Documents*, Simla: Indian Institute of Advanced Study, 1967.

——, *The Mughal and Sikh Rulers and the Vaishnavas of Pindori : A Historical Interpretation of 52 Persian Documents*, Simla: Indian Institute of Advanced Study, 1969.

Grewal, J.S., 'Ganesh Das's Char-Bagh-i-Punjab', *Proceedings of the Indian History Congress* (Patiala: Punjabi University), 1967.

——, 'The Qazi in the Pargana', *Studies in Local and Regional History*. ed., J.S. Grewal, Amritsar: Guru Nanak Dev University, 1974.

——, *In the By-Lanes of History: Some Persian Documents from a Punjab Town*, Simla: Indian Institute of Advanced Study, 1975.

——, *Guru Tegh Bahadur and the Persian Chroniclers*, Amritsar: Guru Nanak Dev University, 1976.

——, *Guru Nanak in History*, Chandigarh: Panjab University, 1998 (rpt.).

——, *The Reign of Maharaja Ranjit Singh: Structure of Power, Economy and Society*, Sita Ram Kohli Memorial Lectures, Patiala: Punjabi University, 1981.

——, *Maharaja Ranjit Singh*, Amritsar: Guru Nanak Dev University, 1982.

——, *The City of the Golden Temple*, Amritsar: Guru Nanak Dev University, 1986.

——, *The Sikhs of the Punjab*, (The New Cambridge History of India. II.3), Cambridge: Cambridge University Press, 1990.

——, *Guru Nanak and Patriarchy*, Shimla: Indian Institute of Advanced Study, 1993.

——, 'Brahmanizing the Tradition: Chhibber's Bansavalinama', *The Khalsa: Sikh and Non-Sikh Perspectives*, ed. J.S. Grewal, New Delhi: Manohar, 2004, pp. 59-87.

——, 'Valorizing the Tradition: Bhangu's Panth Prakash', *The Khalsa: Sikh and Non-Sikh Perspectives,* ed. J.S. Grewal, New Delhi: Manohar, 2004 pp. 103-22.

——, and Indu Banga (eds.). *Early Nineteenth Century Punjab* (*From Ganesh Das's Char Bagh-i Panjab*), Amritsar: Guru Nanak Dev University, 1975.

——, *The Civil and Military Affairs of Maharaja Ranjit Singh: A Study of 450 Orders in Persian,* Amritsar: Guru Nanak Dev University, 1987.

Grewal J.S. and Irfan Habib (eds.), *Sikh History from Persian Sources,* New Delhi: Tulika / Indian History Congress, 2001.

Grewal, Reeta and Sheena Pall (eds.), *Five Centuries of Sikh Tradition: Ideology, Society, Politics and Culture,* New Delhi: Manohar, 2005.

Griffin, Lepel and others, *Chiefs and Families of Note in the Punjab,* Lahore: 1940.

——, *The Rajas of the Punjab,* London: 1870.

——, *Ranjit Singh,* Oxford: Rulers of India Series, 1905.

Gupta, Hari Ram, *History of the Sikhs.* vol. III. Lahore: 1944.

——, *A History of the Sikhs.* vol I. Shimla: The Minerva Book Shop, 1952.

Gurdas, Bhai, *Vārān Bhai Gurdas,* ed. Giani Hazara Singh, Amritsar: Khalsa Samachar, 1962.

Hans, Surjit, 'Prem Sumarg: A Modern Forgery', *Punjab History Conference Proceedings,* Patiala: Punjabi University, 1982.

Hasrat, Bikrama Jit, *Life and Times of Ranjit Singh,* Hoshiarpur: V.V. Research Institute Book Agency, 1977.

Hukamnāme: Guru Sāhibān, Mātā Sāhibān, Banda Singh ate Khālsā jī de, ed. Ganda Singh, Patiala: Punjabi University, 1967.

Hutchison, J. and J. Ph. Vogel, *History of the Punjab Hill States,* 2 vols., Lahore: 1933.

Jaggi, Ratan Singh, *Bhai Gurdas: Jīwan te Rachnā,* Patiala: Punjabi University, 1974.

Janam Sākhī Sri Gurū Nānak Dev Jī, ed. Kirpal Singh and Shamsher Singh Ashok, 2 vols. Amritsar: Khalsa College, 1962, 1969.

Janam Sākhī Sri Gurū Nānak Dev Jī, ed. Piar Singh, Amritsar: Guru Nanak Dev University, 1974.

Kapur Singh, *Parasharprasna or the Baisakhi of Guru Gobind Singh,* Jalandhar, 1959 (reprinted by Guru Nanak Dev University, Amritsar, 1989, 2001)

Khafi Khan, *Muntakhab al-Lubāb,* Calcutta: 1884.

Khushwant Singh, *A History of the Sikhs,* Princeton: Princeton University Press, 1963.

——, *Ranjit Singh: Maharaja of the Punjab,* London: George Allen & Unwin, 1962.

Khushwaqt Rai, *Tawārīkh-i Sikhān,* MS 1274, Khalsa College, Amritsar.

Kirpal Singh, *Life of Maharaja Ala Singh of Patiala and His Times,* Amritsar: Khalsa College, 1954.

——. 'Facts about Guru Gobind Singh's Martyrdom', *The Sikh Review*, Sept.-Oct., 1957, pp. 68-73.

Koer Singh, *Gurbilās Pātshāhī 10*, ed. Shamsher Singh Ashok, Patiala: Punjabi University, 1968.

Kohli, S.S., *Panjābi Sāhit dā Ithās*, Ludhiana: Lahore Book Shop, 1955.

Lahauri, Muhammad Qasim, '*Ibratnāma*, MS 1270, Khalsa College, Amritsar.

Lakshman Singh, *Guru Gobind Singh*, Lahore:1909.

Macauliffe, M.A., *The Sikh Religion*, 6 vols., London: The Clarendon Press, 1909.

Mākhaz-i Tawārīkh Sikhān, ed. Ganda Singh, Amritsar: Sikh History Society, 1949.

Malcolm, John, *A Sketch of the Sikhs*, London: 1812 (reprinted by Asian Educational Services, New Delhi, 1986).

Malhotra, Karamjit K., 'The Earliest Manual on the Sikh Way of life', *Five Centuries of Sikh Tradition: Ideology, Society, Polity and Culture*, ed. Reeta Grewal and Sheena Pall, New Delhi: Manohar, 2005.

McLeod, W.H., *Guru Nanak and the Sikh Religion*, Oxford: The Clarendon Press, 1968.

——, 'The Influence of Islam upon the Thought of Guru Nanak'. *History of Religions*, vol. VII, No. 4 (May 1968), pp. 302-16.

——, *Evolution of the Sikh Community*, New Delhi: Oxford University Press, 1975.

——, *The Chaupa Singh Rahit-Nāma*, Dunedin: University of Otago Press, 1987.

——, *Sikhism*, London: Penguin Books, 1997.

——, *Sikhs of the Khalsa: A History of the Khalsa Rahit*, New Delhi : Oxford University Press, 2003.

Mohan Singh, *An Introduction to Punjabi Literature*, Amritsar: 1951.

Nargis, Narsingh Das, *Gulab Singh*, Jammu: 1961.

Oberoi, Harjot, *Construction of Religious Boundaries: Culture, Identity and Diversity in the Sikh Tradition*, New Delhi: Oxford University Press, 1994.

Pannikar, K.M., *Gulab Singh*, London: 1930.

Purātan Janam Sākhī Sri Gurū Nānak Dev Jī, ed. Bhai Vir Singh, Delhi: Bhai Vir Singh Sahit Sadan, 1999 (rpt.).

Randhir Singh (ed.), *Prem Sumārg*, Amritsar: Sikh History Society, 1953.

Rao, Ram Sukh, *Jassa Singh Binod*, M/772, Punjab State Archives, Patiala.

——, *Fateh Singh Pratāp Prabhākar*, ed. Joginder Kaur, Patiala: 1980.

Sachdeva, Veena, *Polity and Economy of the Punjab During the Late Eighteenth Century*, Delhi: Manohar, 1993.

——, 'The Rule of the Bhangis (1765-1810)', M.Phil. Dissertation, Guru Nanak Dev University, Amritsar.

Sainapat, *Shri Gurū Sobhā*, ed. Shamsher Singh Ashok, Amritsar: Shiromani Gurdwara Prabandhak Committee, 1967. Also, Sainapat, *Shri Gur Sobhā*, ed. Ganda Singh, Patiala: Punjabi University, 1967.

Sarkar, Jadunath, *A Short History of Aurangzeb*, Calcutta: 1930.

Shabdārth Sri Gurū Granth Sāhib Ji, 4 vols., Amritsar: Shiromani Gurdwara Prabandhak Committee, standard editions.

Sharma, Sri Ram, *The Religious Policy of the Mughal Emperors*, Bombay: Asia Publishing House, 1962.

Sher Singh, *The Philosophy of Sikhism*, Lahore: 1944.

Sinha, N.K., *Rise of Sikh Power*, Calcutta: A Mukherjee & Co., 1960 (3rd ed.).

——, *Ranjit Singh*, Calcutta: 1968.

Sohan Singh, *The Seeker's Path*, Bombay: 1959.

Sri Dasam Granth Sāhib, 5 vols., ed. Ratan Singh Jaggi and Gursharan Kaur Jaggi, New Delhi: Gobind Sadan, 1999.

Sri Guru Granth Sahib, tr., Manmohan Singh, Amritsar: SGPC, 1964.

Sri Gurū Granth Sāhib Darpan, 10 vols., ed., Sahib Singh, Jalandhar: Raj Publishers.

Sukha Singh, *Gurbilās Pātshāhī 10*, ed. Gursharan Kaur Jaggi, Patiala: Punjab Languages Department, 1989.

Sujan Rai, *Khulāsat ut-Tawārīkh*, ed. Zafer Hasan, Delhi: 1918.

Suri, Sohan Lal, *Umdat ut-Tawārīkh*, 5 Daftars, Lahore: New Imperial Press, 1888-89.

Surinder Singh, *Sikh Coinage: Symbol of Sikh Sovereignty*, New Delhi: Manohar, 2004.

Swaran Singh, 'Amritsar in Medieval Panjabi Literature: An Historical Analysis' (Punjabi), Ph.D. Thesis, Guru Nanak Dev University, Amristsar, 1994.

Tahmas Khan, *Tahmas Nameh*, ed. Muhammad Aslam, Lahore: Punjab University, 1986.

Talib, Gurbachan Singh, *Guru Tegh Bahadur: Martyr and Teacher*, Patiala: Punjabi University, 1975.

——, *Sri Guru Granth Sahib in English Translation*, 4 vols., Patiala: Punjabi University, 1997, 2001, 2003.

Teja Singh, *Sikhism: Its Ideals and Institutions*, New Delhi: Orient Longman Ltd., 1951.

—— and Ganda Singh, *A Short History of the Sikhs*, New Delhi: Orient Longman Ltd., 1950 (reprinted by Punjabi University, Patiala, 1989).

Trilochan Singh, *Guru Tegh Bahadur*, Delhi: Delhi Gurdwara Parbandhak Committee, 1967.

Wilson, H.H., 'Civil and Religious Institutions of the Sikhs', *The Sikh Religion: A Symposium*, Calcutta: Sushil Gupta Private Ltd., 1958.

Index